This book, *Unleashing Heali..*
Emotions, tackles a very difficult subjec.. ....
depth, transparent testimony, and clear instruction for the journey of
what it means to be truly *"lead by the Spirit of God"* (Rom. 8:14).

Drs. Virkler and Kayembe have the breadth of their decades of
experience in bringing healing to the human soul and give a fresh perspective of what is possible for Christian believers to walk in the power
of the Spirit in our emotions. This work is valuable for anyone who
desires wholeness in their soul. It is also a valuable tool for counselors,
pastors, and anyone who seeks to help others.

This will be used as reference reading in Randy Clark's Global
School of Supernatural Ministry, where Dr. Virkler is a faculty member.

DR. MIKE HUTCHINGS
Director, Global School of Supernatural Ministry and Global
Certification Programs

When understood and applied, these vital truths about Kingdom
emotions will release new life and power into the church! *Unleashing
Healing Power Through Spirit-Born Emotions* by Mark Virkler and
Charity Kayembe is an exceptional and much needed work that not
only reveals the difference between carnal emotions and the fruit of the
Spirit but also teaches how to tap into Spirit-born emotions in everyday
life and for ministry.

DRS. DENNIS AND JEN CLARK
Senior Pastors of Kingdom Life Church
Founder/Directors of Full Stature
Ministries and TEAM Embassy School
Bests-selling authors of
Releasing the Divine Healer Within and
Self-Deliverance Made Simple

Mark Virkler and his daughter Charity have done it again!
Unleashing Healing Power Through Spirit-Born Emotions is an

amazingly practical book that will take you on a spiritual journey to emotional healing. I am unaware of any other book that focuses on our emotions to this depth.

Everyone has a soul, which is what we think (mind), how we choose (will), and what we feel (emotions). Sadly, most of us have damaged souls, including very unhealthy emotions. Charity and Mark go deep into the Scriptures and show how God is not only the originator of our emotions but has made a way for us to have healthy emotions. I love the progression in the book that takes us from what our emotions are, to how they are healed, to learning how God tunes us to know His heart for others.

Jesus knew that compassion was one of Father God's triggers for engaging into ministry. We too can develop our skills to know when Father God is positioning us to be just like Jesus and partner with Him to bring healing and restoration to others. Well done, Mark and Charity!

STEVE LONG

Senior Leader, Catch the Fire Toronto

Author of *My Healing Belongs to Me*,
On the Run, and *The Faith Zone*

Dr. Mark Virkler's material has played a huge role in the development of not only my life but the life of the students of the Global Fire School of Supernatural Ministry and Kingdom Life Institute in Murfreesboro, Tennessee. I've always believed that as Spirit-filled Christians we are capable of producing anything we have a passion for. Being made in the image of God, we have the same divine component to feel, sense, and create just as He does. Our thoughts and actions are the seeds that hold the power to create and reproduce the supernatural in our life. When that seed is mixed with the desire of strong emotion, a conception takes place that leads to birthing! I call this the "Kingdom Law of Reproduction." Scripture tells us in Proverbs 23:7 that as a man thinks (and feels) in his heart so he is (so he will become). Miracles manifest by faith through our emotions! This is simply the *power of agreement* or the principle of "If any two of you agree touching anything it will be done for you." When your emotions agree with your thinking it shall be done for you!

Dr. Mark Virkler has beautifully opened the truth of the Gospel to a life of miracles in this new book. If you are hungry for the supernatural and glory of God then you will want to ingest and digest the contents of this amazing new book. I want to highly recommend this book to you as it holds the power of revelation to completely change your life for the Kingdom of God.

JEFF JANSEN
Founder of Global Fire Ministries International
Author of *Glory Rising* and *The Furious Sound of Glory*
Senior Leader of Global Fire Church

The moment I picked up this book I could feel that it had the Spirit of revelation all over it. The idea of "heart coherence" flowing out of our glorious new-creation identity is profound. But the concept of engaging Kingdom emotions as a precursor to the flow of divine healing is revolutionary!

It all makes such perfect sense, especially with Jesus as our example of releasing heaven on earth. Everything in Jesus was in perfect heavenly alignment, most notably His emotional state of perfect heart coherence through His intimate union with the Father. Jesus radiated the perfect "Shalom" of heaven on earth, and that is more than just peace; it is divine well-being and health. He said, "My shalom I give to you!" (see John 14:27).

This book is cutting-edge revelation at its absolute best! My friends Mark Virkler and Charity Kayembe are a dynamite team who write edge-of-your-seat practical theology that both challenges and equips all at once.

I heartily commend this book to you as a significant breakthrough in the science of releasing heaven on earth. It has stirred me deeply to seek to engage more fully in heaven's flow of compassionate supernatural healing. I don't just want to heal the sick; I want to be moved with the Father's compassion to heal the sick!

PHIL MASON
Spiritual Director: Tribe Byron Bay, Australia
Author: *Quantum Glory: The Science of Heaven Invading Earth* and the four volume *Supernatural Transformation* Series
www.philmason.org

We have known Mark for over 20 years and have greatly valued his teaching gift in pioneering the transformational truth that we can clearly hear the voice of God as we pay attention to His presence and the moving of His Holy Spirit. On first hearing Mark teach, we have found that hearing God has brought more glorious freedom, direction, wisdom, and security, as well as inner healing and transformation. Our shelves of journals overflow!

His teaching has always been fully supported with Scripture, confirming how God can lead and direct our lives. In this book, *Unleashing Healing Power Through Spirit-Born Emotions*, Mark and Charity support their very practical teaching thoroughly with biblical context and application. However, *Spirit-born Emotions* brings a whole new level to the ministry and power of the Holy Spirit being released within us.

On reading each chapter, we could literally see the effect of Mark's joy, hope, faith, and love lifting up and transforming our present, our past, and our future! Sickness, trauma, brokenness—all candidates for healing and the miraculous as, through communion with God, His Spirit takes over our old self, awakens our spiritual senses, and matures Kingdom emotion within us.

TREVOR and SHARON BAKER
Revival Fires
Dudley, England

Fascinating! In only the last year or two, God has repeatedly highlighted to me how *He* chose to use Kingdom emotions such as peace, love, joy, compassion, and many others to expand and *heal* His Kingdom here on earth. Mark Virkler, one of the most superb teachers of the Word of God, has published a *great work* in this book, *Unleashing Healing Power Through Spirit-Born Emotions*.

Listen to me. (I mean, listen to Mark!) Jesus, when moved by *compassion*, healed the multitudes and left no one out. We all want that in our lives—the love, compassion, healing power, all of it, right? Then get a copy of this book and put it into practice immediately! I'd recommend it for your study groups too.

STEVE SHULTZ
Founder, The Elijah List

Dr. Mark Virkler and his daughter, Dr. Charity Kayembe, have done it again. Their book, *Unleashing Healing Power Through Spirit-Born Emotions*, gives great biblical principles by which to live, be healed, and heal others.

I have personally benefited from the powerful declarations they encourage us to make. The action exercises, classroom activities, and follow-up steps are all practical and helpful. This book is an excellent course for a person to be healed in spirit, soul, and body.

Drs. Mark and Charity make it remarkably clear that joy strengthens us, peace rules us, love compels us, and compassion moves us. I highly recommend this book to all pastors and leaders and the Body of Christ.

REV. RONALD V. BURGIO, D.MIN
Lead Pastor, Love Joy Church, Lancaster, New York
President Emeritus, Elim Fellowship, Lima, New York

unleashing

HEALING
POWER

through

SPIRIT-BORN EMOTIONS

MARK VIRKLER AND
CHARITY VIRKLER KAYEMBE

unleashing

HEALING
POWER

through

SPIRIT-BORN EMOTIONS

MARK VIRKLER AND
CHARITY VIRKLER KAYEMBE

DESTINY IMAGE® PUBLISHERS, INC.

P.O. Box 310, Shippensburg, PA 17257-0310

"Promoting Inspired Lives."

This book and all other Destiny Image and Destiny Image Fiction books are available at Christian bookstores and distributors worldwide.

Cover design by Eileen Rockwell

Interior design by Terry Clifton

For more information on foreign distributors, call 717-532-3040.

Reach us on the Internet: www.destinyimage.com.

ISBN 13 TP: 978-0-7684-1795-1
ISBN 13 eBook: 978-0-7684-1796-8
ISBN 13 HC: 978-0-7684-1798-2
ISBN 13 LP: 978-0-7684-1797-5

For Worldwide Distribution, Printed in the U.S.A.

1 2 3 4 5 6 7 8 / 21 20 19 18 17

MARK'S DEDICATION

Thank you to my wife Patti, who has stood by me for 45 years of marriage and loved me through all my transitions, a few of which are described in this book.

Without her love, patience, and understanding heart, I would not be who I am today.

CHARITY'S DEDICATION

To my amazing husband, Leo.
I have found the one whom my soul loves.
Thank you for doing life together with me!

ACKNOWLEDGMENTS

We are grateful to our friend Pastor Phil Mason and his outstanding revelation on the New Creation miracle, as well as quantum physics and how it correlates to our walk in the Spirit. He has expertly unpacked many hard-to-understand concepts, bringing science and the supernatural together in a powerful way. What a gift!

We also appreciate our friend Dr. Jim Richards and his excellent insights on how so much of what improves the quality of our life is a state and not a goal and for providing a key component to our understanding that the language of the heart is personal, positive and present tense.

Finally we are thankful for the teaching of Dr. Caroline Leaf. She has made complex neuroscience accessible to all and shown how it is relevant to our everyday lives and most importantly to our relationship with God.

We have been inspired by these leaders and this book has been influenced by the unique revelations they carry.

We also want to acknowledge the awesome publishing team that is Destiny Image: Larry, John, Brad, Sierra, Meelika, Patti, Wil, Christian, Cavet and everyone who has partnered with us in getting this message out. We appreciate your wonderful contributions and all your hard work on this project. Thank you very much!

CONTENTS

Joyfully gazing upon images of God's promises,
as already fulfilled, releases those miracles
into my life. What I see is what I get.

A joyful heart is good medicine
—PROVERBS 17:22

FOREWORD

In early childhood, through adolescence, and into my twenties, I wore my emotions on my sleeve and I was definitely both controlled and motivated by my emotions (or lack of them). I remember my mother, teachers, spiritual leaders, and others telling me not to be so emotional. As a result, I had a deeply engrained negative perspective on the value of emotions, and when I emoted I often felt inner condemnation strike at the core of my being.

I also experienced times of flat-lining on the emotional monitor and discovered quickly that I hated the lack of emotions more than the dramatic and uncontrolled emotions I experienced. What a dilemma! I was convinced that I was defeated when I emoted and defeated when I didn't. It felt like a lose-lose battle.

The night I was born again was a very emotional night as I was alone in my living room reaching out to Him for salvation. I felt Jesus come into my heart like "liquid love" as He miraculously removed all my sin, guilt, and shame. I felt so clean inside.

I wept and wept all night long. The more I felt His love the more I wept. It was so beautiful, and I came to a realization that night that He loved my emotions...and I loved them too. I loved Him like I had never known or experienced love before. I felt alive, fully accepted, and celebrated.

As I grew in the Lord I was blessed with loyal friends who influenced me in my maturing process. I received healing for past emotional pain, deliverance from demonic control that had found a landing strip in my life, and valuable wisdom and insight on how to embrace God-inspired and Spirit-led emotions.

I began to enjoy spiritual encounters and I became familiar with God's emotions too. He is full of vibrant, life-filled emotion. He laughs, He cries, and He experiences a full range of emotions such as compassion, delight, righteous anger, love, and sadness.

I came to realize that I am emotional because He is emotional. I am created in His image and likeness. I experienced healing through emotional encounters in His presence and I received deliverance on many occasions in the midst of both weeping and laughing through His inspiration. I love Spirit-born emotions!

I am grateful that Dr. Mark Virkler and his lovely daughter Charity wrote this amazing book. What freedom the revelation it contains will bring to you and what a tool it will be in your hand as you reach out to others.

May you receive valuable keys and insights into the heart of God and the ways of His Kingdom as you journey through the pages of this Spirit-inspired work.

PATRICIA KING

HOW GOD TAUGHT ME TO HONOR KINGDOM EMOTIONS

*Over my lifetime, I have moved from **scorning** emotions to **accepting** them and, now, to **honoring** them. Now, the challenge is to learn to **feel** and **move** in the power of Kingdom emotions!*

Do you have a theology concerning the role of Kingdom emotions in bringing forth spiritual transformation?

I sure didn't. Actually, I used to scorn emotions as soulish. Thirty-seven years ago, when I began hearing God's voice through two-way journaling, God told me there was a place for emotions. He reminded me that Jesus, moved by compassion, healed (see Matt. 14:14), so I decided to accept emotions. Now, God is taking me one step further, showing me that the Kingdom emotions of compassion and thankfulness are *crucial* in bringing forth the miracles and transformations He has in store for my life.

I have come to the conclusion that faith, when coupled with the Kingdom emotions of compassion and gratitude, brings forth miracles. When used together, the synergy of these elements releases sufficient spiritual power to overcome the hard-wired circuits in my mind and body and produce a life-transforming miracle.

> **Miracles occur when revelation, carried on the waves of compassion, is energized with the spirit of gratitude.**

Wow, from scorn to a celebrated place of importance! It would have been nice if it didn't take 37 years to embrace these changes.

WHAT ARE YOUR DEFINITIONS OF FAITH AND LOVE?

Growing up, my definitions of faith and love did not actually include emotions as a component part of either one. I had defined faith as *allegiance to a creed or statement of fact* and love as a *decision to lay down my life for another.* Were my descriptions of faith and love correct? Were they biblical? You will discover in this book that these definitions needed considerable revamping!

I began searching Scripture to see what it says about emotion. Was I in for a shock! Here is one Scripture which sums things up: "*faith working through love*" (Gal. 5:6). The literal meaning of *working through* in this verse is "energized by." So faith is *energized* by love. Without love, faith doesn't work.

I have come to believe that emotions are the *channel that releases spiritual energy.* The healing power Jesus released rode on the carrier wave of compassion. If I want to see miracles in my life, I need to combine compassion and faith. Compassion toward myself and others and faith that God can do anything He wants!

HOW MUCH TIME SHOULD I GIVE TO EXPLORING FAITH ENERGIZED BY LOVE?

The Bible devotes hundreds of verses to faith, belief, and love and hundreds more to their opposites—fear, doubt, anger, hatred, and judgment. These are enormous topics to wrestle with and to integrate into our lives. I finally took a year to explore the dynamic of *faith energized by love*. I have come to the realization that compassion is the carrier wave on which the power of the Holy Spirit rides. *Faith energized by love releases miracles.*

The devotional "New Creation Celebration: Replacing Emotions"[1] guides you into experiencing "faith, energized by love." It leads you in *honoring* the role of emotions in releasing the Spirit. Try it for seven days and see if you are not experiencing miraculous transformations in your spirit, soul, and body. I have!

The purpose of this book is to help you establish a biblical understanding of the various elements that make up this devotional series, especially the role of emotion in bringing forth transformation. God's Kingdom is defined as *peace* and *joy* in the Holy Spirit (see Rom. 14:17)! These are Spirit-born emotions.

A BRIEF INTRODUCTION TO FAITH ENERGIZED BY LOVE

"Faith working through love" (Gal. 5:6) is a topic that will be expanded in Chapters 5-7 of this book. Here is a brief introduction to

---

1   www.cwgministries.org/emotions

this verse. If healing, transformation, and miracles occur when 1) faith 2) is energized 3) by love, would this mean that everyone, even children, can expect to see miracles if they can tap into these three things—faith, Holy Spirit flow, and love? It is obviously much easier for a child to live in faith, flow, and love than an adult. That is why Jesus instructed us to become like children so we could experience the Kingdom (see Matt. 18:3).

Faith Working Through Love (Chapter 5)

Faith is one of the nine ways the Holy Spirit manifests Himself (see 1 Cor. 12:7-9). So faith is birthed by the movement of God within my heart. The five component parts that build heart faith are modeled by Abraham, the Father of all who believe (see Rom. 4:11,20-21). Faith is not something I muster up, nor is it mental assent to a creed. Faith is the outflow of the presence of the Holy Spirit.

Faith *Working Through* Love (Chapter 6)

The literal meaning of the Greek word translated *working through* in Galatians 5:6 is "energized by." This Greek word, *energeō,* is the Holy Spirit's energy that releases miracles (Strong's G1754). The New Testament teaches us that *energeō* also sustains all life and holds every atom together (see Col. 1:17). In the new birth, the Spirit *indwells us* (see John 20:22). The Holy Spirit then *fills* the yielded and obedient Christian (see Eph. 5:18). Finally He overflows, resting *upon* the believer and anointing them with power to heal and perform miracles (see Acts 2:2-3).

Faith Working Through *Love* (Chapter 7)

The literal meaning of the Greek word for love (*agapē*) is "affection, good will" (Strong's G26). The literal meaning of the closely related word *compassion* (*splagchnizomai*) is "to have the bowels yearn" (Strong's G4697). *Splankna* (the Greek word) can be defined as *"the yearning compassion of God flowing from our innermost beings upon which rides a release of God's mercy, power, and blessing to the person in need.*" Compassion is the carrier wave of the healing power of the Holy Spirit. Compassion is active love. Compassion has a strong emotional content to it. Emotions are a language of the heart. God lives in our hearts, and His Spirit rides out on the waves of Kingdom emotions that flow from our hearts.

So faith produces miracles when it is energized by the Holy Spirit and coupled with the emotion of love. Wow! It has taken me years to gain a revelation about this simple biblical truth! Now the challenge is to live in it, stop being critical, and start loving.

CAN THE EMOTION OF LOVE ACTUALLY BE MEASURED?

In Chapter 11 of this book, we explore an inexpensive heart monitor that lets you know if you are 1) tuned to your heart, 2) feeling emotions of love, gratitude, compassion, joy, and thankfulness, and 3) releasing love to another. Biblically speaking, this posture is called living by the Spirit or abiding in Christ (see Gal. 5:25; John 15:1-4). It is almost unbelievable to me that a heart monitor could actually measure *when* one has entered this state, but after using it 150 times I can guarantee this is exactly what it does. I will discuss this instrument in detail in Chapter 11 as it has been a concrete tool to train me to *feel* and live in Kingdom emotions.

The "New Creation Meditations" discussed in this book will help you release emotions of anger, fear, and separation from God and replace them with the Kingdom emotions of faith, love, and peace. The heart monitor can be an objective tool, training you to experience these Kingdom emotions.

The Key Principle We Will Explore in This Book:

Gazing upon images of God's promises as already fulfilled produces Spirit-born emotions (faith, joy, and gratitude), which unleash healing power (see Gen. 15:5-6; Matt. 14:14; Rom. 14:17).

- There is an increased release of the power of the Holy Spirit.
- Your body's healing genes are "switched on."
- Life becomes exciting, fun, and joy-filled.

RESOURCES FOR INDIVIDUAL AND SMALL GROUP USE

CDs, DVDs, electronic media, and small group activities that correlate with this teaching are available. Please refer to the end of this book for more information.

Part I

THE POWER OF
KINGDOM EMOTIONS

Chapter 1

MY ROCKY RELATIONSHIP WITH EMOTIONS OVER THE YEARS

*A **joyful** heart is good medicine.*
—PROVERBS 17:22

It wasn't just emotions that I struggled with. I struggled with a whole lot of things. As a typical teenager, I was quite sure I knew pretty much everything. The church I was saved in at age 15 was pretty much in the same camp as I was. They were so sure they were the only ones going to heaven that they would not let us marry outside our denomination.

I now look back and realize I was saved into ultra-conservative fundamentalism. Well, we all start off somewhere, and if we look we find that God causes all things to work together for good (see Rom. 8:28). Some of their good things were that they believed in thorough repentance, making Jesus Lord at the point of salvation, water baptism, and that the Bible was the Word of God. So thank You, God, for that wonderful foundation.

I noted this church was not following some very clear biblical commands, like allowing musical instruments to be part of our *a cappella* worship (see Ps. 33:2). Their only answer when I asked them about it at the very mature age of 16 was, "Well, we don't do it that way."

Sorry, that answer has never worked for me. If it's in the Bible, we do it. When the Lord opens my eyes to something in the Bible I haven't seen before, I believe in changing. It's as simple as that as far as I am concerned. Anything the Bible models or instructs me to do, I'm going to pursue. I'm going to change. I have chosen His way over my way, the Bible over my culture or any religious traditions I have been taught or even that I have preached. I sure don't want to be in the group that invalidates the Word of God through my traditions (see Mark 7:8).

I don't mind changing. I love to change. Change is the only constant. I choose to fully manifest Jesus Christ to this world. You know, *"the measure of the stature which belongs to the fullness of Christ"* (Eph. 4:13).

I want everything I say to be grounded in Scripture, so I provide scriptural references throughout my writings. I believe the Bible is the only authoritative gauge for all of life. Even though I took philosophy and psychology in college, these are not authorities in life. I reserve that role for Scripture alone.

ANY LIE WILL DO

Satan says any lie will do as long as he convinces me God's original intent is unobtainable. It never ceases to amaze me how far satan goes to remove the Bible and God's original intent from mankind. God, of course, desired walks with us in the Garden in the cool of the day (see Gen. 3:8). His desire has and always will be communion with His children.

Satan's first lie centered around the claim, "I sure don't need these walks with God where He talks with me and explains His ways and reveals His wisdom." You see, satan says, "*You* can know" (see Gen. 3:5). Well, of course that's true. Of course I can know. I went to school and college.

"You" became humanism, which essentially means living with me at the center of my life rather than Jesus. "Know" became rationalism, which is living life out of my mind rather than my heart (see Prov. 4:23).

Two lies were the first words out of satan's mouth, and yet they are so common it never crossed my mind not to believe them. I believed I could know. It's called reason, logic, rationalism. It's what my culture believes. It's what I believed. I trusted in my theology to keep me safe from error. I tested everything against my theology. Why, the Bible itself says, "*Study to show yourself approved*" (2 Tim. 2:15 MEV).

I suppose there were several reasons that living from my mind was very comfortable for me. I am naturally a thinker, not a feeler. I am left-brained, not right-brained. I live in a left-brain culture that worships rationalism and believes that truth comes through reason. Even my church and Christian liberal arts college agreed. It is all about reason, logic, and theology. So everyone was on board with my setting aside emotions.

MORE LIES TO ENSURE I DON'T EXPERIENCE GOD'S ORIGINAL INTENT OF FELLOWSHIP IN THE GARDEN...

You see, satan doesn't really care which lie of his I believe as long as I believe I can't have the experiences I find recorded in the Bible.

Dispensationalism says I can't live Scripture because these things happened in another dispensation (i.e. a period of time when God interacted with man in a certain way) and they are not available today.

Liberal theology says we can't live it because the Bible is full of myths that must be removed so we can get down to the kernel of truth. Religion says I can't live it because it is too hard; it takes consecutive 40-day fasts, and even then I probably won't be good enough to operate in the gifts of the Holy Spirit (see 1 Cor. 12:7-11). And once I found out how truly easy it is to hear God's voice and see visions, satan told me, "It can't be that easy. This is just you making it up. You need to doubt this."

You know, any of these lies can work, ensuring I will not radiate the power and revelation of the Spirit of God to the world around me. I have believed just about all of those lies at one point or another in my life. I now reject them all in the name of Jesus. They will have no power over me. *I can live Scripture!*

UNQUESTIONED "TRUTH" BECAME LIES

I was too young to even question where the roots of my discomfort with emotions came from. It was the cultural norm, so I unquestioningly accepted it. I was taught emotions were soulish, and soulishness was to be rejected. That was fine with me. I rejected emotions. It never crossed my mind to look to see if there were any verses in Scripture that placed emotions in the spiritual realm. When I looked, I found, much to my amazement, there are verses that locate emotions in man's spirit. For example, Ezekiel says, *"I went embittered in the rage of my spirit, and the hand of the Lord was strong on me"* (Ezek. 3:14). However, I never looked, so I never knew.

In those early years of my Christian life, I even passed out a tract that showed a train consisting of an engine, coal car, and caboose. The engine was "fact" or the Bible, the coal car was our faith, and the caboose was our feelings. The tract stated: *"The train will run with or without the caboose. However, it would be futile to attempt to pull the train by the caboose. In the same way, we, as Christians, do not depend upon feelings or emotions, but we place our faith (trust) in the trustworthiness of God and the promises of His Word."*

The above statement sure appeared correct. My interpretation of it was that I was to live out of my theology, which is not actually what the tract said. I believed it was my carefully constructed paradigms that kept me safe and kept me pure. Emotions played *no* place in my theology. Actually, I did not have a carefully constructed doctrine concerning emotions. I just never noticed that Jesus, moved by *compassion*, healed. Because compassion is an emotion and I didn't have any place for emotions, it went completely over my head that emotion was foundational in the lifestyle of Jesus.

The phrase *felt compassion* is not just a one-time statement. It appears 12 times in the New Testament. Plus, of course, the Kingdom is peace and joy, which are both emotions (see Rom. 14:17). I really didn't have a clear or consistent theology concerning Kingdom emotions. (It's interesting that *Christianity Today* ran an article in 2014 titled, "Emotion Isn't the Caboose to Faith.")[2]

SCIENTIFIC RESEARCH ON THE HEART AND EMOTIONS

I love to review what the most up-to-date science is saying about emotions, health, vitality, creativity, intuition, and living well. HeartMath Institute has compiled more than 20 years of research on these topics, delving into questions such as: Where do emotions

---

2   Owen Strachan, "Tim Keller: Emotion Isn't the Caboose to Faith," ChristianityToday.com, May 30, 2014, http://www.christianitytoday.com/ct/2014/april-web -only/jesus-resonates-with-people.html.

originate? Are they by-products of the mind? Do they flow from our hearts? Do we have a mind in our hearts? The Bible says we do; Mary pondered these things in her heart (see Luke 2:19).

HeartMath has proven that we do have a brain in our hearts, and the brain in our hearts sends more signals to the brain in our heads than the brain in our heads sends to our hearts. Wow! Really? Now, that's mind-bending!

HeartMath.com also explores the power of emotions to improve the quality of one's life. I have worked through their free downloadable compilation of 20-plus years of research, "Science of the Heart," and it is definitely worth the time it takes to at least skim it. It dovetails perfectly with the 1,200 verses on heart and spirit that I have explored.

EMOTIONALISM AND RATIONALISM

The *Merriam-Webster Dictionary* defines emotionalism as "a tendency to regard things emotionally, undue indulgence in or display of emotion."

My take on "an undue indulgence in or display of emotion" was, "If you display more emotion than me, you are into emotionalism." I'm less emotional; therefore, I could attribute emotionalism to most people.

Merriam-Webster defines rationalism as "reliance on reason as the basis for establishment of religious truth, a theory that reason is in itself a source of knowledge superior to and independent of sense perceptions." I love reason, logic, and theology, so for years rationalism suited me just fine.

LEARNING TO BE FLEXIBLE

In my journaling, God told me *I could trust His voice in my heart more than I could trust the reasoned theology of my mind.* I explained to

Him that this wasn't true because I had a verse memorized that clearly says that the heart is deceitful and desperately wicked (see Jer. 17:9 NKJV). Who could trust a voice coming through a deceitful and desperately wicked heart? God patiently explained to me that that verse was not describing my heart, as He had given me a new heart and a new spirit (see Ezek. 36:26-27), and I could trust His voice that flowed out of my new heart more than I could trust the reasoned theology of my mind. Wow!

By accepting this as a true word from the Lord, I changed from living my life headfirst to living heart first. After all, how many of us have felt a thing was true in our hearts before we were able to go to Scripture and find a verse that clearly confirmed it?

DO I TRUST MY MIND, MY HEART, NEITHER, OR BOTH?

Most Christians of whatever stripe are united that the Bible is the final authority for everything it speaks to. The question is, how do we decide what the Bible is actually saying? I realized that if I put my "head" in charge, all I would get is my reason interpreting the Bible for me.

When God started speaking directly into my heart, I developed an understanding of a broader methodology for establishing truth. Now I honor the discernment of my heart (see Mark 2:8). In addition, I ask God to guide my reasoning (see Isa. 1:18; 1 Cor. 2:16), giving me Spirit-anointed reason or reason guided by the flow of His Spirit (see John 7:37-39; 10:27).

I also meditate on Scripture and enjoy that burning sensation in my spirit as He opens Scripture to me (see Luke 24:32). The "truths" I am discovering I then submit to my two or three spiritual advisors for confirmation and see if the fruit released in my life is consistent with what the Bible says I am to be experiencing (see Prov. 11:14; 2 Cor. 13:1; Matt. 7:16).

Of course, dreams, visions, prophecy, and two-way journaling are also integrated into this process (see Acts 2:17; Rev. 1:10-11). This is the essence of my method for discovering truth. I call it "The Leader's Paradigm." It is the collaboration of God confirming His voice through these six means. It is far different from my earlier reliance on the false god of rationalism.

There are no boxes in my worldview. Instead, I have principles from which I live. My key principle is a passion that I grow into the stature of the fullness of Christ. Once I am living as He did, I've arrived! Until then, I am a learner, constantly growing, constantly changing. At age 65, I'm still a learner.

PAUL: "KNOWLEDGE" VERSUS "TRUE KNOWLEDGE"

I lived out of my reasoned, logical theology just like the apostle Paul did. I did exactly what Paul did. He went about killing those he disagreed with. I also left Bible college "killing" (judging and despising) everyone who disagreed theologically with me. I couldn't kill them physically, but I could publically rebuke them, call them a heretic, and I could sure look down my nose in disdain at them.

Paul had an encounter with God on the Damascus road, where he heard God's voice and saw a vision (see Acts 9). I had a similar experience when God woke me up one morning with a booming bass voice and said, "Get up; I am going to teach you to hear My voice." That morning I learned four keys to hearing God's voice: 1) quiet myself down, 2) fix my eyes on Jesus, 3) recognize His voice as spontaneous, flowing thoughts within, and 4) write them down.

Three years later, Paul came out of the wilderness with a brand-new word in his vocabulary. It is *true knowledge* (see Col. 2:2; 3:10 NASB). What's true knowledge? Paul puts it in opposition to man's *knowledge, logic, and reasoning* (see Col. 2:4,8). Really? I would sure like to know what Paul meant when he distinguished between man's knowledge and true knowledge.

I didn't have a definition of "true knowledge" or an understanding of how it is different from knowledge. Whatever it is, it is something Paul picked up during his three years in the wilderness, where, of course, there were no books, no classrooms, no teachers, and only the Holy Spirit to instruct him. Only spiritual revelation was available in the wilderness. So I discerned that for Paul, true knowledge was that which was born by revelation in his spirit. This was different from knowledge that came through the reasoning of his mind.

This startling revelation caused me to go back to explore every verse in the Bible on reason, logic, and theology, *because those were the things I lived out of.* Guess what? Logic and theology don't even show up as words in the Bible. In addition to this staggering fact, there is no command for me to reason. The closest command is, *"Come now, and let us reason **together"** (Isa. 1:18), but that is not reasoning on my own but letting God inject His thoughts into my mind to guide my reasoning process by His Spirit. That allows me to experience what the Bible calls "the mind of Christ" (1 Cor. 2:16). I experience reasoning together with God when I ask for His insight, see Him with me, tune to flowing thoughts, and allow this flow from the river within me to guide my reasoned thoughts. Truly simple and truly effective. I've been doing it now for many years.

You know, when God reasons He goes straight to picturing. *"'Come now, and let us reason together,' says the Lord, 'Though your sins are as scarlet, they will be as white as snow.'"* That is *not* how I was taught to reason. I was taught to use logic, not pictures. Hmmm, I wonder who should change their approach to reasoning—me or God?

At least I knew how to study. The Bible is sure clear about that. *"Study to shew thyself approved unto God"* (2 Tim. 2:15 KJV). That is, until I discovered that this is the *only* command in the Bible to study, and it is a mistranslation of the Greek word *spoudazō*, which literally means "be diligent" (Strong's G4704). The New King James and New American Standard Bible translate it correctly: *"Be diligent to present yourself"* (2 Tim. 2:15).

Wow! So here I had memorized and practiced error for how many years? You have no idea how disgusted and angry that made me! Just to be clear, *spoudazō* appears a total of 12 times in the Bible, and only *once* is it translated "study." The other 11 times it is translated correctly.[3]

Now that my favorite verse, *"Study to shew thyself approved unto God,"* can no longer be used to justify my reason-based theology, as it is a mistranslation, what will I use for my new favorite verse?

Well, here it is: *"Were not our hearts burning within us...while He was explaining the Scriptures to us?"* (Luke 24:32). This is revelation knowledge. God opens up Scripture verses as I meditate upon them (see Josh. 1:8). Yes, He is still speaking. *"My sheep hear My voice"* (John 10:27).

INSTRUCTION FROM THE EXPERIENCES OF LIFE?

Within rationalism, I always let my thoughts lead. However, that approach shipwrecked the apostle Paul, and it was a revelatory experience on the Damascus road that led him off in an entirely new direction.

---

3   See www.cwgministries.org/study for a listing of all 12 times *spoudazō* shows up in the Bible.

Three years of rereading Scriptures in light of his new experience caused him to radically adjust his theology (see Gal. 1:17-18). He reversed his belief system, now accepting that Jesus was the Christ, the Son of the Living God.

So, biblically speaking, it is appropriate to allow the experiences of life (in this case, a direct revelatory encounter with God) to readjust us and cause us to look again at Scripture to see if we may have missed something. I have done this many, many times. Jesus did say we are to test things by their fruits (see Matt. 7:15-20). So if my theology is producing fruit in my life that is contrary to Scripture, then I change my theology.

I have chosen to only teach things that I have first seen proven in the experiences of my life. Living truth! Truth I am personally living.

STAGES TO EMBRACING EMOTIONS

In 1979, when I was 27 years old, I had my major breakthrough in my Christian experience. I learned to hear God's voice clearly, daily, and intimately. I tell this story in my book, *4 Keys to Hearing God's Voice*, available from www.CWGMinistries.org. It was life-changing, and the day I learned to do this I spent five hours hearing from Him and writing out what He was saying. In one of those early visionary encounters, Jesus was holding my head against His chest and caressing my hair. He spoke and said, "Tenderness is OK." Whoa! No man had ever held my head against his chest and caressed my hair. This dramatically changed me.

Jesus went on to say:

> I want to restore emotions to your life and I want you to do three things to restore the emotions. I want you to read through the Gospels and see that I, Jesus, *moved by*

compassion, healed, and that it is OK to have emotions and to let them *lead* in your life and ministry.

Next, I want you to read the Psalms and notice that David had emotions and expressed them *all* to Me, and that was perfectly fine. I can handle all your emotions as you present them to Me. Finally, I want you to notice how tenderly I love you in your two-way journaling, and then I want you to love yourself and others with that same tenderness.

So I did those three things, and God has been continuously restoring emotions to my dry and choleric personality. One immediate result was that my wife said our marriage improved greatly when I learned to hear God's voice through two-way journaling.

Then at 64 years of age, I attended a seminar where I was taught that healing is a result of clear intention coupled with elevated emotion. These two things paved the way for healing power to flow.

I said, "Really? You need elevated emotions for the healing power of the Holy Spirit to ride on? I wonder if that is a biblical concept." I certainly had never looked to see if such a thing were so.

I had zero theology concerning the role of emotions to bring forth a miracle of healing. So I researched Scripture and science while I experimented on myself to see what I would learn. My research and experimentation is what the rest of this book is about. It has been a fascinating experience as I have invested an entire year into exploring this idea in depth.

I have decided that clear intention is what the Bible calls faith. I have faith for a specific thing. I speak to a mountain and see it cast into the sea. If a clear intention is faith, then it is quite easy to build a case for the need for clear intention to be present in order to experience a miracle.

The new part was going to be building a theological understanding for the role of elevated emotions in order to release a miracle. As I explored this, I decided that *elevated emotions* are what the Bible referred to as *Kingdom emotions*. I came to grips with words I had been brushing off, things like the Kingdom of God is *emotions*—peace and joy in the Holy Spirit (see Rom. 14:17). This peace and joy isn't from holding a certain mental construct that makes me peaceful or joyful. It is *peace and joy in the Holy Spirit*. These emotions are spirit realities, coming from the Holy Spirit. They are birthed in my spirit, not my brain. And these are *Kingdom* emotions! Really? Really! So I began building *a theology of Kingdom emotions*. That was something exciting and new.

Then, of course, we have the word *compassion*. Jesus, moved by compassion, healed (see Matt. 14:14)! Up to that point in history, compassion was only a noun. The Gospel writers turned it into a verb to describe the intensity of Jesus' feelings. *They created a new form of the word compassion* because the existing definition was not a strong enough word to describe what Jesus was experiencing. OK, I believe I am gaining a theological grid for the need for emotion in the release of miracles and personal transformation.

Compassion, a Kingdom emotion, led Jesus as He ministered healing. Hard to imagine being led by an emotion as spiritual, isn't it? The healing power of the Holy Spirit rode on this intense emotion—compassion. However, out of a fear that we would let negative emotions lead us, some have taught that no emotions should lead us. But suppose we put Kingdom emotions at the front of the train?

Revivals certainly have emotions. However, because I had not known that emotions could be spirit-level realities, I considered revivals to be displaying soulish emotions and thus emotionalism. However, compassion, joy, peace, and love are fruits of the Spirit, not fruits of the soul (see Gal. 5:22).

Ahab had an emotion in his spirit, which moved him to action (see 1 Kings 21:5), so the Bible clearly teaches that emotions can be present in our spirits. That deepens them from simply being the result of mental constructs or soulishly whipping them up into a frenzy.

Yes, I have been in services where emotions were manipulated to a high level, and that makes me uncomfortable. I would call that soulish. So what do I do in a worship service instead? I fix my eyes on the King, seated on His throne in heaven with the multitudes worshiping before Him (see Rev. 4). I join with them in worship and adoration of my Lord. As I do this, Kingdom emotions arise in my spirit that have not been stirred by a soulish frenzy but have been birthed in my spirit by being in the presence of my King.

GUIDING EMOTIONS

Now that I have let emotions out, can I guide them so they are not all over the place?

Yes, I can. I discovered that emotions are by-products of the pictures I am gazing at. If I picture something terrible happening, then the emotion of fear arises within me. If I see Jesus at my right hand (see Acts 2:25), then peace and calm overtake me. So if I control the pictures I gaze upon, then I can guide my emotional responses.

> *By selecting the pictures I gaze upon,*
> *I guide my emotional responses.*

The best way I know to control my mental pictures is to fix my eyes on Jesus (see Heb. 12:1-2), tune to flow, and ask Him to give me

His pictures for each and every situation. This results in His picture lighting upon my heart and mind (i.e., a vision), and as I embrace it, Kingdom peace floods my soul.

For example, I was picturing our nation's capital as full of spineless, crooked politicians and feeling the emotions of fear and anger. So in my morning devotions, I asked God how He saw my nation's capital. I tuned to flow, and within moments a picture came to me of Jesus enthroned above our Capitol and Congress, with His robes, glory, and power streaming down over them. The flowing thoughts that came to me were, "I rule in your nation's capital." Well, of course He does. He is King of kings and Lord of lords. Instantly the emotions of peace and comfort flooded my soul.

So I am able to instantly guide and control my emotions by asking God to give me His true pictures to replace the unbiblical pictures I am gazing at. How cool is that! If emotions are the channel of the Spirit, I can now enlarge the Spirit's flow out through me by gazing longer and more intently at the divine pictures God gives me. What a priceless revelation!

> *I enlarge the Spirit's flow by gazing longer and more intently at the pictures God gives me!*

READY TO MOVE FORWARD

Now, I believe in the role and power of Kingdom emotions. I believe they do promote healing. I believe the Church has absolutely missed it by not embracing the place of Kingdom emotions to precipitate healing, miracles, and spiritual transformation. We will begin doing so in this book, and we will add the most recent scientific research that correlates with what the Bible says about emotions. For example, you can find thousands of scientific studies proving that a merry heart does good like medicine (see Prov. 17:22 NKJV). Go to PubMed,[4] and in their search bar type in "emotions and the immune system" or "emotions and cancer" or "positive emotions and health."

Are you ready to explore? Do you have an open mind? Are you willing to go to Scripture with me, see what it states, simply say, "Yes, Lord," and try it out to see where it takes you?

The "New Creation Celebration" meditations I have developed to go along with this book draw you into a strong emotional encounter with the Lord Jesus Christ by having you gaze intently on who you are as a new creation in Him. As you take the time to do these devotionals, you will find that your emotions are being transformed by the Holy Spirit. You are coming alive with Kingdom emotions even as you shed unhealthy emotional states. You are promoting a lifestyle of spiritual transformation.

Wouldn't it be nice to see people moved by compassion, praying for healing on the streets and releasing God's miracle-working power just as Jesus did? Is this what our nations need? Would it produce another revival? Is this God's plan? Will you be a part of it? I will!

Let the Church be the Church once again. Let us light our cities with Christ's divine light and healing power. Let us be known as those whose compassionate touch with clear intention to heal sets the captives free. Come. Can you hear Him calling you?

---

4   www.ncbi.nlm.nih.gov/pubmed

ACTION EXERCISES

Review this web link[5] as it introduces you to clearly, easily, and daily hear God's voice and receive His visions. These are skills that the devotionals throughout this book are based on.

Daily Devotional

Complete the "River of Life" meditation each day for the next seven days. This devotional is available as an audio with music in the background. You can listen for free at www.cwgministries.org/SpiritualTransformations. It is also available as part of the "New Creation Celebration" meditations, which can be purchased as a CD set or as individual MP3 files.

Feel the power of the Holy Spirit surge through you as you gaze intently at the River of Life flowing from the throne of God and covering you completely. Prayerfully read and imagine these passages to prepare the eyes of your heart to see this reality: Ezekiel 47:1-12 and Revelation 22:1-2. See yourself as in the upper room of Acts 2:1-4, being immersed in the Holy Spirit. As you *see* this and enter deeply and devoutly into it, the Holy Spirit can and will bring transformation and healing. If you see it clearly, you will feel its transforming power.

Journaling

"Lord, what would You speak to me concerning the truths of this chapter?" Record your journaling in a separate notebook or in a computer file.

Read this web link on every use of the word *spoudazō*: www.cwgministries.org/study. Is it "study" or "be diligent"?

---

5   www.cwgministries.org/4keys

Testimony from Margaret Cornell as she uses the River of Life Devotional

Dear Mark,

This morning when I sat to pray I did your Holy Spirit devotional. I've done it half a dozen times before, but this time rather than using the music with your spoken voice, I simply did it from memory.

The moment I started, my feet became hot and I felt a fire of the Holy Spirit spread throughout my body, and when I'd finished I found my husband and laid hands on him and he felt the fire too, and then we prayed for other people who we know are sick and released to them the fire of the Holy Spirit.

Even now, a little while later, I still feel energized in my body by the Holy Spirit. This is such a good thing to do and such a good thing to feel. Even as I write this testimony, I feel the bubbling up of the Spirit that started when I went to Toronto and experienced the fire of God there.

As I journaled, here is what God spoke to me about this experience:

You are experiencing the baptism of fire that I promised with the baptism of My Holy Spirit. It is a cleansing fire, a holy healing fire, so let your body remain in this state for as long as you can. You have been asking Me for a new anointing to heal the sick, and this is a new beginning, a small beginning of that. This year you will see what you have longed for. Let Me restore your body, soul, and spirit, for this last year has been a battle zone, you have experienced much buffeting, but now it is a new time of grace and progress in all your heart desires.

Chapter 2

WHERE DO EMOTIONS COME FROM? OLD SELF VERSUS NEW SELF

*In reference to your former manner of life, you
lay aside the **old self**, which is being corrupted
in accordance with the **lusts of deceit**.*
—EPHESIANS 4:22

EMOTIONS ARE PRODUCED BY EITHER THE "OLD SELF" OR THE "NEW SELF"

My old self operated when I lived in the kingdom of darkness, separated from Jesus. My new self is the new creation I have become now that I am a part of God's Kingdom. The gods behind one kingdom are in conflict with the God of the other Kingdom. In stepping from my old self to my new self, I am shedding any thoughts and emotions I still have that were part of my former darkened lifestyle where I served the prince of the power of the air, and I am putting on Christ's thoughts and emotions and serving the true risen Lord. Banished are fear, anger, anxiety, unforgiveness, and false guilt.

CHARITY

EMOTIONS: ARE THEY REALLY THAT BIG OF A DEAL?

We may be tempted to disregard or diminish the importance of our feelings, but Scripture has much to say about them. In fact, it turns out emotions are a decidedly key player, not only in our spiritual walk in general but in our spiritual warfare specifically.

Satan is thoroughly defeated and not a threat to us (see 1 John 4:4). We know greater is Holy Spirit in us than any spirit in the world, so how does the enemy end up sneaking into our lives? Where does he get in?

Genesis 3:1 says that the serpent was the most crafty and cunning of all the animals. His strategy is so subtle, the devil and his cohorts prefer we not even realize they are infiltrating. We understand that if we actively engage in sin then we open ourselves up to darkness. If we purposefully practice evil, then our enemy has the legal right to affect our lives and influence us negatively. So we know better than to play with Ouija boards, lie to our bosses, or cheat on our spouses. That's sin, and we don't participate!

WHAT JESUS SAID

But that's an Old Covenant version of sin, and Jesus has a different take on it. In the Sermon on the Mount, Jesus taught, *"You have heard that it was said, 'You shall not commit adultery'; but I say to you that everyone who looks at a woman with lust for her has already committed **adultery with her in his heart***" (Matt. 5:27-28).

Jesus also said, "You have heard that the ancients were told, 'You shall not commit murder' and *'Whoever commits murder shall be liable to the court.' But I say to you that **everyone who is angry** with his brother shall be guilty before the court"* (Matt. 5:21-22).

Jesus wanted us to understand that it's not just outward behavior; it is our inner attitudes and feelings that He cares about. He came to teach us a different way, a different Kingdom. It's an inner Kingdom— the Kingdom of the heart.

We want to live like Jesus, live holy, so that we can be sure the enemy has no hold or claim on us and no power over us (see John 14:30). We're living outwardly holy lives, so why is there a struggle? How do the forces of darkness have any influence? It is true that Jesus disarmed satan and stripped him of power, which means that the only power he has is what we give to him (see Col. 2:15).

We see through these scriptures that it is not only the obvious outward sins that give the enemy access but also the hidden sins of our hearts. The way we feel about our in-laws and our neighbors. The thoughts we think about our pastor and our peers. The emotions we entertain about ourselves and our future. Are they holy and godly and good?

ENTRY POINTS OF EMOTION

James 4:7 promises that if we resist the devil he will flee! But what is the first half of that verse? *Submit yourselves to God*, then resist the devil, then he will flee. Now if we are aware of sin in our hearts and purposefully choose to ignore it, our prayers won't be answered (see Ps. 66:18). So what kind of submission to God are we talking about? What kind of sin should we be on guard against, and where are the enemy's entry points?

1. Harboring Anger

We re-empower the enemy in our lives when we harbor anger and let the sun go down on our wrath. God says that not letting go of anger gives the enemy a foothold in our hearts and lives: *"Be angry, and yet do not sin; do not let the sun go down on your anger, and do not give the devil an opportunity"* (Eph. 4:26-27).

This is encouraging because here we see that anger is not the sin because we are able to be angry and not sin. Harboring the anger, continually living in the anger, and not releasing it to God—that is where the momentary, benign anger crosses the line and becomes unhealthy, dangerous, sinful anger that allows the enemy a place in our lives.

Ecclesiastes 7:9 says we must not let anger lodge within us or else we are fools. So while we may experience a rush of anger in the heat of the moment, we do not let it live and dwell and abide and get comfortable taking up residence inside our hearts.

2. Indulging in Anxiety

Anxiety is another way we let the enemy influence our lives. We may not consider worry to be a sin, but if we are worrying we are not expressing faith in God. And anything not of faith is sin (see Rom. 14:23).

Jesus Himself actually had quite a bit to say about this seemingly inconsequential emotion in Matthew 6:25-34:

> *Therefore I tell you, do not worry about your life, what you will eat or drink; or about your body, what you will wear. Is not life more than food, and the body more than clothes? Look at the birds of the air; they do not sow or reap or store away in barns, and yet your heavenly Father feeds them. Are you not much more valuable than they? Can any one of you by worrying add a single hour to your life?*
>
> *And why do you worry about clothes? See how the flowers of the field grow. They do not labor or spin. Yet I tell you that not even Solomon in all his splendor was dressed like one of these. If that is how God clothes the grass of the field, which is here today and tomorrow is thrown into the fire, will he not much more clothe you—you of little faith?*
>
> *So do not worry, saying, "What shall we eat?" or "What shall we drink?" or "What shall we wear?" For the pagans run after all these things, and your heavenly Father knows that you need them. But seek first his kingdom and his righteousness, and all these things will be given to you as well. Therefore do not worry about tomorrow, for tomorrow will worry about itself. Each day has enough trouble of its own* (NIV).

We see here that worry is not as harmless as the enemy would lead us to believe. When we allow ourselves to entertain anxious thoughts and feelings, we are basically saying, "God, I don't believe that You will provide for me. I don't believe You will take care of me." We are telling God that we don't trust Him, and without faith it is impossible to please Him (see Heb. 11:6).

3. *Entertaining Fear*

We also re-empower the enemy through our fear (see Heb. 2:15). This is a big one! We need to understand that fear is simply faith in reverse. Another way to say it is that fear is faith in satan.

Our faith is incredibly strong. We move mountains with it (see Matt. 17:20). Therefore, we are responsible to pay close attention to how we wield such a mighty weapon by carefully considering where we place our faith. We must not have more faith in the power of the devil to get us than we have faith in the power of our heavenly Father to protect, provide, and care for us.

Job said, *"What I feared has come upon me; what I dreaded has happened to me"* (Job 3:25 NIV). He was expecting the worst, and according to his faith it was done unto him (see Matt. 9:29).

The story of Job was written as an example to us, showing why we never want to indulge ungodly fear in our hearts or in our minds. Ever.

4. *Withholding Forgiveness*

One of the most dangerous ways we inadvertently re-empower the enemy is when we walk in unforgiveness. The Bible says that we are creating a space in our lives for the devil to come in if we entertain unforgiveness in our hearts.

> But one whom you forgive anything, I forgive also; for indeed what I have forgiven, if I have forgiven anything, I did it for your sakes in the presence of Christ, so that no advantage would be taken of us by Satan, for we are not ignorant of his schemes (2 Corinthians 2:10-11).

Satan is called the accuser of the brethren, and he constantly accuses others to us (see Rev. 12:10). He lies and twists truth and tries to make us see others through a distorted lens, tempting us to walk in bitterness, judgment, and resentment toward them.

In the sixth chapter of Matthew we find the Lord teaching His disciples how to pray. Jesus then makes a very direct, unmistakable declaration: *"For if you forgive other people when they sin against you, your heavenly Father will also forgive you. But if you do not forgive others their sins, your Father will not forgive your sins"* (Matt. 6:14-15 NIV).

Clearly, walking in unforgiveness is not an option. This is more than enough reason to forgive everyone of everything at all times! However, as if to drive the point home, just a few chapters later Jesus underscores this when He shares the parable of the unforgiving servant in Matthew 18. The ungrateful servant was forgiven his enormous debt, yet instead of being thankful he turned around and demanded payment from his fellow slave of a much lesser debt.

In the parable, the servant's master was moved with anger over this injustice and had the unforgiving servant turned over to the tormenters to be tortured. Jesus taught that we must extend mercy and forgive each other from our heart, otherwise we too will experience torment (see Matt. 18:21-35). Therefore we see how withholding mercy, compassion, and forgiveness opens the door to pain and allows the enemy into our lives.

5. *Accepting False Guilt*

A fifth way we let the enemy into our lives is through false guilt. Essentially, guilt is not forgiving ourselves, so this is closely related to unforgiveness. However, it seems as Christians we are often much better at forgiving our family, friends, and even our enemies than we are at forgiving ourselves.

We experience false guilt when we still feel bad over something for which we have already confessed and repented. Once we have repented of a sin, God no longer remembers it (see Heb. 10:17). As far as the east is from the west, so far has He removed those transgressions from us (see Ps. 103:12).

Again, it is the accuser of the brethren who heaps condemnation upon us and makes us feel guilty about things that God has chosen to forget. Sometimes we need to be more like our heavenly Father and develop a case of holy amnesia!

The apostle Paul reminds us that there is now *no condemnation* for those who are in Christ Jesus (see Rom. 8:1). Therefore, we must not denigrate Jesus' sacrificial death by presuming our sin is more powerful than His cleansing blood. It is finished, so we can let go of false guilt and be set free from condemnation. Hallelujah!

TAPPING INTO GOD'S PEACE AND JOY

As we can see, far from being unrelated to our walk with God or disconnected from our spirituality, emotions are absolutely central to it. In fact, because emotional freedom is vital to our well-being, I have co-written a book on emotional freedom techniques. *EFT for Christians: Tapping into God's Peace and Joy* explores one more gift of healing God gave us in the form of energy psychology.

EFT is a God-created physiological technique that empowers us with liberty and choice concerning our feelings and how we experience them. It involves tapping gently on acupressure points of the face and upper body. This tapping can release, via the neurological system, pent-up emotional stress of daily and long-term events and memories.

Hundreds of university research projects show why EFT works so well and the extraordinary testimonies are moving. From returning combat soldiers to Rwandan refugees to school shooting survivors, EFT has been exceptionally effective in releasing various traumas including anxiousness, fears, and persistent sadness. Indeed, Dr. Joseph Mercola, founder of the most visited natural health website in the world, describes the immediate and powerful results he witnesses from tapping as "therapy at the speed of light."[6]

We all have stress of varying degrees in our lives, and stress is not all bad. It's our reaction to the stress, when we allow it to cause us to be stressed, that becomes a problem. So whether it's the traffic commute, an upcoming exam, or a challenging co-worker, we want to neutralize the effects of unhealthy stress before it causes damage in our relationships, in our spiritual life, and in our bodies.

KINGDOM OF EMOTIONS

As discussed in the first chapter, there are various reasons we have developed this wrong idea that we are not supposed to live by emotions. However, as we will continue to learn, according to Scripture they are positively central to our lives!

Joy strengthens us (see Neh. 8:10). Peace rules us (see Col. 3:15). Love compels us (see 2 Cor. 5:14). Compassion moves us (see Matt. 9:36). What part of compassion, peace, and joy do we not feel?

I love what Pastor Kris Vallotton of Bethel Church says about Romans 14:17. Because righteousness, peace, and joy in the Holy Ghost are the Kingdom of God, that means that "two thirds of the Kingdom is felt!" Obviously this demonstrates that Father cares much about our feelings and desires greatly for us to feel what He feels. It is His good pleasure to give us the Kingdom, and that includes all of His holy, healing Kingdom emotions.

---

6   Dr. Joseph Mercola's *Emotional Freedom Techniques*, Disc 1, Introduction. See www.GloryWaves.org/survivor for more information.

MARK

SPIRITUAL SOURCES

Flowing thoughts in our minds come from *two* primary *spiritual sources* (see John 7:37-39).

Satan brings to the battlefield of our minds flowing thoughts that are congruent with his nature. He is the accuser of the brethren, the father of lies, the adversary and the enemy and a thief who comes only to steal and kill and destroy my faith, hope, love, and life (see Rev. 12:10-11; John 8:44; Matt. 13:39; John 10:10). So any spontaneous thoughts lining up with the nature of satan I reject, as they are coming from demons.

The Holy Spirit reveals to us our new nature in Christ, flooding our minds with *flowing* thoughts that are congruent with His nature. He is the Comforter; the Spirit of Truth; the One who convicts (convinces) without condemning; the one who edifies and comforts; whose voice is loving, gentle, patient, and filled with mercy (see John 14:16; 16:13; 16:8; 2 Cor. 7:3; 1 Cor. 13; 14:3; Gal. 6:1; 1 Thess. 5:14; 2 Cor. 1:3). All spontaneous thoughts lining up with the nature of Christ I accept, as they are coming from the Holy Spirit.

ANALYTICAL THOUGHTS

Analytical thoughts are connected and constructed with my brain, thus coming from *self.* Logic and reasoning controlled by self would be considered my thoughts; for example, 2 + 2 = 4. Another way of saying this is that man's reasoning is the reasoning he does when outside God's sanctuary or when not in the presence of the Holy Spirit (see Ps. 73:16-17). When Asaph reasoned outside the sanctuary, he reasoned himself into a pit of despair (see Ps. 73:1-15). When he finally came into the presence of the Lord, he *perceived.* He received revelation knowledge, and his depression was replaced with God's truth (see Ps. 73:18-20).

I used to spend 80 percent of my time living in negative, accusative thoughts. Now I spend about 98-plus percent of my time living in positive, uplifting thoughts because I have taken every thought captive to the obedience of Christ (see 1 Cor. 13:13; 2 Cor. 10:5). Everyone needs a revelation of the following:

Stepping from the Old Self to the New Self: Satan's Lies versus God's Truths

	OLD NATURE LIES TO "PUT OFF"	NEW-CREATION TRUTHS TO "PUT ON"
1	*I can't...*	I can do all things through Christ who strengthens me (see Phil. 4:13).
2	*I lack...*	My God shall supply all my needs according to His riches in glory in Christ Jesus (see Phil. 4:19).
3	*I fear...*	God has not given me a spirit of fear, but of power and of love and of a sound mind (see 2 Tim. 1:7).
4	*I don't have faith.*	God has given to me a measure of faith (see Rom. 12:3).
5	*I'm weak.*	The Lord is the strength of my life (see Ps. 27:1).
6	*Satan has really got me.*	Greater is He that is in me than he that is in the world (see 1 John 4:4).
7	*I'm defeated.*	God always causes me to triumph in Christ Jesus (see 2 Cor. 2:14).
8	*I don't know what to do.*	Christ Jesus is made unto me wisdom from God (see 1 Cor. 1:30).
9	*I expect to get sick once in a while.*	By His stripes I am healed (see Isa. 53:5).
10	*I am so worried and frustrated.*	I can cast all my cares upon Him, because He cares for me (see 1 Pet. 5:7).

	OLD NATURE LIES TO "PUT OFF"	NEW-CREATION TRUTHS TO "PUT ON"
11	*I'm in bondage.*	Where the Spirit of the Lord is, there is liberty (see 2 Cor. 3:17).
12	*I feel so condemned.*	I experience no condemnation because I am in Christ Jesus (see Rom. 8:1).

Putting Off the Old Self and Putting On the New Self

	LIVING SEPARATE FROM JESUS PRODUCES THE "STRESS RESPONSE"— PROMOTES ILLNESS. WE "PUT OFF" THIS OLD SELF.	LIVING AWARE OF JESUS PRODUCES THE "RELAXATION RESPONSE"—PROMOTES HEALTH. WE "PUT ON" THIS NEW SELF.
Beliefs and Pictures	Not enough, overwhelmed, griping, blaming, timid, rushing, distracted, and other demonic beliefs.	Believer in God's goodness, receiver of mercy, adopted, enabled, victorious, blessed, protected, cared for, and other godly beliefs.
Resulting Emotions	Fear, anger, insecurity, worry, anxiety, guilt, shame, depression.	Fruits of the Spirit, compassion, gentleness, gratitude, love, joy, peace.
Resulting Health	Digestive problems, insomnia, hypertension, heart disease, cancer, ulcers, arthritis, colds, to name a few.	Healthy digestion, restful sleep, vitality, energy, robust heart, strong immune system, pain-free body and joints, to name a few.

THE CROSS WAS ENOUGH

For by one offering [sacrifice] *He* [Jesus] ***has perfected forever*** *those who* ***are being sanctified*** (Hebrews 10:14 NKJV).

In the spirit world, the perfection is *already completed*. It endures even while we are in the process of working out our salvation (see Phil. 2:12-13). If I acknowledge the following 12 things as already completed and finished and speak them forth as my personal, present-tense, positive reality, I *write them upon my heart*.[7] This allows me to experience these truths.

I am complete in Jesus Christ. Jesus has provided me: restored fellowship, new heart desires, His righteousness, power over sin, His glory, the Holy Spirit, health, prosperity, hope, joy, peace, adoption into His family and eternal life.

Watch this music video by MercyMe[8] as they show how the cross has made you "Flawless." It is awesome and has already been listened to over 15 million times. We have their album *Welcome to the New* and have listened to it at least 100 times. They have a revelation of *grace-based living*, and hearing it releases tremendous life. It captures the fact that Jesus has done it all on the cross. We can relax and go with the flow. He's got us!

GOING DEEPER: THE 12 THINGS JESUS ACCOMPLISHED FOR US ON THE CROSS

Calvary is the central event in history. What Christ provided is extremely positive and worth pondering and visualizing and feeling. These gifts cover *every* area of our lives, making us complete in Christ (see Col. 1:28).

---

7   See Chapter 21 of *The Anatomy of a Miracle* by Dr. Jim Richards.
8   www.youtube.com/watch?v=wjLlLPZderk

1. *Jesus took my rebellion and independence and restored to me daily fellowship with God.*

All of us like sheep have gone astray, each of us has turned to his own way; but the Lord has caused the iniquity of us all to fall on Him (Isaiah 53:6).

The glory which You have given Me I have given to them, that they may be one, just as We are one (John 17:22).

- My lack and need: rebellion, independence
- Jesus' gift: restored fellowship
- Kingdom reality established: I have fellowship with God, Eden restored, walks in the garden in the cool of the day.
- Kingdom emotions experienced: I feel loved, accepted, warmed, and inspired.

2. *Jesus removed my darkened heart, and I have a new heart ablaze with God's desires.*

*He was crushed for our **iniquities*** (Isaiah 53:5).

Moreover, I will give you a new heart and put a new spirit within you (Ezekiel 36:26).

- My lack and need: heart's iniquities
- Jesus' gift: a new heart and new spirit
- Kingdom reality established: I have a new, soft heart that hungers after God.
- Kingdom emotions experienced: I feel peace, passion, holiness, joy, and contentment.

3. *Jesus removed my sinfulness, and now I wear Christ's robe of righteousness.*

> *He made Him who knew no sin to be sin on our behalf, so that we might become the righteousness of God in Him* (2 Corinthians 5:21).

- My lack and need: sins
- Jesus' gift: His righteousness
- Kingdom reality established: I put on Christ's shining white robe of righteousness.
- Kingdom emotions experienced: I feel clean, peaceful, grateful, overflowing joy.

4. *Jesus removed the power of sin and now I have a power and passion to live in holiness.*

> *He Himself bore our sins in His body on the cross, so that we might die to sin and live to righteousness; for by His wounds you were healed* (1 Peter 2:24).

- My lack and need: defeat by the power of sin
- Jesus' gift: power to live righteously
- Kingdom reality established: My compulsion toward sinful desires is removed.
- Kingdom emotions experienced: I feel free, released, joyful, and full of peace.

5. *Jesus has taken my shame and now I radiate His glory.*

> *Jesus, the author and perfecter of faith, who for the joy set before Him endured the cross, despising the shame* (Hebrews 12:2).

The glory which You have given Me I have given to them, that they may be one, just as We are one (John 17:22).

- My lack and need: shame

- Jesus' gift: God's glory

- Kingdom reality established: I radiate the shekinah glory of God.

- Kingdom emotions experienced: I feel peace, joy, excitement, honor, acceptance.

6. Jesus removed the curse I deserved, and I now walk by the Spirit experiencing God's blessings.

*Christ redeemed us from the **curse of the Law**...in order that in Christ Jesus the blessing of Abraham might come to the Gentiles, so that we would receive the promise of the Spirit through faith* (Galatians 3:13-14).

- My lack and need: curse

- Jesus' gift: God's blessing, the Holy Spirit

- Kingdom reality established: I have a new Resident living within—the Holy Spirit.

- Kingdom emotions experienced: I feel empowered and energized with joy unspeakable.

7. Jesus has taken my sickness, and I now live in divine health.

*By His **wounds** you were **healed*** (1 Peter 2:24).

- My lack and need: wounds

- Jesus' gift: healing

- Kingdom reality established: I am healed.

- Kingdom emotions experienced: I feel healthy, joyful, thankful, content.

8. *Jesus has taken my poverty and I now live in abundance.*

For you know the grace of our Lord Jesus Christ, that though He was rich, yet for your sake He became poor, so that you through His poverty might become rich (2 Corinthians 8:9).

- My lack and need: poverty
- Jesus' gift: His riches
- Kingdom reality established: I have more than enough.
- Kingdom emotions experienced: I feel secure, peaceful, grateful, and excited.

9. *Jesus has taken my sorrow and regret of what could have been; now hope fills my heart daily.*

*Our **sorrows** He carried* (Isaiah 53:4).

*Christ in you, the **hope** of glory* (Colossians 1:27).

- My lack and need: sorrows, regrets
- Jesus' gift: hope
- Kingdom reality established: God makes everything work out for good for me!
- Kingdom emotions experienced: I feel peaceful, relaxed, joyful, calm, and thankful.

10. *Jesus has taken my anxiety; now joy and peace guard my heart.*

> *In everything by prayer and supplication with thanksgiving let your requests be made known to God. And the peace of God, which surpasses all comprehension, will guard your hearts and your minds in Christ Jesus* (Philippians 4:6-7).

- My lack and need: anxiety
- Jesus' gift: joy, peace
- Kingdom reality established: I know God hears and answers my prayers.
- Kingdom emotions experienced: I feel peace, joy, excitement, honor, acceptance.

11. *Jesus has removed my fear of rejection and adopted me into His family, passionately loving me.*

> *About the ninth hour Jesus cried out with a loud voice, saying, "Eli, Eli, lama sabachthani?" that is, "My God, My God, why have You forsaken Me?"* (Matthew 27:46)

> *He predestined us to adoption as sons through Jesus Christ to Himself, according to the kind intention of His will* (Ephesians 1:5).

- My lack and need: rejection, fear
- Jesus' gift: adoption as a son of God
- Kingdom reality established: I am adopted into a wonderful, supportive, multi-gifted family.
- Kingdom emotions experienced: I feel accepted, encouraged, loved, and nurtured

12. Jesus experienced my death, and I now have eternal life.

For the wages of sin is death, but the free gift of God is eternal life in Christ Jesus our Lord (Romans 6:23).

- My lack and need: death

- Jesus' gift: eternal life

- Kingdom reality established: I spend eternity in the presence of God.

- Kingdom emotions experienced: I feel peace, joy, excitement, honor, acceptance, and love.

HOW MUCH BETTER?

If positive thinking has value, then how much more powerful is it to ponder the new Kingdom realities established at Calvary?

If positive visualization has value, then how much more powerful is it to use godly imagination and see the Kingdom realities established at Calvary?

The cross was enough. I believe, speak, and hold in my imagination the reality that *the cross has made me flawless!* I put on what Christ provided.

TWO-WAY JOURNALING EXERCISES[9]

Consolidating, Expanding, and Living in These Truths

Considering the greatness of God's sacrifice to allow His beloved Son to come to earth to experience this terrible death and separation, as well as the pain and suffering Jesus was willing to experience to

---

9   www.cwgministries.org/4keys

purchase these victories for me, it is proper that I take the time to fully internalize these realities so I can *live* them.

I find the easiest way to do this is to journal about each of them, asking God for a picture concerning what my life looks like when I am walking in each. Then, if I can see these images as one magnificent picture, the image will stay with me and I will be able to easily memorize the vision and walk in it, living and walking by the Spirit (see Gal. 5:25). Perhaps get an artist to do your picture justice. I also choose to spend more time journaling about each of these 12 blessings of Calvary so God can let me see them in fullness and walk in them in completeness.

Visions and Journaling Concerning the 12 Provisions of Calvary

	PROVISION OF CALVARY	GOD'S VISION	GOD'S RHEMA
1	Spiritual intimacy with God: *"They may be one, just as We are one"* (John 17:22).	A silver cord connecting God's Spirit to my spirit.	This is the cord that cannot be broken. All that I am flows through it to you. Tune to this life flow within, constantly.
2	A healed heart: *"I will give you a new heart and put a new spirit within you"* (Ezek. 36:26).	God giving me a heart transplant.	This new heart is not wounded, proud, resistant, or broken. Cherish it. Love it. Depend on it.
3	Adorned with Christ's righteousness: *"We might become the righteousness of God in Him"* (2 Cor. 5:21).	A white, clean, spotless robe that He puts on me.	You are adorned as a bride on her wedding day, made pure and holy by what I have given you—My righteousness. Wear it proudly.

	PROVISION OF CALVARY	GOD'S VISION	GOD'S RHEMA
4	Power over sin: "*He Himself bore our sins in His body on the cross, so that we might die to sin and live to righteousness*" (1 Pet. 2:24).	Satan's head crushed by Christ's heel.	Satan withers in defeat under My heel. He no longer has any power to defeat you. Do not welcome him in.
5	Divine glory: "*The glory which You have given Me I have given to them*" (John 17:22).	I exude a radiant glow for all to see.	I have made you completely new. You now shine with My glory. Radiate My Spirit.
6	The Holy Spirit: "*We would receive the promise of the Spirit through faith*" (Gal. 3:13-14).	A ball of light is residing in my belly.	I have placed My Spirit within you as a permanent resident. Draw from Him and yield to Him.
7	Physical healing: "*By His wounds you were healed*" (1 Pet. 2:24).	A whipped body purchased my healing.	I paid a huge price to ensure you would walk in divine health.
8	Financial prosperity: "*You through His poverty might become rich*" (2 Cor. 8:9).	A seesaw with an empty money sack on the low end and a full sack on the high end.	Everything is a divine exchange. I gave up all My riches so you could have abundance. Receive the abundance that is yours.
9	Hope: "*Christ in you, the hope of glory*" (Col. 1:27).	My mind shines with the light of hope.	In a world of hopelessness, you offer hope to all you touch.

	PROVISION OF CALVARY	GOD'S VISION	GOD'S RHEMA
10	Peace: *"In everything by prayer and supplication with thanksgiving let your requests be made known to God. And the peace of God, which surpasses all comprehension, will guard your hearts and your minds in Christ Jesus"* (Phil. 4:6-7).	A protective shield of peace covers my heart and my mind.	I hear and respond to each and every request, granting My grace to meet the need. So trust in Me and you will walk in peace.
11	A family: *"He predestined us to adoption as sons through Jesus Christ to Himself"* (Eph. 1:5).	A happy family unit enjoying a meal together.	I have given you a loving family to respond to all your needs. Reach out to them and receive.
12	Eternal life: *"The free gift of God is eternal life through Jesus Christ our Lord"* (Rom. 6:23).	Forever together in heaven.	Life on earth is a speck in eternity. Keep your eyes fastened on the goal.

Your Turn: Visions and Journaling Concerning 12 Gifts Provided at Calvary

Journaling question: "Lord, what would You like to say to me concerning the new realities You provided for me at Calvary? Please grant me a clear picture of each of these 12 realities and what they look like as they are lived out in my life. I want to see these pictures clearly so I can live continuously and only in them, beholding them day and night."

	PROVISION OF CALVARY	GOD'S VISION	GOD'S RHEMA
1	Spiritual intimacy with God: *"They may be one, just as We are one"* (John 17:22).		
2	A healed heart: *"I will give you a new heart and put a new spirit within you"* (Ezek. 36:26).		
3	Adorned with Christ's righteousness: *"We might become the righteousness of God in Him"* (2 Cor. 5:21).		
4	Power over sin: *"He Himself bore our sins in His body on the cross, so that we might die to sin and live to righteousness"* (1 Pet. 2:24).		
5	Divine glory: *"The glory which You have given Me I have given to them"* (John 17:22).		
6	The Holy Spirit: *"We would receive the promise of the Spirit through faith"* (Gal. 3:13-14).		
7	Physical healing: *"By His wounds you were healed"* (1 Pet. 2:24).		
8	Financial prosperity: *"You through His poverty might become rich"* (2 Cor. 8:9).		
9	Hope: *"Christ in you, the hope of glory"* (Col. 1:27).		

	PROVISION OF CALVARY	GOD'S VISION	GOD'S RHEMA
10	Peace: *"In everything by prayer and supplication with thanksgiving let your requests be made known to God. And the peace of God, which surpasses all comprehension, will guard your hearts and your minds in Christ Jesus"* (Phil. 4:6-7).		
11	A family: *"He predestined us to adoption as sons through Jesus Christ to Himself"* (Eph. 1:5).		
12	Eternal life: *"The free gift of God is eternal life through Jesus Christ our Lord"* (Rom. 6:23).		

ACTION EXERCISES

Read these articles:

- www.cwgministries.org/FaithAndLove
- www.cwgministries.org/DemonicThoughts

Journaling: "Lord, are there any old nature beliefs (lies) that are still resident within me?" List any that come to you (you can review the chart above, "Old Nature Lies," and the article above on demonic thoughts). Complete a "New Creation Celebration: Replacing Beliefs"[10] (22 minutes) for any/each lie. You will find that God may want to come

---

10 www.cwgministries.org/beliefs

back and discuss the same topic daily, hitting it from different angles each day and deepening it until the old nature belief is completely *out* of your life. Follow the leading of the Holy Spirit. He knows best.

Read www.cwgministries.org/PerfectPeace and begin imagining yourself clothed in the 12 provisions of the cross. How does that feel? Bask in the vision and the feeling. Journal what God is speaking to you about putting on these 12 provisions of Calvary. Make sure to listen to the free online music video that puts these truths to music in a very powerful way.

The above application exercises may take you several weeks to complete. That is fine. Continue on with this assignment even as you move forward reading the following chapters.

Chapter 3

STEPPING FROM OLD SELF TO NEW SELF

*I am transformed as I **gaze upon** who I am in Christ. Transforming power is released as I look.*

Have you noticed how you are changed by what you are looking at? When we engage in worship, lifting up our eyes and beholding Christ's glory, we are transformed into His likeness. Peace, comfort, and rest fill our soul. We are kept in perfect peace when our imagination is fixed on God.[11]

On the other hand, we can imagine in our minds that our spouse or friend who is late arriving home has been in an auto accident, and as we gaze at that picture we become filled with fear and worry.

The Bible tells us clearly that we are transformed *while we look* (see 2 Cor. 3:18; 4:18). The Israelites in the wilderness *looked* at their

---

11 For more on this, see www.cwgministries.org/PerfectPeace.

adversities rather than at the assurance of the Lord that *He had given them the Promised Land.* As a result of where they fixed their eyes, they were moved to fear and unbelief and they *died* in the wilderness rather than receiving the destiny God had said was theirs (see Heb. 3-4).

So we have choices. We could contemplate our sin, and sinfulness could grow within us. We could consider the weakness of our flesh and become depressed. We could focus on the antichrist, and fear would grow within us. We could observe the evil in the world, and despair, rage, and feelings of helplessness would grow within us. We could gaze upon the shortcomings of others and judge these, and these same shortcomings will grow within us.

We become that which we gaze upon and judge, which is why we are told to fix our eyes on Jesus and judge not (see John 5:30; 12:47; 2 Cor. 10:12; James 4:11; 5:9), but instead to honor all (see 1 Pet. 2:17). I know, because I have tried each of these erroneous ways of living.

Jesus said, *"Take care what you listen to"* (Mark 4:24). *Take care* is *blepo* in the Greek, and it means "see and feel" (Strong's G991). This verse instructs us to envision the words God is speaking to us. Take time to 1) listen with the ears of our heart, 2) see with the eyes of our heart, and 3) feel God's resulting emotions in our heart. *This is biblical meditation.* God is granting supernatural understanding! I hear, see, and feel His heart toward me. I then speak and act from a heart burning with revelation (see Luke 24:13-25). This is life as it is meant to be!

In the "New Creation Celebration" meditations,[12] we spend time *gazing upon* who we are in Christ. We also spend quite a bit of time hearing from the Lord and obeying what He says. That is why they are so transformational. We become reflections of the One we gaze upon.

---

12   www.cwgministries.org/emotions

> *God's promises, seen as already fulfilled,*
> *produce faith, attracting miracles.*

Jesus lived in the midst of an evil generation, an evil government, and a legalistic, pharisaical religious sect, and yet He walked in peace, power, and authority. He wasn't down, depressed, upset, or frustrated. Where were His eyes fixed? Where was He looking that allowed Him to live in peace, power, and authority? Ever wonder if the Church can do the same thing today? Amidst the 24-hour newscasts of all satan is doing, can we live in peace, releasing miracles and His Kingdom everywhere we walk? I believe we can.

NEW CREATION: POSITIONAL REALITY, PROCESS, OR BOTH?

Let's see if we can answer this question.

Becoming a New Creation Happened in the Past

> *Therefore if anyone is in Christ, he **is** a new creature; the old things passed away; behold, new things **have come*** (2 Corinthians 5:17).

At the point of your salvation, were some sins miraculously, *instantly* removed from your life? Can you remember this occurring? Can you recall something that immediately dropped out of your life? How about something that instantaneously became new?

Becoming a New Creation Is Also an Ongoing Process

> ***Put on*** *the new self who* ***is being*** *renewed to a* ***true*** *knowledge [i.e., knowledge birthed by the Spirit] according to the image of the One who created him* (Colossians 3:10).

> ***Work out*** *your salvation...for it is God who is at work in you* (Philippians 2:12-13).

The Israelites fought to receive their Promised Land, which God had said was theirs. So too, we fight to experience our promised destinies. Healing, freedom, and deliverance are most often a process. These things were legally provided for us by Christ's death on the cross, but now we have to fight to establish them in our lives.

Here is a verse which perfectly sums up the two truths: *For by one offering* [sacrifice] *He* [Jesus] *has perfected forever those who are being sanctified"* (Heb. 10:14 NKJV). So yes, jurisdictionally it is complete, but practically we are working it out. We are becoming who we are.

WHY WOULD GOD MAKE THIS A GROWING PROCESS?

As the Israelites fought to enter into their promised blessings, we too must learn to put on our new-creation personalities daily. God explains *why* He makes this a process:

> ***I will not drive them out*** [i.e., their enemies] *before you in a single year, that the land may not become desolate and the beasts of the field become too numerous for you. I will drive them out before you* ***little by little,*** *until you become fruitful and take possession of the land* (Exodus 23:29-30).

Wow! That explains a lot. God will not give me freedom in an area where I am not ready to maintain that freedom, because if He did numerous "beasts" would encroach and I would not have the capacity to deal effectively with them. Reminds me of Jesus saying if you cast out a demon and don't fill the area with righteousness, seven times more demons come back (see Luke 11:24-26).

Not all of our enemies are removed at the point of salvation.

TRANSFORMATION FLOWS FROM THE SPIRIT

So is this transformation something I do or something He does as I open myself to Him?

> *Be renewed in the **spirit** of your mind, and **put on the new self*** (Ephesians 4:23-24).

Spiritual transformation is not forced external obedience to rules but a changed heart and mind through the indwelling work of the Holy Spirit as you encounter God. In Romans 12:2 it says, *"Be transformed by the renewing of your **mind**."* Here is a verse explaining how our minds are renewed.

> *Then He **opened their minds to understand** the Scriptures* (Luke 24:45).

So we see this transformation comes as I present myself to God and experience Him, His revelation, and His life-changing power.[13]

Another time the word *transformed* appears in the New Testament is, *"But we all, with unveiled face, beholding as in a mirror the glory of the Lord, are being transformed into the same image from glory to glory, just as from the Lord, the Spirit"* (2 Cor. 3:18).

---

13 See *The Supernatural Transformation Series* by Phil Mason, especially Volume 3: *The Heart Journey.*

This verse clearly says the transformation process involves seeing and holding an image before us using the eyes of our hearts. As we behold, we are transformed into that which we are gazing upon. This is really awesome, and really different from me attempting to change myself by memorizing a rule and then trying to obey it.

The Greek word in the above passages is *metamorphoō* (Strong's G3339), which is where we get the word *metamorphosis*. This metamorphosis is taking place *"while we look not at the things which are seen, but at the things which are not seen"* (2 Cor. 4:18).

The only other place in the New Testament that *metamorphoō* is used is when Jesus was "transfigured" before the disciples and His face and garments shone (see Matt. 17:2; Mark 9:2).

CHARITY

CHASING BUTTERFLIES

I love the revelation that Dr. Jim Richards, creator of Heart Physics, shares on transformation in his excellent book, *Moving Your Invisible Boundaries*:

> There is no promise of transformation apart from some type of meditative process.... This is not the kind of change where you are trying to become something you are not. It is the process whereby what you are changes you. The caterpillar doesn't *become* a butterfly. The caterpillar *is* a butterfly in a different state. When we yield to the righteousness of God, already in us, it transmutes us to manifest outwardly what God has already made us to be inwardly.

Amen! That is such a powerful picture to help us understand our new-creation reality. God confirmed this insight one evening when I fell asleep and had a dream. Through it, Holy Spirit reminded me that the heart of this book and message is all about transformation. We meditate in order to experience Kingdom emotions because those Kingdom emotions transform us.

In my dream I was a teaching assistant, but I kept telling the students the wrong thing. The main teacher explained what I really needed to do was have all the kids go chase butterflies. So I told them to, and they did!

As we teach in our book *Hearing God Through Your Dreams: Understanding the Language God Speaks at Night,* we can easily translate the dream message by asking a few key questions, such as what is the main action in the dream?[14] Well, in this dream I was teaching. Next, I just match that up with my waking world by asking, where am I teaching someone something? This pinpoints the area of my life to which the dream is speaking.

As I mentioned, the setting of the dream—that is, what was going on in my waking life when I had the dream—was that I was meditating on this writing project. Now before publication, the working title of this book was *Spiritual Transformations.* So in waking life I am "teaching" through this book, and the main Teacher, who is the Holy Spirit, is leading and guiding me on what's most important.

UNPACKING THE DREAM

The most important and impactful symbol was the butterflies. Butterflies, to me, are the perfect picture of transformation. Indeed, the

---

14   For more on this DAESI Dream Work Method, see www.GloryWaves.org/daesi.

Greek word used in Romans 12:2 for *transformed* is the same one we get our English word *metamorphosis* from.

God was reminding me that what we're really after is *transformation*. That is our focus, and the best part about transformation is that it's something that is done to us. Transformation is an inside job. The caterpillar doesn't struggle and strive in its own strength to will itself into a beautiful butterfly. He rests and abides and, through God's creative miracle, emerges as a brand-new creation.

Just like us. We are new creations and old things have passed away. We don't work hard to change ourselves outwardly. We are transformed from the inside out. And when are we transformed? While we look (see 2 Cor. 3:18).

We have already been made in God's image; He sees us as we are in Him, the very righteousness of God in Christ Jesus (see 2 Cor. 5:21). All we need to do is work out that perfect salvation and transformation, and it's actually easier than we have thought. Because it truly is Holy Spirit who is at work in us to accomplish this, so all we must do is see ourselves the way God sees us. Glimpse His version of us by gazing through the lens in which He is looking.

OBSERVATION CAUSES TRANSFORMATION

We want to explore some of the fascinating ways quantum physics correlates with our walk in the Spirit in general and our times of meditation and spiritual transformation specifically.[15]

One of the most mysterious yet foundational principles in the field of quantum physics is the *observer effect*. A simplified version of this

---

15   www.GloryWaves.org/quantum

principle is that when we look at something, we change it. Our very act of observing it affects it.[16]

The physicists are referring to invisible waves of energy in the quantum realm. All probabilities and possibilities are distributed along the wave. However, the wave remains in a state of potential until it is observed. When the wave is observed and measured, it "collapses." It is changed from being an invisible wave and collapses into our physical dimension as a manifested particle, such as a photon or electron—the stuff light and matter are made of.

This phenomenon is called *wave function collapse*, so for our purposes we want to understand that "collapse" means to move something from the invisible realm into the visible realm. To move something from the unseen to the seen, from the supernatural to the natural, from the spiritual to the physical, from heaven to earth.

Another exciting aspect of the quantum realm is that it is a world of potential, where any possible outcome is available at every moment in time. That is actually what the physicists tell us; that is how they define the quantum dimension.

Well, that sounds familiar to us! That's the world of faith, where all things are possible to them that believe and nothing is impossible with God (see Mark 9:23; Matt. 19:26). We know that God already gave us everything when He gave us Christ. Jesus is our Healer, He is our Provider, He is our Peace. It's all in Him and it's all ours, available right now. We have *already* been blessed with every spiritual blessing. Where? In heavenly places (see Eph. 1:3). We have *already* been given all things for life and godliness (see 2 Pet. 1:3). So all we need to do now is collapse these promised resources of the Kingdom into our everyday lives.

---

16   See Phil Mason's excellent book *Quantum Glory: The Science of Heaven Invading Earth.*

How do we do that? Through the observer effect. Hebrews 11:3 speaks to this understanding of wave function collapse when it says that *"we understand that the worlds were prepared by the word of God, so that what is seen was not made out of things which are visible."* What is seen—matter, particles, this natural world—is made out of what is unseen—waves of potential energy in the invisible spirit realm.

We see that wave function collapse is a picture in the natural world of what happens when we pray. In the realm of the spirit, every possibility is available to us in Christ—healing, provision, divine perspective. But we want to bring those heavenly resources into our physical dimension. We want these infinite possibilities of blessing in the spirit to collapse and materialize in our tangible world. Through our practiced observation and vision, these heavenly waves of glory collapse into a definite manifested miracle, a "particle" of healing or blessing, something that is concrete and available in our localized dimension of time and space.

A Real-Life Example

I explore other aspects of the supernatural science of quantum physics in our book *Hearing God Through Your Dreams,* but I want to share one more example here to illustrate this principle as it relates to our visionary prayers. I believe in your times of intercession you are already collapsing glory waves of blessing into the world, and I want to explain from a quantum scientific angle what is happening and why it's working so that you continue to do it!

One of my grad students is a medical missionary overseas. She had given a little girl all the medicine she had available, yet the child only continued to grow weaker. Having done all she could in the natural, she sent the two-year-old home with her family. And then she prayed.

In a vision, she saw Jesus go to the girl's home, lay His hands upon her, and heal her. She was in the spirit with Jesus and prayed into that vision, agreeing with what Jesus was doing and speaking life over the little girl as well.

She became the quantum observer of Jesus and collapsed that wave of potential healing from heaven into the physical world. Her visual agreement with the spirit realm became a bridge for the supernatural blessing to cross and become manifest as a miracle in the natural world.

The next day she called to check on the girl and confirmed that at the very hour she had been with the Lord and the girl in spirit—she was healed. All of a sudden, she had awakened, jumped out of bed full of energy, and begun to happily play with the other children for the rest of the day. It was an instantaneous miracle, and they were so grateful to have their little girl back!

In this way we see the observer effect in action as we walk by the Spirit, because when we observe something we change it. My student saw the wave of glory and changed it so it was no longer just a potential reality in heaven, but now it collapsed into a manifested reality on earth. Observation caused transformation.

WITNESSING HISTORY IN THE MAKING

If we have the opportunity of seeing a significant event play out on the national or international stage, commentators will often describe it by saying, "We are witnessing history in the making!" Obviously, we understand this to mean that we are privileged to watch a great feat take place or see something happen for the very first time. We are witnessing it; we are observing it.

Next we want to look at how Jesus Himself actually called us to be observers. The way He put it is that we are His witnesses. After Jesus died, was buried, resurrected, and then came back to earth He gave some final instructions to His disciples. Right before He ascended to heaven, He told them to wait for the promise of the Father.

We know the last thing someone tells us right before they leave is most important. Well, the last thing Jesus said was, "Guys, don't go *anywhere* until you've been baptized with the Holy Spirit." Now why would that be? Jesus went on to explain that once Holy Spirit came and baptized them, they would have power to be His witnesses (see Acts 1:1-8).

ANOINTED TO BE OBSERVERS

Normally we Christians understand witnessing to be something we do with our mouth, yet everyone else knows that it is something we do with our eyes. That's the dictionary definition—we witness and see something. So it's all about observing, just like eyewitness news shows us an event on TV. Or if we are a witness in a courtroom, it's because we saw a crime or saw an accident take place. First and foremost, in order to be a witness we must be an observer and a seer.

Jesus taught us that the baptism of the Holy Spirit opens the eyes of our hearts to the supernatural world that is all around us. It unlocks the spiritual dimension to us, so we have the power to see the spirit realm that permeates and infuses the physical realm. Holy Spirit anoints us to observe the Kingdom of heaven that is so close, it's actually inside us (see Luke 17:21).

We know this is how Jesus lived. He said, *"I can do nothing on My own initiative"* (John 5:30). He also said He only did what He saw the Father do and said what He heard Him say (see John 5:19-20). So for us to model Jesus, we need to be able to see what He and Father are doing and hear what Holy Spirit is saying. Right now, we are real-time witnesses and present-tense observers of the activity of heaven; that's what Jesus was talking about in Acts 1:8.

WITNESSING JESUS

This is the kind of witness the apostle Paul was. We know that Jesus had already ascended to heaven by the time of Paul's conversion. So when Paul saw Jesus, it was the same way we see Jesus—in the invisible dimension of heaven. He looked with the eyes of his heart into the spirit realm and observed Jesus (see Eph. 1:17-18).

In Acts 22, Paul recounts the counsel given him by Ananias: *"Then he said: 'The God of our ancestors has chosen you to know his will and to see the Righteous One and to hear words from his mouth. You will be his witness to all people of what you have seen and heard"* (Acts 22:14-15 NIV).

We understand from these verses that in order to be a witness we must be tuned in to the supernatural realm, constantly looking and listening to see what the company of heaven is doing. When we see Jesus with us at our right hand, our observation collapses His presence, peace, and power more fully into our world.

THE SECRET

This is *how* we are able to fix our eyes on Jesus, how we are able to set our mind on the Spirit, and how we are able to look at the eternal things that are unseen (see Heb. 12:2; Rom. 8:5-6; 2 Cor. 4:18). Acts 1:8 is our how. We receive power when the Holy Spirit has come upon us to be His witnesses. Witnesses of Jesus. Seers of Jesus. Lookers and watchers and observers of Jesus.

Jesus wants a witness to His life—the one He's living right now.

Now we understand that when we see the potential God is showing us through our times of meditation and visions by day and by night, we create a visual agreement. This agreement is a bridge upon which these promises of heaven can cross. However, they remain in a spiritual state of possibility until someone on earth sees what God has made available—until someone observes it.

NEW-CREATION OBSERVATION

Likewise, in our times of meditation we observe our new-creation selves. This is God's version of us, and He sees us as perfect. We are inside of Christ, and because of this we are holy and happy and healthy. We are creative and favored and brilliant and strong and loved. That is who Jesus is, and He is in us and we are in Him. That is how God sees us, so that is how we must see ourselves too.

Because of the observer-effect principle, we now understand that when we observe this truth we collapse it. We change it from being just a spiritual reality to being a physical reality as well. As we behold Jesus, we are transformed by the power of the Spirit into His glorious image, His version of us (see 2 Cor. 3:18). His glory waves of potential and promise collapse into our hearts and change our lives, because observation causes transformation.

MARK

Spiritual transformation occurs when I look to see God's reality, experience His energizing power, and am transformed into that which I am gazing upon.

Christian transformation is not a result of cognitive reasoning or setting my will and striving. It is a result of steadfastly looking at true spiritual reality, and being energized to become these things. In our "New Creation Celebration" meditations, we have you spend a lot of time gazing upon who you are in Christ. In this way, you are "putting on Christ." This is Spirit-born transformation from the inside out. As mentioned earlier, another common example of this transforming process is that when we are caught up in worship and are beholding the Lord, we are changed. We feel love, joy, peace, and power flood our hearts.

Revelation-based learning results in what Paul called "*true* knowledge," which was the knowledge Paul received by the Spirit when he spent three years in the Arabian wilderness. When Paul discusses "true knowledge" in Colossians, it is knowledge *infused by love* and it produces our new self in the image of Jesus Christ (see all of Colossians 2, and especially Colossians 2:2 and 3:10). Peter also tells us that "true knowledge" is birthed by God's divine power operating within us, and it increases Christlike qualities through us (see 2 Pet. 1:3,8).

True knowledge is what you experience when a verse leaps off the pages of Scripture and directly into your spirit, making your heart leap and burn. I know you have experienced that.

> **True knowledge is knowledge birthed in revelation.**

My freedom from slavery to sin comes through the power of the in-working Holy Spirit.

> *Our old self was crucified with Him...so that we would* **no longer be slaves to sin** (Romans 6:6).

> **By the Spirit** *you are putting to death the deeds of the body* (Romans 8:13).

So rather than striving to overcome a sin issue, I turn to the power of the indwelling Holy Spirit, which is experienced as an energizing life flow within (see Rom. 8:2). As I call it forth, it becomes strong enough to confront and overcome the hardwired responses of my old self with its bent toward sin. Now I am free! I have just worked out my salvation, for it was Christ who was at work within me (see Phil. 2:12-13).

Spiritual transformation occurs when the energy of the Spirit within becomes strong enough to confront and overcome the energy of the hardwired responses of my old self. Christ is now living through me by His indwelling Spirit:

> *I have been crucified with Christ; and it is no longer I who live, but **Christ lives in me*** (Galatians 2:20).

> *The one who joins himself to the Lord is **one spirit** with Him* (1 Corinthians 6:17).

If I 1) believe Christ is my life through the energizing of His Spirit within, 2) *set my gaze upon this truth*, and 3) speak it as my current, personal reality while 4) living tuned to the river (flow) of the Holy Spirit within, *then* I experience it (see John 7:37-39). I experience life in the Spirit (see Gal. 5:25; 1 Cor. 12:7-11). I must believe, see, speak, and tune to His flow.

EXPERIENCING RESURRECTION POWER

> *Not that I have already obtained it...but **I press on** so that I may lay hold of that* (Philippians 3:12).

Yes, He is there in my heart. The river of the Holy Spirit is flowing, and I am learning more each day how to lean upon and trust His flow within, so let's discard the old so I can embrace the new. I discard fleshly logic and reason and self-effort and instead see Jesus at my right hand and His power within flowing as a river, and I tune to this flow and live from it.

I *must* throw away my old self's security, strength, and wisdom in order to gain the Spirit. This is an intense concept to wrap our heads around. God is looking for us to stop trusting in our flesh's abilities and put our *complete trust* in His abilities. A mixture of our best efforts and our thoughts about how to implement His vision for our lives is *not* acceptable. He wants us to put away the old man and rely completely on His Spirit.

Abraham combined his best thoughts with God's voice and produced Ishmael, which messed everything up (see Gen. 12:1-3; 15:1-5; 16:1-4; 17:18-19).

Moses sensed he was to be a deliverer, so using his strength and wisdom he went out and killed an Egyptian who was harassing an Israelite (see Exod. 2:11-14). God said, "No, this is not the way," and removed him to the back side of the wilderness for 40 years until he learned to hear God's voice and see God's visions (see Exod. 3). Then Moses returned in the power of the Spirit to accomplish the supernatural. He manifested God's wisdom and power and, as such, became as God to Pharaoh (see Exod. 7:1).

> *As we pursue the call of God upon our lives,*
> *we must cast down our strength and wisdom*
> *and choose to lean totally on His.*

God has called me to saturate the world with the message of communion with God. Rather than concocting a master plan of my own devising, I have sought His leading step by step. For the entire first year after my commission, all God would say to me about it was to *love my wife*. Apparently He felt a really strong marriage was an essential foundation for conducting a worldwide ministry. I agree. Had I devised my own plan for how the ministry should grow and expand, I probably would not have begun with a focus on strengthening my marriage.

THE RIGHT AND WRONG APPROACH TO TRANSFORMATION

In Mark 10 we see two individuals come to Jesus to receive blessing and transformation. One experiences the desired change because he is willing to discard his old nature and accept a new life. The other does not receive transformation because he is unwilling to lay aside his old nature. We must put off our old self before we can receive our new self (see Col. 3:8-10).

The Rich Young Ruler Loses Out with Jesus

The rich young ruler asked for eternal life and Jesus was willing but instructed him not to cling to his Old Self—his dependence upon money. He went away grieving, because he was not willing to give up his false identity—in this case, his trust in uncertain riches (see Mark 10:17-22).

> *Jesus' Mark 10:30 Principle: When I give up self-reliance and trust in Christ, I receive a hundredfold return of His empowering, His energizing, and His resources.*

Blind Bartimaeus Receives His Miracle

The second individual in Mark 10, blind Bartimaeus, fared better. Bartimaeus began with a personal revelation of the ability of Jesus to transform him. He declared that Jesus is the Son of David, and thus the

Savior. Bartimaeus added to this revelation intense, passionate emotion demonstrated by him *crying out loudly*. This caught Jesus' attention, and Jesus stopped and invited Bartimaeus to come to Him (see Mark 10:46-52).

Bartimaeus *leapt up* to go to Jesus and *threw aside his cloak*. His beggar's coat had kept him warm when nights were cold, it was the bed he slept on, and it was what he laid on the ground to catch alms people tossed to him. His cloak was crucial to his old identity (that of a beggar), but would not be needed with his new identity—that of being a seeing man.

Jesus asked Bartimaeus what he wanted, and Bartimaeus, calling Him Rabboni (meaning Lord/master), asked to receive his sight.

> *Jesus said to him, "Go; your faith has made you well."*
> *Immediately he regained his sight and began following*
> *Him on the road* (Mark 10:52).

LET GO OF THE PAST

I must let go of my past so I can embrace God's miracles for my future!

Do not cling to your past, to your sins, your inferiorities, self-consciousness, or your inabilities. Give them all to Jesus. Let Jesus save you from your puny self-efforts. Then you can receive His limitless power.

I cannot experience my new-creation self
if I cling to my old self's security.

75

Our *New Creation Celebration: Replacing Emotions*[17] devotional takes you through the steps of discarding your old self's beliefs and emotions and embracing your new self's beliefs and emotions.

SURRENDER

I *must* surrender self-effort if I am to receive divine empowering!

I want miracles! I want spiritual transformation! Like Paul, I fight against the sinful desires of my flesh (see Rom. 7), sickness in my body, and lack in my life. I agree with Paul's conclusion: I cannot overcome the flesh using the power of the flesh. *Only* the power of the Spirit can work a miracle of transformation (see Rom. 8). To access this power, I need to surrender self-effort because that stands in the way of divine enabling. I need to stop striving if I am going to make it in life! Wow, now isn't that just a bit counterintuitive?

> *The flesh cannot overcome the flesh—only the Spirit can! I shift my faith from depending on self to depending on God. Trusting completely in God's power allows transformation to occur.*

TWO-WAY JOURNALING: *RHEMA* FROM THE SPIRIT

Mark, that which is of the flesh is of the flesh and will not overcome that which is of the spirit.

---

17 www.cwgministries.org/emotions

Heart issues are interwoven with spirit issues. You will not overcome issues of your heart or the meditations of your heart with the will of your mind or mental self-control.

Your mind does not have the power necessary to overcome the power of the spirit world. Only the Spirit of God can overcome the damages wrought by satan's kingdom. He is the adversary, he and his cohorts—principalities, powers, and evil spirits. These will *not* be overcome by the mind or the setting of man's will. These will only be overcome by the power of My Spirit.

So as you come into My presence, you experience My mercy and My manifest power. You are enabled to operate in the power of My Spirit. This happens through the *"law of the spirit of life in Christ Jesus."* It is the energizing that your spirit feels when in My presence, the presence of the King, the most powerful One in the universe. His rays, My rays, penetrate and transform you and the deceitfulness in your soul. *That is where the victory is won. That is where the victory is won. That is where the victory is won.*

So come to Me. Enter into My presence, and ask of Me and draw upon Me and you shall receive life, My life, My power, My Spirit. That is what overcomes the flesh. *Nothing else* accomplishes this. So teach people to come into My presence.

Lord, how do we come into Your presence?

By beholding Me, by seeing Me. By coming before Me and honoring Me and worshiping Me as your Life and your Source of all. I am your Lord and your Savior. Those who recognize that and who enter before Me into My courts receive from Me. Those who don't struggle on their own, looking to their own flesh and their own strength to accomplish, and they do not receive from Me.

So come before Me, receive of Me, and your joy will be full. Come, stand, and worship in My presence, for there your triumph is made complete. It is perfected praise that brings forth My victory.

10 STEPS TO EXPERIENCING SPIRIT-BORN TRANSFORMATION

Simple, thorough steps for you to be transformed from the inside out, not as religious self-effort but from the Holy Spirit within!

1. **I ask for God's help** and receive it. I pray, asking God to intervene, to release His Kingdom on earth in this situation.

   Therefore let us draw near with confidence to the throne of grace, so that we may receive mercy and find grace to help in time of need (Hebrews 4:16).

2. **I receive revelation, spiritual seeds, which I plant for my miracle.** I choose to be like Jesus and do only what I hear and see my Father doing.

   *Truly, truly, I say to you, the Son can do nothing of Himself, unless it is something He **sees** the Father doing.... As I **hear**, I judge* (John 5:19,30).

3. **I *cease* my own laboring.** I stop exerting my strength to get the job done, knowing the efforts of the flesh accomplish nothing, or even worse, create Ishmaels, which bring about consequences lasting thousands of years.

Let us be diligent to enter that rest (Hebrews 4:11).

It is the Spirit who gives life; the flesh profits noth-ing; the words (rhema) *that I have spoken to you are spirit and are life* (John 6:63).

4. **I fertilize these seeds of revelation with faith.** Note: The promise, or potentiality, of blessing was available but not realized because they did *not* believe it was part of their future.

    It shall be done to you according to your faith (Matthew 9:29).

    The word which they heard did not profit them, not being mixed with faith...although the works were finished from the foundation of the world (Hebrews 4:2-3 NKJV).

5. **I think *only* of the promise fulfilled.** I bring every thought captive to God's revealed will. The spiritual warfare I fight is largely in my mind where I destroy every thought that does not line up with God's revealed word, and I insist every one of my thoughts agree with and obey what Christ has spoken to me.

    We are destroying speculations...and we are taking every thought captive to the obedience of Christ (2 Corinthians 10:5).

6. **I picture *only* the promise fulfilled, which releases Kingdom emotions** of thankfulness and joy that I have *already* triumphed in Christ. My spirit is saturated with true gratitude that God's revealed blessings are already present in my life. I experience this by

continuously gazing upon His revealed blessings until my emotions are caught up with what I am seeing with the eyes of my heart.

> *Thanks be to God, who always leads us in triumph in Christ, and manifests through us the sweet aroma of the knowledge of Him in every place* (2 Corinthians 2:14).

7. **I praise passionately, saying, "The promise is fulfilled."** I silence unbelieving thoughts by seeing and speaking, "The promised blessing is already done."

   > *Hold fast the confidence and the rejoicing of the hope firm unto the end...lest there be in any of you an evil heart of unbelief, in departing from the living God* (Hebrews 3:6,12 KJV).

8. This perfected praise provides the spiritual energy to release the miracle. "*Out of the mouth of babes and nursing infants You have* **ordained strength**" (Ps. 8:2 NKJV). Note how Jesus quotes this verse, changing two words: "*Out of the mouth of babes and nursing infants you have* **perfected praise**" (Matt. 21:16 NKJV). So we praise God for already accomplishing that which He has said He has done. We see it, feel it and speak it. *This perfected praise* sends out streams of faith, drawing God's miracle to us (see Mark 11:20-22).

9. I sense the energy of the Spirit flowing within—a divine energizing within that transforms me. "*The law of the Spirit of life in Christ Jesus has set you free*" (Rom. 8:2).

10. **I act in accordance with the Spirit's power and revelation.** The spiritual and emotional energy growing within me moves me to action. The proof that my faith is alive is that I act on God's instructions. *"Faith without works is dead"* (James 2:26).

11. **I put on God's protective armor,** which is faith, hope, love, and peace. I put on Christ's righteousness and battle fear and doubt by speaking the *words* I have received from the Lord. I energize myself by praying in the Spirit. This, the Bible calls the armor of God (see Eph. 6:10-18; 1 Thess. 5:8) and can be summed up as "putting on Christ." This is what we do in our "New Creation Celebration" meditations.

To fully implement God's truths in your mind, you want to use His process of biblical meditation to successfully complete the process. So take Scriptures and meditate upon them for two months so that the revelation God is asking you to walk in becomes fully yours!

But his delight is in the law of the Lord, and in His law he meditates day and night. He will be like a tree firmly planted by streams of water, which yields its fruit in its season and its leaf does not wither; and in whatever he does, he prospers (Psalm 1:2-3).

When you renew your mind, you are removing treelike substances from your brain and growing new treelike substances in your brain.[18] Watch these amazing online videos by Dr. Caroline Leaf and get excited about the science, simply explained, concerning what takes place within your brain as you renew your mind by the power of the Holy Spirit.[19]

---

18 www.youtube.com/watch?v=kazIKVxVo94

19 www.youtube.com/watch?v=_kR56Zp_VyA

ACTION EXERCISES

My declaration: I experience daily Spirit-empowered transformation because:

1. **I ask** You, heavenly Father, for Your wisdom continuously.

2. **I receive** Your spoken words, visions, and emotions.

3. **I trust** completely in Your power.

4. **I believe** what You have spoken.

5. **I ponder** only Your promises to me.

6. **I see** Your promises already fulfilled.

7. **I speak** Your promises as my personal, present-tense reality.

8. **I feel** Your Spirit's energy within me.

9. **I act** on Your spoken words.

10. **I stand** protected by faith, hope and love.

Journaling

Lord, which of the above ten steps involved in transformation do You want to discuss with me now? What would You like to say?

Lord, what security blanket would You have me cast down now, so I can pick up Your supernatural, empowering grace to succeed?

Do one or both of these "New Creation Celebration" meditations over the next week:

1. There will be a lie (false belief) connected to any security blanket you have had, so complete a "New Creation Celebration: Replacing Beliefs"[20] (22 minutes) and replace that lie with truth. You may find God wants to speak with you concerning removing this lie several days in a row, hitting it from all angles and deepening the new truths He is replacing it with. So do the "New Creation Celebration: Replacing Beliefs" five times, allowing God to bring up any lie He desires each of these five times or the same lie all five days.

2. Perhaps God is leading you to put on Christ in a deeper way. That means you could complete the "New Creation Celebration: Putting on Christ"[21] (13 minutes).

River of Life As You Drift Off to Sleep

As you lay in bed drifting off to sleep, softly play the *River of Life,*[22] a 12-minute meditation where you are immersed in the River of the Holy Spirit. Feel the power of the Holy Spirit surge through you as you gaze intently at the River of Life flowing from the throne of God and covering you completely. Prayerfully imagine the scriptural reality described in Ezekiel 47:1-12 and Revelation 22:1-2. See yourself as in the Upper Room, Acts 2:1-4, being immersed in the Holy Spirit. As you

---

20 www.cwgministries.org/beliefs

21 www.cwgministries.org/christ

22 www.cwgministries.org/immersed

see this and enter deeply and devoutly into it, the Holy Spirit can and will bring energizing, transformation, and healing.

I have found it a great way to focus myself on the Holy Spirit as I drift off to sleep. Of course, also do this devotional while awake and alert to receive an even fuller impact.

Chapter 4

CULTIVATING KINGDOM EMOTIONS AND HEIGHTENED KINGDOM EMOTIONS

Kingdom emotions put your body in the state of healing while heightened Kingdom emotions open you up for miraculous transformations.

PERFECT PEACE WHEN YOUR IMAGINATION IS...

*"The steadfast of **mind** You will keep in perfect peace, because he trusts in You"* (Isa. 26:3). The word mind is actually the Hebrew word *yêtser* (Strong's H3336). I memorized this verse as "the steadfast of *mind*," but it is correctly translated "the steadfast of *imagination* You will keep in perfect peace, because he trusts in You." Out of nine times *yêtser* appears

in the Bible, it is translated correctly as "imagination that frames up your reality" seven of these times. We explore this word in depth here: www.cwgministries.org/PerfectPeace.

Suffice to say, the Bible, written as a book of stories, is constantly guiding my imagination, so I am seeing God in action in the affairs of mankind. When I present the eyes of my heart to the Holy Spirit, He enlightens them, allowing me to see in the spirit world (see Eph. 1:17-18). So the Bible promotes proper use of the eyes of my heart and godly imagination, which I define as picturing things God says are true. When I see properly, I find the Kingdom emotions of peace, faith, gladness, thankfulness, and compassion are produced.

How to Promote Kingdom Emotions

Engaging in throne room worship, singing in tongues (see 1 Cor. 14:2,4,15), experiencing a soaking session, attending a revivalist healing service, experiencing deliverance, roaring at the enemy (see Isa. 31:3-4), crying out to God, completing a "New Creation Celebration: Replacing Emotions" meditation—all of these activities will stimulate Kingdom emotions in your heart. We will explore each of these in this book.

Devotionals That Build Kingdom Emotions

The meditations that comprise the *New Creation Celebration series* contain music with voice-over as well as accompanying prayer guides. They draw you into interaction with Jesus so you experience miraculous transformation. These encounters range in length from nine to forty minutes, depending on the specific meditation you select. You are putting off your old self and putting on your new self in Christ. You may hit the pause button on your listening device anytime you need more time in the devotional to interact with God.

The resulting increase in faith and gratitude becomes God's magnet, which attracts His blessings, anointings, and provisions to your life.

This allows you to experience the destiny the Lord has planned for you, which includes health, wisdom, provision, achievement, leadership, and abundance (see Deut. 28:1-14). This also allows you to walk through persecution and suffering with your eyes fixed on Jesus and experience His peace and miracles in the midst of life's storms (see Matt. 5:10; Acts 5:41; 8:1).

The purpose of this chapter is to give you deeper comprehension of each aspect of the "New Creation Celebration" meditations so you can do them with greater intention and reap greater results.

The 12-minute meditation "River of Life" provides an experience where you are immersed in the River of the Holy Spirit. Don't worry, as in a dream, you can breathe under water! As you experience this scene prayerfully, you are likely to find your body shaking as the power of the Holy Spirit flows through you and you leave the encounter empowered and filled with peace.

"New Creation Celebration" Meditation Comes in Four Versions

- "New Creation Celebration: Replacing Emotions" (40 minutes)

- "New Creation Celebration: Replacing Beliefs" (22 minutes)

- "New Creation Celebration: Putting on Christ" (13 minutes)

- "New Creation Celebration: Possessing Your Promised Land" (9 minutes)

Access and download *all* of the above meditations[23] along with a printout of the prayer guides that accompany each one.

---

23   www.cwgministries.org/SpiritualTransformations

You Choose!

Utilize any part for your daily devotional. You may choose to begin in the evening with the "River of Life" segment playing as you drift off to sleep, and in the morning select the "New Creation Celebration" segment that meets the call of your heart and the Holy Spirit.

For example, I ask, "Holy Spirit, what is on my heart that needs to be dealt with today?" If I am feeling fear or believing a lie (something contrary to Scripture), then I will complete the meditation that deals with replacing emotions or the one dealing with replacing beliefs.

If I need re-affirmation of who I am in Christ, I do the meditation "Putting on Christ." If I am waiting for a Promised Land destiny to manifest in my life, I could do the meditation "Possessing Your Promised Land," as it reminds me of the steps I am to be taking as I press forward in faith and obedience.

The First Time Is Always Awkward

We are asking that you try each of the meditations four to six times so that you get beyond any awkward stage, which is standard when attempting anything new. Completing each of these five devotionals six times each means 30 sessions or one month of daily meditation. This gives you powerful tools you will be able to use as needed throughout your life, as well as bring great transformation to you over the next month.

The "New Creation Celebration: Replacing Emotions" meditation begins by asking the Lord what emotion He would have you let go of and then tracing that emotion back to its roots. Using God's wonderful counsel, you remove *all* contributors to this stressful emotion and *replace it* with His Kingdom emotions of love, joy, peace, compassion, faith, and thankfulness. The reason it takes 40 minutes is because you are experiencing major heart surgery.

LIVES HEALED AS PEOPLE EXPERIENCED THE *New Creation Celebration* MEDITATIONS

- **Emotionally impacted:** "I was moved to tears. I sensed His presence in a new and fresh way."
  —Pastor Keith Carlisle

- **Seeing myself as a new creation:** "I love going through this and hearing the Lord speak. Learning to see myself as the new creation that I am is a process. I just realized this morning that my concentration is much better since I began using the devotional. My mind is not jumping around from one thing to another. I can stay in the Word longer and actually read with more focus." —Judy Young

- **Healing:** "What a blessing this devotional has been to me. The 'River of Life' has brought healing to me physically. It is gradual, but I crave that healing flow of the water of the Holy Spirit. I listened to it twice during the early hours of this morning. The 'New Creation Celebration' has brought an encounter with the Lord every time I have listened to it. Revelation has come to me through the whole session. God is using it to heal me." —Judith Johnson

- **Cellular cleansing:** "It was a kind of mini-*Prayers that Heal the Heart* and really worked for me. The added features of cleansing the cells and genes are very good." —Jessie Mejias

- **Freedom in Christ:** "This devotional is incredibly powerful. It is a tremendous guide to lead people into

the freedom in Christ that Jesus has already paid the price for. I will certainly recommend it to others."
—Brenda Brown

- **Improved counseling:** "It is very helpful in my own life and it has had a significant impact on my counseling ministry." —Rev. Paul Stanton

IS 40 MINUTES TOO LONG FOR A HEART TRANSPLANT?

Healing comes through prayer (see James 5:15). People like Heidi Baker, with her awesome healing ministry, spend three or more hours a day in prayer, as have most all great healing evangelists throughout history. I just never knew what to do in a one-hour prayer time that would make it life-giving and life-transforming. Well, the "New Creation Celebration: Replacing Emotions" will make your hour of prayer flash by in what seems like a moment.

You will come out of your time of meditation radiating faith, joy, hope, and gratitude into the world. This attracts God's blessings into your life. His provision and favor will manifest in any area that you express the Kingdom realities of faith and compassion. You will move from radiating fear to radiating faith, peace, and positive expectation for whatever specific issues you have processed in depth. Fear draws lack into your life; faith draws abundance into your life. You will feel energized, Spirit-empowered, and transformed. Guaranteed! Try the "Replacing Emotions" meditation daily for a week and see if you don't notice a big difference.

You will drop depression, negativity, sickness, and ineffectiveness and step into the realities of Kingdom health, Kingdom emotions, Kingdom power, and Kingdom wisdom.

Jesus asked the disciples, *"Could you not watch with Me one hour?"* (Matt. 26:40 NKJV).

It sure beats an hour in front of the TV or an hour on the Internet. This will become the most transformative hour of your day!

TWELVE UNIQUE FEATURES

The reason the "New Creation Celebration: Replacing Emotions"[24] meditation is so life-changing is because it combines all these activities into a single devotional time.

1. I begin by getting "in Spirit," which is crucial (see Rev. 1:9-11).

2. I am guided into hearing God's voice and seeing His visions, which are both foundational to transformation (see Gen. 12:1-3; 15:5-6; Matt. 6:22; 2 Cor. 3:17-18; 4:17-18).

3. I incorporate revelation from my dreams. Our day begins in the evening. "Evening and morning" is the way the Bible describes a day (see Gen. 1:5,8,13,19,23,31).

4. I experience prophetic prayer counseling. The meditation begins with God speaking, bringing up an area He would like to transform. This area is processed throughout the devotional with His voice leading all the way.

5. I process one emotion (or an aspect of one emotion) per session. This could be viewed as daily sanctification (see Heb. 12:14) or as a tune-up using these seven

---

24 www.cwgministries.org/emotions

prayers—breaking generational curses, severing ungodly soul ties, identifying and repenting of ungodly beliefs and inner vows, inner healing, healing cellular memories, and deliverance.

6. I throw off self-reliance (see Jer. 17:5; Hab. 1:11; Prov. 3:5-6).

7. I surrender fully to the power of Spirit. It is the Spirit who gives life; the flesh profits nothing (see John 6:63-64; Hab. 3:19; Exod. 15:2).

8. I "put on Christ" by gazing upon my new self in Him (see Rom. 6:1-23; 8:1-13).

9. I practice "walking by the Spirit" by picturing three moments of time in my upcoming day and seeing my "new self in Christ" responding in each situation.

10. I experience Kingdom emotions. Emotions are the language of the heart, and they are crucial in bringing forth change. When faith and emotions agree, transformation occurs.

11. I ask for a confirming sign from God, which will let me know I am on the right path.

12. Faith grows, attracting God's blessings and miracles (see Rom. 10:17; Matt 9:29; Mark 9:23).

WAYS TO TUNE TO YOUR SPIRIT

Being "in Spirit" and "in the moment" is where miracles occur. Following are some approaches to help us move into the posture of being "in spirit" so we can experience His flow within (see Rev. 1:9-11).

Put a check mark next to the approaches you have found successful in quieting yourself to hear from your heart and a plus mark next to the approaches you would like to explore.

1. __ **Relax, become calm:** Put a smile on your face. Use stillness or soaking music. Breathe as deeply and slowly as you comfortably can as you become aware of your love for God (see Deut. 28:47). Move into the present moment (see Exod. 3:14).

2. __ **Two-way journaling:** You can easily hear God's voice by 1) quieting yourself down, 2) seeing Jesus at your right hand, 3) tuning to flow, and 4) writing. His voice comes as flowing thoughts that light upon your mind as your eyes are fixed on Jesus. Explore this more deeply in the book *4 Keys to Hearing God's Voice*.[25]

3. __ **Pray or sing in tongues:** Tongues allows your spirit to commune with God and be strengthened with divine energy, revelation, and passion (see 1 Cor. 14:1-4,15)

4. __ **Throne Room Worship:**[26] See yourself worshiping with the multitude before God's throne in heaven. See an example here[27] (start 12 minutes in).

5. __ **"Sea of Galilee"**[28] meditation, which can be used in two ways: 1) Begin the music at the beginning, with the five-minute introduction where you are taken on a walk with Jesus along the Sea of Galilee. This is

---

25 www.cwgministries.org/4keysbook
26 www.cwgministries.org/throne
27 http://bit.ly/HinnVideo
28 www.cwgministries.org/galilee

followed by 25 minutes of soaking music, which you listen to as you journal. 2) When you want music only, simply begin six minutes into the track.

6. ___ **"River of Life"**[29] meditation can be completed in 12 minutes and takes you into an awareness of the Holy Spirit who surrounds and permeates you.

7. ___ **Additional approaches** include flagging or dancing in His presence. Those comfortable with EFT[30] can use this method to enter the heart level. HeartMath's emWave®2 heart coherence monitor is another tool we will explore in Chapter 10.

MIRACLES PLUS GIFTS OF HEALINGS

*God has appointed in the church...**miracles, then gifts of healings*** (1 Corinthians 12:28).

My Confession

I maximize health by pursuing both miracles and gifts of healings.

Miracles

Because the "New Creation Celebration" meditations include the hearing of God's voice and conclude with you spending a significant period of time gazing on how you look, act, and feel now that you have put on your new self in Christ, *faith arises* in your heart. *Faith is a magnet* that draws God's miracles to your life. So this devotional promotes miracles by enlarging faith.

---

29 www.cwgministries.org/immersed
30 www.cwgministries.org/eft

Gifts of Healings

How does the "New Creation Celebration: Replacing Emotions" promote "gifts of healings"? Gifts of healings include healings that occur as you use the many additional modes of healing compatible with Scripture. One of these modes would be the healing that is expedited as one experiences what has been called "the relaxation response." The Bible calls this "entering into rest" or "ceasing your labors" (see Heb. 4:10-11).

As you know, living in stress damages your health. On the other hand, experiencing God's emotions of compassion, joy, peace, and thankfulness promotes healing by shifting you from the "stress mode" to the relaxation response. This releases you from the damages of living in the stress mode and turns on healing responses throughout your body. Chapter 8 examines the stress mode and the relaxation mode in much greater detail and shows how the relaxation mode signals new genes in new ways, thus promoting millions of healing chemical reactions within your body *every moment* that you live in this state!

Because up to 90 percent of adult doctor visits have an emotional root,[31] you have just promoted restoration and health to your entire being by 1) receiving revelation from the Wonderful Counselor; 2) moving from stress to peace; as well as 3) believing, speaking, and seeing the miracle already done. You can expect physical healing to follow (see 3 John 2).

As you experience the "New Creation Celebration: Replacing Emotions" meditation for several days or weeks, you will be replacing stressful emotions with Kingdom emotions. You will be undermining stress piece by piece until it is *fully* removed. This results in healing and transformation springing forth. Kingdom emotions produce Kingdom health.

---

31   http://bit.ly/SickStress

> *If Kingdom emotions create the state of healing within our bodies, what might heightened Kingdom emotions produce? The state of breakthrough miracles!*

KINGDOM EMOTIONS AND HEIGHTENED KINGDOM EMOTIONS BOTH PROMOTE HEALING

Compassion is an example of heightened Kingdom emotion. This word *compassion* literally means "to have the bowels yearn."

When He went ashore, He saw a large crowd, and felt compassion for them and healed their sick (Matthew 14:14).

In miracle services, people experience *heightened* Kingdom emotions as they hear passionate preaching about the healing Jesus has purchased for them (see Isa. 53:5). This is interspersed with prophecy and times of healing prayer as well as testimonies of healing that others are experiencing. These all lead to *intensified* faith, hope, love, compassion, and thankfulness.

When I was a student at Roberts Wesleyan College (1970-1974) I wrote a research paper on "Revivals" in which I said, *"Revivals are intensely emotional* and Christological in focus." Unfortunately, I disdained emotions at that point in my life, so my summary decision after writing this paper was, "I will never be able to be part of a revival since I would never lower myself to emotionalism, plus I love preaching about theological doctrines, so just focusing on Jesus is not where I am at." I have since repented of both of these beliefs.

In her book *EFT For Christians: Tapping into God's Peace and Joy,* Charity writes, *"Feelings are the filter* that allows energy to move in and out of our spirit...and our cells.... Emotion is the energy that activates and releases the spirit." And Dr. Jim Richards, in his book *Wired for Success, Programmed for Failure*, says, *"Emotion plus information* is the doorway to the heart."[32]

Heart faith requires we use the language of the heart, not the language of the mind. The language of the heart includes emotions, pictures, flow, meditation, and pondering. We can only change our state of being when we're functioning on our heart level. The Holy Spirit spills life and revelation directly into our hearts (see 1 Cor. 6:17).

Any intense experience, if maintained for more than half an hour, can leave permanent changes in the neural circuits involving emotion and memory.[33]

> *Emotions are the channel of the spirit, so expect more of God's life-transforming, miracle-working power when releasing heightened Kingdom emotions.*

ROARING AT YOUR ENEMY INVOLVES HEIGHTENED KINGDOM EMOTIONS

Use heightened Kingdom emotions when you need a breakthrough and standard Kingdom emotions have not achieved the transforming miracle you are seeking.

Roaring is one possible element within biblical meditation. The word *hâgâh* (pronounced haw-gaw, Strong's H1897) occurs 24 times in the King James Version of the Bible and is translated six of these times

---

32   James B. Richards, *Wired for Success, Programmed for Failure* (Traveler's Rest, SC: True Potential Inc., 2010).

33   Andrew Newberg and Mark Robert Waldman, *Born to Believe* (New York: Free Press, 2008), 183.

as "meditate." Other times it is translated with various words for the activities that compose the various parts of biblical meditation. These include *speak, mutter, talk, utter, mourn, study,* and *roaring.*

In Isaiah 31:4, the King James Bible translates this word as "roaring."

> *For thus hath the Lord spoken unto me, Like as the lion and the young lion **roaring** on his prey.*

So part of meditating on and appropriating the promises of Scripture in our lives involves roaring. Wow! Let's explore what this looks like so we can begin doing it. Remember how athletes come on the field with a roar? Yes, that does seem to put more energy in the atmosphere.

Let's say you have a situation in your life that is contrary to the rule and reign of God. In Isaiah 31:3, the Egyptians looked to the strength of their army as their god. So the true God was going to come and roar at this army, this false reality set up by satan, and fight against it and destroy it (see Isa. 31:5).

That is exactly what the Lord wants us to do over the ungodly situations in our lives. These situations could be a lingering sickness, infirmity, sin, fear, doubt, unbelief, anger, poverty, disunity, an emotional block, etc. Anything in your life that is contrary to the word of God is an enemy the Lord of Hosts wants to come down and destroy.

> *So shall the **Lord of hosts come down to fight** for mount Zion, and for the hill thereof. As birds flying, so will the Lord of hosts **defend Jerusalem**; defending also he will **deliver it**; and passing over he will **preserve it** (Isaiah 31:4-5 KJV).*

As you battle against this problem in your life, why not get really involved and roar at it? Yes, I really mean *roar* at it. Get emotionally passionate! Get loud! Get intense! Even get angry! And because it is the Lord of Hosts joining with you in doing the battle, you might just as well see this with the eyes of your heart. It is Jesus, as the Lion of Judah, standing there with you, roaring at this problem and commanding it to be gone *now!*

Of course, begin by asking Jesus what your emotional response should be toward everything. If He is laughing at it, then we should be laughing also. If He is roaring, then we too should be roaring. You notice in Isaiah 31:4 it says, *"The **lion** and the **young lion** roaring on his prey."* Jesus is the Lion of the Tribe of Judah who is roaring, and I see myself as the young lion standing next to Him roaring also. Of course, I recognize the most powerful of these two roars is the roar coming from Jesus. By doing what I see Him do, I am releasing His Kingdom on earth (see Matt. 6:10).

I see roaring as an application of this principle: *"The kingdom of heaven suffers violence, and violent men take it by force"* (Matt. 11:12).

Tim Madden Roared at Lyme Disease and Experienced a Miracle!

For example, my friend Tim Madden, a YWAM Crossroads Discipleship Training School leader in Kona, shared this story with me in January of 2013. He had suffered with Lyme disease for several years, and the Lord told him in his journaling time that it was OK to get angry at the devil. He was quite surprised because he had grown up in an angry home and had made a point of avoiding anger when raising his children. Anger was not something he felt right about using in everyday life, but he decided to take God at His word and obey.

So Tim went for a drive in his car with his windows rolled up so no one could hear him shout at the devil and the Lyme bacteria that were causing his illness. He did this on several different days over a several-week period, and sure enough the Lyme disease left his body and his health was restored! I have checked with Tim over the last four years, and Lyme disease is still gone.

Sometimes we simply tolerate these situations rather than getting passionate and intense about the fact that they will no longer be allowed in our lives because they are contrary to the Word of God! Instead, let's obey God's command to roar at our enemies until they have fled in terror.

Begin by asking God to identify an issue in your life that is contrary to His Word. Then go ahead and join with the Lion of Judah, seeing the two of you roaring in unison at this enemy and scaring the wits out of it until it flees and the situation in your life comes into full alignment with the Word of God.

When God Roars, Things Happen

> The **Lord roars** *from Zion and from Jerusalem He utters His voice; and the shepherds' pasture grounds mourn, and the summit of Carmel dries up* (Amos 1:2).

> The **Lord roars** *from Zion...and the heavens and the earth tremble* (Joel 3:16).

> The Lord will go forth like **a warrior,** *He will arouse His zeal like a man of war. He will utter a shout, yes,* **He will raise a war cry.** *He* **will prevail against His enemies** (Isaiah 42:13).

> The **Son of God** *appeared for this purpose, to* **destroy the works of the devil** (1 John 3:8).

I decree from His Presence and Things Happen

> *You will also* **decree a thing,** *and it will be established for you; and light will shine on your ways* (Job 22:28).

*The righteous are **bold** as a lion* (Proverbs 28:1).

*Let the **high praises** of God be in their mouth, and a two-edged sword in their hand, **to execute vengeance on the nations** and punishment on the peoples, **to bind their kings with chains** and their nobles with fetters of iron, to execute on them the judgment written; this is an honor for all His godly ones. Praise the Lord!* (Psalm 149:6-9)

REFLECTIONS CONCERNING ROARING

Roaring is a powerful tool in defeating the enemy. *Intensity, determination, and passion* are wound up in these mighty roars. These attitudes are important in winning a battle. Roaring emboldens faith in the one who roars and instills fear in the adversary. Seeing Jesus roaring together with you emboldens faith even more. Always intersperse the name of Jesus as you rebuke the enemy. For example, after you roar several times, then command "In Jesus' name, demons, be gone." Repeat two or three times. Then repeat the entire process a second or third time until you feel in your spirit the victory is won.

Once you have done a couple of practice roaring sessions and realize you can do such a thing as "roar at the enemy" and it doesn't break you, it only stretches you, now it is time to integrate roaring into your armory of warfare tools you use when you battle the enemy (see Eph. 6:10-18).

You may be led by the Holy Spirit to incorporate "roaring at the enemy" alongside of any of the Spirit-led devotionals you do. It is especially appropriate to incorporate roaring whenever you are stuck and need a breakthrough!

Consider roaring a *prophetic action that releases spiritual energy* similar to Joash being told by Elisha to strike the ground five to six times so he could soundly defeat the enemy (see 2 Kings 13:14-19). So roar five to six times in faith and get your victory. See this as a prophetic act that is releasing the power of God into the situation.

TESTIMONIES FROM OTHERS WHO ROARED AND EXPERIENCED BREAKTHROUGHS

Cameron Batten

I wanted to share with you something that happened to me as we were participating in the roar exercise. When I asked the Lord what He wanted to change, He clearly and immediately said He wanted to destroy the hold that the adversary had over me because I had harbored a lie that I was rejected and always would be. As I was still, I saw Jesus run up to me, but He stopped short by about ten feet. And with the anxiousness and intensity of a linebacker, waiting for the ball to snap, He was waiting on something—me!

As I began to "roar" and go after that stronghold, He instantly ran and dove into my wounded heart, He uprooted and drove out the lie and replaced it with His love and presence. He was waiting for me to cooperate with Him. He used my mouth to turn His power loose to heal my wounded heart! That happened in my seat! I wasn't in a prayer line. Jesus communicated His desire for me, and we worked together to accomplish His work. If Jesus can accomplish that by my just cooperating with Him at the seminar, how much more can we accomplish every day, now that I've learned to hear Him!

I am free, more so than I have ever been. I realized when I took my place, stood my ground on the Word, that the

Lion of the Tribe of Judah "roared" with me, and the walls that held me captive came tumbling down. I will never be the same because of this message. I have finally discovered Christianity with a living Jesus, and not just a silent historical Jesus! I will be eternally grateful! I go now to share this message. God bless you on your mission.

A Roaring "Practice Session" Produces a Breakthrough

At a seminar in Raleigh, North Carolina, I lead a group in practicing "roaring" at sickness within their bodies (sickness is an enemy of the Lord's). We roared and commanded it to leave our bodies and commanded divine healing to occur in Jesus' name. I had just finished teaching that biblical meditation includes roaring; this was simply a practice session on how to roar.

A little bit later a woman came to the front and shared her testimony. She had had pain in her knee for two years as a result of ligament surgery. The pain completely left as she roared at it and commanded it to leave in Jesus' name! Thank You, Jesus!

From now on, I am going to consider these sessions more than simply "practice sessions." I am going to enter them with faith for miracles to take place, and I will regularly lead people into roaring at their sicknesses. How about we all begin to lead people into roaring exercises where they roar with the Lion of Judah and come against infirmity in their bodies? Let's watch the Lion of Judah win some battles for us as we agree with Him in His roars!

I was with Tim Madden again in January of 2016 teaching his YWAM Crossroads group, and we did a practice roaring session. I encouraged everyone to choose an enemy and roar at it, suggesting it could be sickness, fear, doubt, or unbelief. One senior citizen testified to the group that she was too weak and full of pain to roar, so she asked her classmate to roar for her at the pain in her body. She did, and now her body is completely pain-free! I have seen similar things occur in every practice roaring session I have conducted. So why not go ahead and have a roaring session and roar at the enemy?

"Crying out" Is Another Example of Heightened Emotions

I saw that the Bible makes a distinction between "prayer" and *"crying out"* to God.[34]

Note the *emotional intensity* alluded to in the definition of this Hebrew word *qârâ': "to cry out, proclaim, utter a loud sound"* (Strong's H7121). This Hebrew word for "call" or "cry" shows up in the following verses:

> *The Lord is near to all who* **call** *upon Him, to all who* **call** *upon Him in truth. He will fulfill the desire of those who fear Him; He will also hear their* **cry** *and will save them* (Psalm 145:18-19).

This same Hebrew word appears in Jeremiah 33:3, Psalm 18:6, as well as 734 other times in the Old Testament. The Greek New Testament has two similar words for calling out to God (Strong's G2896 and G994), which occur over 60 times. Consider the emotional intensity in the story of blind Bartimaeus who *cried out and would not be silenced* (see Mark 10:46-52). Also consider the *crying out* found in Matthew 15:21-28—the Canaanite woman who cried out persistently and the deliverance she received.

Jesus Himself provided a parable teaching that we are to cry out to God day and night until God answers: *"Will not God bring about justice for His elect who* **cry to Him day and night**, *and will He delay long*

---

34 Bill Gothard, *Power of Crying Out: When Prayer Becomes Mighty* (Colorado Springs, CO: Multnomah Books, 2002), loc. 125-126.

*over them? I tell you that **He will bring about justice for them quickly***" (Luke 18:7-8).

God meets us in two places—in our faith and in our confession of weakness. Crying out, saying, "Lord, I don't understand why Your deliverance tarries. Please come to me now" may not be the most conducive way to build faith and trust. It may be a rant of fear or desperation. It is best when my cry is a heartfelt cry of passionate belief that God's Kingdom be manifest now! However, sometimes I may begin with the cry of weakness, lack of understanding, and/or impatience. David certainly cried out in both of these ways in the Psalms. As with David, our prayer is to *end in thanksgiving* that God has heard and it is finished (see Phil. 4:6), and we declare, *"It is done."*

The question I know to be asking is, "Lord, why is Your promised provision not yet manifesting in my life? What do I need to do differently in order to see it manifest? What do You want me to be doing to precipitate the release of this miracle?" Then I listen, hear, and obey what He speaks. I conclude by thanking Him for His love, provision, and wisdom as to how to move forward.

*Righteousness must accompany one's crying out: "The eyes of the Lord are toward the **righteous** and His ears are open to their **cry**"* (Ps. 34:15). *"The **righteous cry**, and the Lord hears and delivers them out of all their troubles"* (Ps. 34:17). Ongoing sin is a barrier to God answering one's cry (see Judg. 10:9-16).

Crying Out Multiple Times in a Day

- *"Evening and morning and at noon I will pray, and cry aloud, and He shall hear my voice"* (see Ps. 55:17 NKJV). Biblically speaking, the day begins in the evening (see Gen. 1:5).

- Elijah prayed *earnestly* seven times in one day before his answer came (see James 5:17-18; 1 Kings 18:41-45).

So cry out intensely to God three or more times a day, while asking for His revelation and then acting on it.

Where could roaring or crying out take place?

Intense, revivalist healing services are surely one place where crying out to God and receiving from Him can happen. It can happen in your prayer closet or in your car or in the woods behind your home, and as we have seen in the above stories, even in the marketplace. I do practice roaring sessions in my seminars and people love it and feel the release. Every time, someone is healed of something. It is truly amazing. By all means try it!

PROPHETIC GESTURES

A prophetic gesture releases spiritual energy, and when done in faith and passion, releases *more* spiritual energy.

> *"You must strike the Syrians at Aphek till you have destroyed them." Then he said, "Take the arrows"; so he took them. And he said to the king of Israel, "Strike the ground"; so he struck three times, and stopped. And the man of God was angry with him, and said, "You should have struck five or six times; then you would have struck Syria till you had destroyed it! But now you will strike Syria only three times"* (2 Kings 13:17-19 NKJV).

What do we discover from the above story?

1. Prophetic gestures release spiritual power.

2. When done in faith and with passion, they release more power.

3. When done halfheartedly, they release less power.

Am I making some assumptions as I read the Bible story and come up with the above three conclusions? Yes, I am. I am picturing a king who is following the instructions of a prophet in a halfhearted way. If I were going after my enemy to defeat them, I would bash them into the ground over and over until I was exhausted. I sure wouldn't tap the ground three times. So, yes, I am assuming a halfhearted response, and this translated into a lesser release of God's power as the enemy now would not be fully defeated.

WHOLEHEARTEDNESS IS A HEIGHTENED KINGDOM EMOTION

Journaling

Mark, I have told you to seek the Lord with your whole heart and then you will find Me (see 1 Chron. 28:9). Wholeheartedness is good and is to be directed *only* toward Me. Wholeheartedness involves filling all five senses of one's heart fully and *only* with Me. That includes the eyes of your heart, the ears of your heart, the mind of your heart, the will of your heart, and the emotions of your heart.

Wholeheartedness involves:

1. Hearing *only* My thoughts, no matter where you are.

2. Seeing *only* My visions—learning to see Me everywhere.

3. Pondering *only* My thoughts while taking all others captive.

4. Speaking *only* My purposes with a singleness of heart.

5. Feeling *only* My emotions, which move you to action.

The more passionate, full, and complete the above process is, the more wholehearted one is and the more of My Spirit's transforming power they experience. It can come in bits and pieces, or it can come in like a flood. For My Son, it came in like a flood. For many others, it comes in as bits and pieces.

It is as simple as that. Don't make it any more difficult.

Thank You, Lord. (We will talk more about the above five senses of one's heart/spirit in the next chapter.)

Notice that *all* wholehearted activities in the Bible are directed God-ward:

- Love (Deut. 6:5)
- Serve (1 Chron. 28:9)
- Observe and keep His law (Ps. 119:34)
- Listen to His voice (Deut. 30:2)
- Pray (Ps. 119:58)
- Search (Jer. 29:13)
- Trust (Prov. 3:5-6)
- Praise (Ps. 9:1)
- Return (2 Chron. 6:38)
- Do your work as unto the Lord (Col. 3:23-24)

KINGDOM EMOTIONS COMPARED TO HEIGHTENED KINGDOM EMOTIONS

1. *Love* is a Kingdom emotion and *compassion* is an intensified Kingdom emotion. In Chapter 7, we see that compassion is defined as *"to have the bowels yearn."*

2. *Peace* is a Kingdom emotion and *joy unspeakable* is a heightened Kingdom emotion. Holy laughter probably falls in the category of joy unspeakable.

3. *Prayer* involves trust and *peace*, while an intensified state of prayer is *crying out*.

4. *Prayer* can also be intensified with *fasting* (see Matt. 17:21). The stimulus to engage in fasting could be heightened Kingdom emotions. A fast can be one way to return wholeheartedly to the Lord (see 2 Chron. 6:38; Jonah 3). I will say that during the fast emotions are generally not heightened as the body is weakened from the fast.

5. *Biblical meditation* and pondering is generally quiet and reflective, and yet one form of meditation is to *"roar* at your enemy," which would be a heightened Kingdom emotion.

6. My love for God calls me to *pursue godliness*. Intensified Kingdom emotions cause me to *fight violently* and take the Kingdom by force (see Matt. 11:12). This births a *passionate commitment* for a complete breakthrough that destroys any blockage in the way. *I will not settle* for anything less than a full

experience of all God has said is mine! Period! I am in all-out war! Whatever needs to change, it will change.

7. Worship produces *peace*, while wholehearted praise such as revival praise and throne-room praise produces heightened intense emotions (see Ps. 9:1), which can manifest as *shouting, declaring, roaring, dancing, falling down, holy laughter,* and many other manifestations we have seen in revivals in Scripture and throughout Church history.

8. *Agreeing with a prophecy* produces a Kingdom emotion of thankfulness, joy, peace (see 1 Cor. 14:3), but it requires a heightened Kingdom emotion to *act out a prophecy* with passion by engaging in a prophetic gesture as your response to the prophecy. It appears this king did not do the prophetic action with passion and thoroughness, as he was rebuked (see 1 Kings 13:17-19). Had he done it with passion and thoroughness, the power of the Spirit of God would have ridden out on this prophetic action and transformed his future.

> *If Kingdom emotions have not released the transforming miracle you seek, use intensified Kingdom emotions to achieve your breakthrough.*

Both Kingdom Emotions and Heightened Kingdom Emotions Have a Place

Both are powerful. From my understanding and experience, I would like to suggest that Kingdom emotions put one's body in the state of healing, while *intensified* Kingdom emotions open one up to the possibility for an instantaneous miracle, a breakthrough! This breakthrough can be for physical healing, emotional healing, divine intervention, etc. Seeking God wholeheartedly, repenting of sin wholeheartedly, and experiencing deliverance from demons should be anticipated as wholehearted activities that release miraculous, instantaneous transformation (see Luke 8:2). Remember that any intense experience maintained for more than *half an hour* can leave permanent changes in the neural circuits involving emotion and memory.

A transforming miracle takes place the moment the energy of the Holy Spirit is experienced with enough force to override and replace the energy that has maintained the hardwired responses of my old self.

Kingdom Emotions Flow from Your Spirit, Not Your Soul

Emotional responses can be born in either your spirit or your soul. God instructs us to live and walk by the Spirit (see Gal. 5:25). The fruit of the Spirit includes Kingdom emotions of love, joy, peace (see Gal. 5:22). This fruit of the Spirit comes from fixing our eyes on Jesus. In times of tribulation, I have looked to see Jesus and seen Him walking on the waves toward me, shining with light, and speaking words of peace and comfort to my heart in the midst of the storm I was experiencing.

Fear is replaced with peace as I gaze at Christ walking calmly toward me in the storm of the night. Peace equips me to walk on the water with Him without being afraid. Peace clears my mind so I may be upset that my child just broke something precious, but rather than burst out in anger I can take a deep breath, quiet down into my spirit, ask for and receive God's counsel (as flowing thoughts, pictures, emotions, and power), and then release the fruit of the Spirit (love, joy, peace, patience).

SAYING THE PRAYER VERSUS BECOMING THE PRAYER

If we pray for peace for our city, peace will descend upon the city during our prayer time and then peace may lift from our city after the prayer time is over. However, if we get up from our prayer time transformed by having become peaceful ourselves, we then *carry that spirit with us* as we walk, and peace continues in our city even after the prayer time is over because we never quit praying.

We are "praying without ceasing." We have *become* the prayer. We become peace. We are carriers of God's peace into our city. We have put on the new creation in Christ. We are abiding in Christ, the Prince of Peace, and He is abiding in us. We radiate continuously who we are. In this case we are carriers of His peace, so that is what we radiate. Research along this theme can be found on page 97 of *Science of the Heart*[35] on the HeartMath website.

Press in Until Healed

> *Is anyone among you sick? Then he must **call for the elders** of the church and they are to pray over him, anointing him*

---

35 www.heartmath.org/research/science-of-the-heart/

> *with oil in the name of the Lord; and the prayer offered
> in faith will restore the one who is sick, and the Lord will
> raise him up, and if he has committed sins, they will be
> forgiven him. Therefore, **confess your sins** to one another,
> and **pray for one another** so that you may be healed. The
> **effective prayer of a righteous man can** accomplish
> much. Elijah was a man with a nature like ours, and he
> prayed **earnestly** that it would not rain, and it did not
> rain on the earth for three years and six months* (James
> 5:14-17).

So we are advised to get additional spiritual insight and counsel
concerning sins that are blocking the healing, release, or destiny and
then confess these sins to one another and pray for one another so
that we can experience God's full blessing. I surely have seen this process work successfully in many, many cases. Let's walk in humility and
restore this practice!

The "New Creation Celebration" meditations are designed to guide
you into intimacy with God where He creates Kingdom realities within
you, which you become. You leave the prayer time not just knowing how
to live but *feeling* the experience so deeply that your neural circuits are
rewritten and you live a new way. When you leave your prayer times,
you take with you this new, sustainable presence of the Holy Spirit.

> *We must become the things we hope to
> experience in our world. Jesus walked in
> peace and brought peace to the world.*

ACTION EXERCISES

1. Read this article: www.cwgministries.org/blogs/high-praises-his-presence-roaring.

2. Personal journaling questions: "Lord, what do You want to speak to me about becoming the prayer? Lord, what would You say to me about Kingdom emotions versus heightened Kingdom emotions?"

3. Meditation exercise: For each of the next five days, complete both of the following two devotionals: "River of Life" and "New Creation Celebration: Replacing Emotions." These can be done back to back or you can split them up, doing each one at a different time of the day. You can try "River of Life" as you are lying in bed falling asleep. However, you may fall asleep halfway through, so it is also very good to do this while sitting in a chair so you experience the full impact of it. There are streaming audio versions with background music and downloadable worksheets.

   ▪ "River of Life,"[36] a 12-minute meditation where you are immersed in the River of the Holy Spirit.

   ▪ "New Creation Celebration: Replacing Emotions"[37] (40 minutes)

Do what works for you. You can use the worksheets alone or the audio alone or the worksheets and audio together.

Technical tidbit: When using the downloadable interactive journaling worksheets, you can do a "save as" and give the file a new file name

---

36 www.cwgministries.org/immersed
37 www.cwgministries.org/emotions

when the day's devotional is done. This keeps your original devotional worksheet clean and ready for you to use on another day.

If you are stuck and need a miracle to transform your body, emotions, thought processes, or gain a breakthrough, use *heightened* Kingdom emotions—one or several days. Record your results.

Part II

FAITH, ENERGIZED BY LOVE, RELEASES HEALING, MIRACLES, AND KINGDOM PROVISION

Chapter 5

Faith: Agreeing with God's Intention to Perform a Miracle

*"**Faith** energized by love".*
—see Galatians 5:6

Faith is one of the nine ways the Holy Spirit manifests.
—see 1 Corinthians 12:9

Gazing at my new state in Christ causes faith to arise in my heart. This signature of faith impacts people, events, and matter, causing each to align with the faith I am sending out!

My Outer World Conforms to What I Believe

Some days my faith has been that I will not make it. I will fail. I will go broke. I will be rejected. I cannot perform or get the job done. These are ugly, disgusting days that I hope are forever behind me, as they draw the kingdom of darkness, fear, and failure to my side.

Now if I wake up with such a thought or emotion, I simply do a "New Creation Celebration" devotional and let God speak to me, reminding me of who I am in Christ. I receive a new faith signature (See Phil. 4:13; Deut. 28:1-14; 8:18; Col. 1:28). I declare:

> *I can do all things through Christ who strengthens me. God has given me the power to create wealth. I am complete in Christ.*

Wow! Once again I have put on my new self and am radiant with His divine life. I find it beneficial to have such devotionals that can easily and quickly take me through the steps of restoration, so I don't need to wallow in misery for a day while I attract demonic negatives to my life! I interact with Jesus throughout the "New Creation Celebration" meditation, so my faith is then based on what He is speaking and revealing within my heart.

Faith comes by hearing and hearing by the *rhema* (the spoken word) of Christ (see Rom. 10:17). I agree with what God is revealing, and declare, *"It is so, it is done, according to Your word. Thank You, Lord. I receive what You have spoken."* This response of faith, obedience, and thankfulness releases the power of the Holy Spirit. My outer world *will conform to the message that is written on my heart*, whether that message be old-creation realities or new-creation realities. What I see, believe, intensely feel, and speak is what I receive (see Mark 11:22-24).

THE LANGUAGE OF OUR HEARTS

The language of our minds will not register as meaningful to our hearts. To impact our hearts we must use the language of our hearts. The language of the heart incorporates the following seven elements:

1) it begins with the voice of the Holy Spirit, which is embraced as we choose to 2) affirm it as 3) a personal and 4) present-tense reality. In addition, the heart's language is 5) visual, 6) emotional, and 7) utilizes biblical meditation to frame in our spirits the things God desires to birth in our lives.

You can read through the Psalms to see how often David prays using 1) *affirmative* statements that are 2) *personal* and 3) *present tense.* A few examples from Psalm 3 will get you started:

> *You, O Lord, are a shield about me* (Psalm 3:3).

> *The Lord sustains me* (Psalm 3:5).

> *You have smitten all my enemies* (Psalm 3:7).

SEVEN ELEMENTS IN THE LANGUAGE OF OUR HEARTS

1. *Revelation Birthed by the Spirit*

The Holy Spirit, the River flowing within our innermost being (see John 7:37-39), communicates to our hearts through flowing thoughts, flowing pictures, and flowing energy. The spoken word of God within our hearts (*rhema,* see Rom. 4:17) provides revelation and power (see 1 Cor. 12:7-11).

2. *Personal Truth*

Truth that is not personally acted upon is dead and worthless (see James 1:26; 2:17). Jesus told the lame man to get up. The lame man stood, thus making God's power personal and real to him (see Matt. 9:6-7). Meditation on the word of God must result in us *applying it* in order for it to benefit our lives (see Josh. 1:8). Christ's death on the cross will not benefit anyone who does not personally apply His blood to wash away their sins.

3. *Present-Tense Truth*

We know the spirit world is present tense only, for in the spirit world there is no past or future. God, who is Spirit (see John 4:24), says; *"I AM WHO I AM"* (Exod. 3:14). He is not an "I was" or an "I will be." He is always present tense. Time is part of our world but not part of the spirit world. When we are meditating and lost in spirit, time disappears from our awareness. Our hearts are energized as our spirits communicate present-tense spiritual realities.

4. *Positive Affirmations*

As we thank God that the promised miracle is *already provided,* we open the door for it to be realized. Mark 11:22-24 instructs us to pray, asking, believing, and *speaking that it is done.* Negativity is prohibited. Those who are not thankful lose everything (see Deut. 28:47-48). Instead, an attitude of gratitude and thankfulness is commanded (see Col. 3:15-16; 2:7; Heb. 12:28). *In* everything we give thanks and *for* everything we give thanks because we know that God is big enough to work everything out for good (see 1 Thess. 5:18; Eph. 5:20; Phil. 4:6; 2 Cor. 2:14; Rom. 8:28).

- The statement, "I am sick" is affirmative, but it is affirming the kingdom of darkness' "facts" rather than the Kingdom of God's Truth (see Isa. 53:5).

- The statement, "I am not sick" is a Kingdom truth, but it is not stated in the affirmative.

- "I am healed and walking in health" is a positive, affirmative Kingdom truth.

5. *Truth Visually Seen*

We are to pray that the *eyes of our hearts* would be enlightened (see Eph. 1:18). A picture is worth a thousand words. Pictures move the heart, and ideas move the mind. Jesus spoke to people's hearts, so He constantly taught using parables, which are picture stories (see Matt. 13:34). The Bible is a picture book, painting the stories of people's lives. Holding a picture of the promise fulfilled promotes faith and release of a miracle (see Gen. 15:5-6; 21:1-2).

6. *Emotionally Felt*

We have emotions in our hearts. God was grieved in His *heart* (see Gen. 6:6). Emotions are very often by-products of pictures. If I choose to imagine God's pictures, I am framing up pictures that produce peace and faith for a miracle (see Gen. 15:5-6). If I choose to imagine satan's pictures, I am framing up pictures that produce fear and bring destruction (see Exod. 14:11-12,35).

> *A steadfast imagination produces an emotional response of perfect peace, which in turn frames up and creates my reality.*

Thoughts of our minds are powerless against the pictures we hold in our hearts. I can declare a thousand times that I am the righteousness of God in Christ, but if I am picturing myself as a miserable sinner, the picture wins over the thousandfold confession.

Inner healing requires the use of the language of the heart. In inner healing, we invite Jesus to show us where He is in the trauma and what He is saying and doing. We tune to flowing thoughts (His voice) and flowing pictures (His visions), and we say, "Yes, Lord" to what He reveals, thus taking on His response toward the individual or situation.

> *Embracing this new picture, which contains Jesus alive and ministering God's response, heals our hearts in ways words never can.*

7. *Meditation*

Meditation is something we do in our hearts (see Ps. 19:14; 49:3; Josh. 1:8). "Imagine" is part of the definition of the Hebrew word for "meditate" (Strong's H1897). Meditation involves prayerfully reflecting and allowing the Holy Spirit to illumine the eyes of our hearts so we see from God's perspective (see Eph. 1:17). Our hearts burn with revelation as Jesus opens Scriptures to us (see Luke 24:32).

Meditation frames God's pictures in our spirit so they can be birthed through our spirit into our world. Biblical meditation promotes miracles. Rather than meditate on God's promised provision half the day and satan's fear of failure the other half of the day, we choose to be steadfast and single-minded, meditating *only* on God's promise visually seen as being fulfilled. No double-mindedness because that means I get nothing (see James 1:6-8). A seven-step approach to meditation can be explored here.[38]

> *To write a message on our hearts we utilize the language of our hearts, meaning that the message is birthed by the Spirit and spoken as personal, present-tense, positive reality, which is visual, emotional, and continuously pondered.*

THE FATHER OF FAITH BIRTHS A MIRACLE

An example of a message of faith being written on one's heart is that of Abram, the father of faith. At age 99, God spoke and changed Abram's name to Abraham, which means *father of many nations* (see

---

38   www.cwgministries.org/meditation

Gen. 17:5). This was at a time when Abraham had no children through his wife.

When Abraham thought of or spoke his name, saying, "I am Abraham," he was writing God's promise on his heart by 1) making God's spoken word to him 2) personal, 3) affirmative, 4) present tense, 5) visual (God said he would have as many children as there are stars), which evoked 6) a deep emotional response within Abraham, and 7) Abraham pondered God's promise (see Rom. 4:17-22). He didn't spend his days thinking, "This will never happen."

Notice Abraham was not saying, "I have a *goal* of being the father of..." nor was he saying, "I ought to be..." nor was he saying, "I am becoming...." Each of these statements push the transformed reality off to some future date, and in reality you are telling yourself, "I am not this now."

Instead, Abraham said, "I *am* the father of a multitude of nations." He entered the state of *heart faith*. He heard a promise from God, saying this was his destiny, and he saw a vision from God as the promise fulfilled (see Gen. 12:1-3; 15:5-6). He chose to ponder it, speak it, and act in faith. Now in the fullness of time, God can bring it forth. Isaac was born to his wife one year later, and the earth was blessed through his seed about 1,500 years later when Jesus was resurrected from death at Calvary.

GOALS MISS THE MARK

As Dr. Jim Richards teaches, rather than having goals, we have states.[39] Abraham didn't say, "I have a *goal* of being the father of many nations." So I would not want to say, for example, "My *goal* is vibrant health." Instead, I say, "I live in the *state* of vibrant health" (see Isa. 53:5).

---

39   See Chapter 3 of *Wired for Success, Programmed for Failure* by Dr. Jim Richards.

By His stripes I *am* healed. It's accomplished! It's my reality! It is the state I am living in as far as faith, pictures, and emotions are concerned.

Gazing steadfastly upon God's pictures deepens faith and emotions.

God gave Abram a vision of the promise fulfilled—millions of stars representing millions of children. The next verse says Abram believed (see Gen. 15:5-6). Faith grew as a result of beholding God's pictures of the promise fulfilled. When I see Jesus' scourged body, it is a powerful picture of the extreme price Jesus paid to purchase my healing. This picture inflames faith within me and makes me *emotionally passionate* to receive this precious gift, release it to others, and to live in the state of health. That picture produces heightened Kingdom emotions, and heightened Kingdom emotions precipitate a breakthrough.

Seeing myself living in the state of health until at least 100 years of age makes me aware of what I as a healthy person think, feel, and do. This moves me to action (see James 2:26), and I eat properly, exercise regularly, process emotional upsets, etc. I am living in that reality and sending out a faith signature to every cell of my being and the world around me that says, "I live in the state of health."

Additional pictures enlarge faith, emotions, and the release of the Spirit's power.

Faith and emotions both are channels that release the Spirit's power. Gazing steadfastly at God's pictures enlarges faith and Kingdom emotions. This results in speeding up spiritual transformation.

So if I add some detailed, powerful pictures concerning the lifestyle I experience if I achieve the state of health, this adds *more power* to fulfill this lifestyle. So below, we write these truths upon our hearts by stating them as our personal, present-tense truths.

I live in the state of vibrant health, which means I get to:

- Fulfill my God-given destiny, which is to...

- Be in good health to celebrate my grandchildren, which means I...

- Enjoy my golden years by doing...

- Live on a cruise ship rather than in a nursing home.

- Skip doctors' offices, hospitals, operations, and degenerative diseases.

- Feel good about the way I look, which results in joy and positive self-esteem.

- Have energy to perform each day's activities.

- Have a great sex life.

Well, you get the point. Continue on, painting powerful pictures that are meaningful to you.

Now I have numerous powerful pictures that I can gaze upon, which generate faith and strong emotional responses, releasing the power of the Holy Spirit to stimulate transformation. I am living by the Spirit (see Gal. 5:25).

If I'm not doing it, then I don't really believe it.

The Bible is clear that my faith is perfected by the works I demonstrate (see James 2:22). So if I have faith that I am to live a healthy life and my actions show something different, then my faith is dead (see James 2:17,20,26). I don't really have faith. I am deceiving myself. So that means I will go back through the seven steps that Abraham, the father of faith, took in establishing biblical faith. I will carefully follow the model he left me so I live and walk as a child of faith and do not deceive myself.

ABRAHAM, THE FATHER OF FAITH, MODELS THE INGREDIENTS OF HEART FAITH

1. **I *hear* God's voice.** God speaks a promise and faith is ignited in my heart. Abram's faith walk began when God spoke to him (see Gen. 12:1-3). Faith comes by hearing *rhema*, which is God's voice in our hearts (see Rom. 10:17). God's voice is simple enough for children to receive. It comes effortlessly as spontaneous thoughts. I ask with a pure, obedient heart and I receive (see Matt. 21:22; James 4:3; 1 John 3:22).

2. **I *see* God's vision of the promise fulfilled.** God showed Abram millions of stars as a picture of Abram's millions of descendants. Beholding God's pictures engages my emotions and enlarges faith (see Gal. 15:6). One of the meanings of the word *meditate* is to "imagine" (Strong's H1897). Visions come effortlessly as spontaneous pictures. I ask with a pure, obedient heart and I receive.

3. **I *ponder* God's *rhema* and vision in my heart** (see Rom. 4:20-21). To ponder or to meditate is to roll it over and over as we imagine it. Biblical meditation employs both left and right brain functions as well as engaging the heart. As we meditate, we destroy every unbiblical thought and picture, tearing down these strongholds, and plotting a new course in the Spirit (see 2 Cor. 10:5-6).

    So throughout the day, we *continue* to believe, see, feel, and speak the completed, promised reality God has for me. I do not spend part of my day reverting

back to gloom, fear, lack, or pessimism. I am not double-minded (see James 1:6-8). I maintain *one* clear focus throughout the entire day and as I fall asleep. This
focus is *belief* that God's promise is real and present
tense joined to an *emotion* of thanksgiving and gratitude that it is done!

4. **I *speak* God's promise as my personal, positive, present-tense** reality. In Genesis 17:5 Abram's
name was changed to Abraham, meaning "father of
a multitude." His belief and confession became, "*I am
Abraham,*" or to be crystal clear, he was saying, "I am
the father of a multitude." This obviously was a personal, positive, present-tense reality he was speaking.
The results were that one year later Isaac was born,
meaning the spiritual reality began to be birthed in
the physical realm.

Derek Prince defines a "right confession" as "saying only what God says about our situation and keep
on saying it." When he had an incurable illness, the
Lord told him to confess healing Scriptures over himself three times a day, just as a doctor would prescribe
taking your medicine three times a day. He did and he
was healed.

Part of being passionate is to pray morning, noon,
and evening (see Ps. 55:17). Biblical meditation involves a state of prayer, imagining, and speaking or
muttering. It is most powerful if you speak God's
promises over yourself while you are relaxed, in the

spirit, in a prayerful attitude. The scientific community would define this as being in the alpha state.[40]

5. **I *act*.** Emotions move me to action, and you will recall that emotions are the by-products of the pictures I am gazing upon. When I gaze steadfastly at the promise of God as being already fulfilled in my life, the energy this generates within me becomes strong enough to overwhelm any energy that would seek to block the fulfillment of the promise.

God's energy moves me to take the action God is asking me to take. In Genesis 17:10-23, God spoke and Abraham acted by obeying that very same hour. If my actions are not consistent with what I say I believe, then the Bible says *my faith is useless and dead* (see James 2:20,26).

Over 250 times when the New Testament speaks of knowing, it uses a form of the Greek word *ginosko*, which is an *experiential knowing*. This is the same word used for a man knowing his wife and bearing a child.

> *Biblically speaking, to "know" something,*
> *means information that is revealed,*
> *felt, embraced, and acted upon.*

Knowledge cannot simply be head knowledge. That is why the Bible can demand I have works to go along with my faith or else my faith is dead. I may say I know (intellectually) that by Jesus' stripes I am

---

40 www.cwgministries.org/Brainwaves

healed (see Isa. 53:5), but it is when I see it, believe it, say it, feel it, act on it, and experience it that I really know it (see James 2:17-22).

When new information is *not* integrated through action it is lost within 12 hours. More than being lost, it works against our progress as it gets categorized by our brains as "useless information." The same is true with information I try in some half-baked attempt and it does not work. Again, it is categorized as "useless information" and set aside. *No halfhearted attempts allowed!*

6. **I avoid injecting my ideas into God's plan.** Jesus did nothing on His own initiative (see John 5:30; 8:28,32; 12:49; 14:10; 16:13). Abram and Sarai came up with their *own idea* of how to fulfill the promised miracle of a child. Sarai gave Abram her handmaid to have a child through her. Well, they did get a male child, but God was unwilling to bring the promised miracle through this child (see Gen. 16:2; 17:18-19).

    The principle is we don't add our good ideas to God's revelation. We follow only His instructions. His instructions can come through your *conscience*, which registers in your heart as a "yes" or a "no," or through the voice of God in your heart, which can easily be heard using *two-way journaling*. Another way the Spirit speaks is through *inner peace* as opposed to unrest. If there is not peace in your heart, don't move forward.

7. **In the fullness of time, God brings forth the miracle.** Some miracles are instantaneous, while many

healings are progressive. Achieving your destiny is progressive. Release from captivity came to the Israelites after four generations of slavery, because "the iniquity of the Amorites" was not yet complete (see Gen. 15:16). Yikes! Obviously this means the delay may not always be because of us.

Jesus came forth in the fullness of time (see Gal. 4:4). The fullness of time meant, in part, that Rome had taken over the world and Roman roads were now ready to carry the message of Jesus to the furthest parts of the earth. So we trust in the goodness of God's timing.

Getting a grip on the timeline—Abram received the promise and vision from God when he was 75 years old. He was told to begin confessing it was true when he was 99, and he received the miracle when he was 100.

IDENTIFYING YOUR PROMISED LAND

God has destined for each of us our own "Garden of Eden" where He communes daily with us in the cool of the day and we celebrate His love, kindness, and blessings toward us. From this Garden He speaks to us of our "Promised Land," which He has ordained for us. Let's have these walks in the garden and believe what He says so we inherit our promised destinies and don't die in the wilderness (see Num. 14:28-30).

God generally takes a person through wilderness experiences because that is where they learn key lessons of trust and abandonment to God. I believe we should accept this as part of life.

> *God spoke to me, "Whatever you fix your eyes upon grows within you; whatever grows within you, you become." This transformed what I have chosen to fix my gaze upon.*

I no longer look at disease, self-effort, lack, weakness, or law. Now I only fix my eyes on Jesus and His spoken promises and visions to me, and these grow within me and I step into these realities (see Heb. 12:1-2; Acts 2:25; Ps. 16:8). I am healed! I am blessed! I have favor everywhere I go! I release effective ministry to those I touch! I have a blessed marriage and family! Thank You, Lord, for these amazing gifts!

FAITH: A GIFT FROM GOD'S SPIRIT

Faith is a *gift*, deposited by God into our spirits (see 1 Cor. 12:9). It's a union of belief and emotion (head and heart) that forms as we *fix our attention on God's realities* in the supernatural realm (see 2 Cor. 3:17-18; 4:17-18). It is beholding true spiritual reality as real, finalized, and present tense. I am healed. Everything I put my hand to prospers. My enemy is defeated. I have the gifts of the Holy Spirit operating within me making me more than adequate to get every job done! I win. Yay, God! When there is absolute harmony between beliefs and emotions, transformation occurs.

> *The inner state that releases miracles is established and maintained as I see God's promise to me as already fulfilled. This produces Kingdom emotions of hope, joy, and thanksgiving. This brings my future into my present, releasing a miracle (see Matt. 14:14; 6:22; Phil. 4:6-8).*

Teaming Up

I find miracles happen even more readily when several people join in unity to focus faith, compassion, and gratitude for a miracle (see Eccles. 4:9-12). For example, when we gather around a person, sitting comfortably, and lay hands on them and soak them in God's healing rays for 15 minutes, miracles happen.

We all simply tune to flowing thoughts, flowing words, and flowing pictures and pray and speak as the Spirit is guiding. It is an amazing, life-giving, and miracle-infused time. Try it. It is an incredibly easy and simple process. Those doing the praying get healed as well as the one being prayed for. We call this *healing soaking prayer*.[41]

Your body's own self-healing mechanisms are activated *while you look*. Holding the picture of what your life looks like and what you look like as fully healed, releases in your body a cascade of chemical reactions that activate your body's own healing response. Your body doesn't know the difference between a picture on the screen in your mind and seeing the real, physical thing. It responds to both. For example, a scary dream causes your heart to race and palms to sweat just as if the threat was in your waking world.

CHARITY

CHANGE YOUR FEELINGS, CHANGE YOUR LIFE

In his book *Breaking the Habit of Being Yourself,* Dr. Joe Dispenza cites some incredible research that is pertinent to both our meditation and dream times with the Lord.

---

41 www.cwgministries.org/soak

The study of epigenetics has shown us that our emotions can radically alter our physical health on a biochemical level. Science has demonstrated that emotionally charged experiences, *even ones experienced in our dreams*, change our physiology. We can literally rewire our neural pathways, influencing the cascade of hormones and neurotransmitters released into our system, which then upregulate and downregulate gene expression in our cells.

What does that have to do with anything? That's a scientific glimpse into supernatural transformation. When we become a Christian our spirits are 100 percent saved; however, we also know that we are to work out our salvation together with Holy Spirit who is working in us (see Phil. 2:12-13).

Dream work and meditation are powerful ways we do that as we observe and collapse that healed and whole version of ourselves into this world. Indeed, that is one of the most beneficial yet least understood blessings of dream work—the ability to experience and truly *feel* how it feels to live in God's version of reality.

The truth of our new-creation miracle is wonderful, but so often we don't understand what that actually looks like in the real world. Like Paul, we want to "know Christ and the power of His resurrection." That sounds great on paper, but what does it mean in our everyday lives and, more importantly, how does it feel?

We can know how it feels as we experience our new-creation selves in the spirit realm through our visions by day and by night. As we ponder those pictures God gives us, we feel their truth. This in turn changes our physiology by switching on healthy genes that unleash healing flow, thereby flooding our bodies with renewed life and energy, regenerating us from the inside out.

MEMORIES OF THE FUTURE

We live out of whatever picture we are holding in our hearts, so we want to hold on to God's pictures. We do this through our visionary prayers. Last summer my husband Leo and I attended a Quantum Glory conference with Phil Mason, spiritual director of Tribe Byron Bay in Australia. He shared many profound insights, but the revelation that impacted us the most was that *"Prophecy is memories of the future."* Yes, that's it!

Indeed, God lives in timelessness, so something we may consider still off in the distance He sees as present-tense reality. In our times of meditation, we do too. We ponder the "memories of our future" that God has given us, His prophetic promises to us. We meditate on those memories and memorize our future. We "remember" His version of our future as we live into the eternal now of God, the great I AM.

When we're in the spirit and in that state of potential manifested and promises realized, we are naturally filled with joy and thankfulness. *Our signature of faith attracts the blessing, and our practiced observation collapses it.* All we need to do is get inside of God's pictures of us through our dreams, visions, and meditations and live to that truth. Live to the memories of our future.

COLLAPSING HIS GLORY

As we have discussed, according to the observer effect in quantum physics, when we observe something, we change it. Just our very act of looking at it affects it. This is an important principle, and we want to revisit it to be sure we appreciate its powerful implication in our lives.

Physicists demonstrate how we can "transform" invisible waves of energy into localized particles of matter—electrons and photons in our natural world—simply by observing them. This is called wave function collapse, and as we have said, for our purposes *collapsing* simply means moving something from the invisible to the visible, from the unseen realm into our seeable, tangible world.

We understand how this principle correlates to our walk in the Spirit because God has a heavenly image of us in His invisible spiritual world. His version of us is in Christ, radiating life and light and the very glory of God because we are in Him and He is in us and our spirits are one with His Spirit (see 1 Cor. 6:17). We participate in His divine nature and are filled up with the fullness of God (see 2 Pet. 1:4; Eph. 3:19). That is His version of who we are right now.

But if we don't see what He sees, the "best us" is only seen in heaven. We need to collapse that blessed new-creation version of ourselves into our current lives here and now. In order to accomplish this, we just need to see what God is seeing, which brings us to another dream I had.

"Papa"razzi

The night after I dreamt of chasing butterflies (mentioned earlier in this book), I had a seemingly unrelated night vision. In my dream, I was eating junk food in a grocery store. I was called outside, and there a photographer took my picture over and over and over again. Different angles, fabulous shots. My clothes were perfect, my hair was styled just right, and I smiled brightly for the camera, realizing what awesome photos these were going to be.

We can decode the symbolism by seeing that the junk food store was a place of unhealthy temptation—of indulging in garbage within like unhealthy thoughts, feelings, pictures. Papa God was the paparazzi photographer! He brought me out of that unhealthy place, and then He took my picture (see 1 Cor. 10:13). That represents Him giving me His version of myself. He showed me His angle and how I look to

Him—how He sees me. I could see myself through the lens of heaven and how I am His image.

First Corinthians 11:15 says a woman's hair is her glory, and in this dream my hair was amazing. This was a picture of God's glory being perfected in me—perfect style, cut, highlights, a "glamour shot." When we see Him as He is, we will be like Him (see 1 John 3:2). And as I looked at Him, I was changed into His image from glory to glory (see 2 Cor. 3:18).

We are in His image. We are His image. We must see ourselves the way He sees us—His image, shot, version, and perspective of us. Through His lens, from His point of view. What is He focused on? What is He totally overlooking? What is He highlighting and "zooming in" on? What's His angle? Collapse His vision and version of our new-creation selves. Collapse the best us, the Christ-us, into this reality and dimension.

PROUD PAPA

Another encouraging reminder this dream gives about God's perspective of us is felt when we consider the question, "What do you even bother to photograph?" It's only things that you value, cherish, and love. You take pictures of what you're proud of and want to show off and share with others. God is proud of us! We are that special to our heavenly Father, worthy of photographing and focusing on and treasuring.

Through our visions by day in meditation and our visions by night in dreams, we are able to see ourselves through the lens of Heaven, through God's eyes. He too is a witness of us, observing us. This is how we exist at all, because God is the Ultimate Observer.[42]

---

42 See Chapter 5 of *Quantum Glory* by Phil Mason.

To bring His reality into our natural world, we simply agree with what He shows us and see the same thing too. Just as the word *confess* means "to say the same thing as" God is saying, we also want "to see the same thing as" God is seeing. And in that place of meditation we will find ourselves transformed as we look, overflowing with peace, joy, gratitude, and every Kingdom emotion.

When we see snapshots of the spirit realm we are able to agree with them, unleashing God's blessing into our lives as manifested miracles. We live to the reality of our new-creation selves and Holy Spirit's anointing within us and upon us. We observe every good gift Father has given to us and release those resources of the Kingdom into our world, collapsing the invisible into the visible, collapsing the unseen into the seen, collapsing the glory—bringing heaven to earth.

MARK

GAZE UPON MY NEW SELF

Because I become what I gaze upon, I want to gaze upon my new-creation self—who I am in Christ. The text below comes from a "New Creation Celebration" worksheet. It guides you into *taking time* to hear from God and then to *gaze* upon your new self in Christ and experience the rush of spirit emotions and spirit power that leave you elated, empowered, and overjoyed. Plan on experiencing what Peter called "*joy inexpressible* and full of glory" (another heightened Kingdom emotion) and this obtains for us salvation (1 Pet. 1:8-9). The Greek word for "salvation" in the New Testament is *sōtēria* and is defined as deliverance, preservation, safety, salvation, and includes healing (Strong's G4991).

New Creation Celebration: Putting on Christ

*Jesus, let me see and feel my new creation in You. What does it feel like to release the **fruit** of Your Spirit*[43]*—to love everyone I meet? How do I act when I'm walking in forgiveness and patience and kindness toward all, including myself? What does it feel like to have joy flood my soul and overflow, bathing others in its cascade and laughter? My heart is so merry; it's having a continual feast. Others get caught up in my joy; it's contagious. And your peace—it sweeps over my soul; I feel such deep contentment. Every part of me is at rest in You.*

Lord, I receive Your equipping[44] *for the issues I will be encountering today. I see myself releasing Your **insight and wisdom** to meet each issue. What does it feel like to release Your wisdom? Your gift of **faith is arising within me**. What does faith that moves mountains feel like? I see myself as more than a conqueror, always triumphing in Christ. What does it feel like to be on the winning team? I see myself releasing **Your healing and miracles** to others. How do I feel? I sense just the **right words** bubbling up within me, which I share to minister life to those I meet. I **feel their hearts' needs** and minister directly to them. I notice how it feels to be equipped by the Holy Spirit. How do I act when anointed and empowered?*

How do I feel being free, being inspired, being creative? What choices do I make now that I'm not afraid? How do

---

43   Galatians 5:22-23: love, joy, peace, patience, kindness, goodness, faithfulness, gentleness, self-control.

44   1 Corinthians 12:7–11: word of wisdom, word of knowledge, faith, gifts of healings, working of miracles, prophecy, the discerning of spirits, various kinds of tongues, interpretation of tongues.

I look enveloped by God's presence? What does His delight over me feel like? How does experiencing His tender compassion make me feel? How do I live life with God at my right hand, knowing I will not be shaken? How does it feel to be forgiven? And healed? What can I do now that I'm strong and healthy? What kind of decisions do I make knowing my Dad is the King of kings? How does being royalty make me feel? What choices do I make knowing that I can do all things through Christ? What does being strengthened by His Spirit in my inner man feel like? What does confidence feel like? How grateful am I, knowing that my steps are ordered of the Lord and He is working all things for my good? How do I feel knowing God always has my back and He is always watching out for me? What kinds of prayers do I pray or decrees do I make from my position with Christ on His throne?

When I do this exercise, I get up from my devotional time charged with the energy of God! Try it. Make it part of your practice, especially on any day you need to put on Christ and be charged with His energy. I'm going to guess that is most days.

Activate both miracles and gifts of healings by taking ten to fifteen minutes to process the above as part of your daily devotions. As you gaze upon your new self in Christ, you are creating and sending forth a signature of faith that is powerful in attracting God's miracles to your life. You are releasing to your body God's natural *and* supernatural healing processes. How cool is that!

HOW MUCH OF THE TIME DO WE LIVE IN FAITH, HOPE, AND LOVE?

If I see myself healed, restored, at peace, functioning in my God-ordained destiny during my morning devotions and then I spend the remainder of my day seeing and feeling the opposite, what do you think I should expect as a result? Would this be what the Bible calls double-minded? What exactly does a double-minded man receive from God?

> *Ask in faith, with no doubting, for he who doubts is like a wave of the sea driven and tossed by the wind. For let not that man suppose that he will receive anything from the Lord; he is a double-minded man, unstable in all his ways* (James 1:6-8 NKJV).

I must come to see one reality, not two. When your eye is single, see what happens. *"The eye is the lamp of the body; so then if your eye is clear, your whole body will be full of light"* (Matt. 6:22). So I choose to see only my new self in Christ with His promises fulfilled *now*. This releases a stream of divine light, flooding my entire being with light all day if I gaze upon this picture all day.

*"But if your eye is bad, your whole body will be full of darkness. **If then the light that is in you is darkness, how great is the darkness!**"* (Matt. 6:23). There is no reason for me to look away from God's promises and see satan's darkness, as that contaminates my entire being with darkness, sickness, hopelessness and death. Trust me, I have done this and it is not fun.

So if I am single-minded for 3 percent of my day (during my devotional time), holding the picture of my destiny and then the remainder of the day I hold another picture, another thought, another emotion, thinking, "It's never going to happen," would you say I was single-minded or double-minded? Will I get my healing or not? Will I achieve my destiny or not?

I will not receive my miracle because I am still signaling my mind, heart, and spirit in two opposite realities. Part of the day I am signaling my genes to fulfill God's destiny of health and blessing, and the other part of the day I am signaling my genes for stress and death. Will that mixed signal restore my body to health? Will that mixed faith produce a supernatural miracle? I don't think so.

Healing occurs when you get beyond the state of duality.

Trusting self produces the stress mode while trusting in God produces a relaxed mode. Your heart and mind note if you are in stress or in relaxation. For example, when you are upset, your stomach doesn't digest food well. When you are at peace, you have good digestion. Your emotional state affects your body, its functions, and its health.

Remember, most adult diseases have an emotional root. Wouldn't it be nice to be signaling your genes for healthy responses 100 percent of the day rather than 3 percent? Every second, 25 million cells are dying and being replaced by 25 million new cells. One cell experiences 100,000 to 6 trillion functions per second. There are 70 trillion cells in your body. Your heart and mind are controlling all these bodily responses.

"What I see is what I get."

Imagine how much healing is pouring into your body as you experience God's emotions, which is exactly what you are training yourself to experience in the "New Creation Celebration" meditations. We can learn to live this new-creation reality continuously!

CLEAR INTENTION PRODUCES GREATER RESULTS!

It has been discovered that if we do an activity with clear understanding, intention, and belief, we will experience better results. Faith works and signals your body to perform in light of what we believe for.

For example, 84 hotel cleaning ladies were discovered to be putting in enough daily bodily exercise through their job to be losing weight, and yet they weren't. However, when half were told that they were doing sufficient exercise to be losing weight, they did their cleaning with the intention of losing weight, and they lost weight and lowered their blood pressure.[45]

The goal of this book is to help you have clear intention concerning the power and the value of Kingdom emotions and know how to live continuously in them.

> *As I gaze upon images of God's promises to me as already fulfilled, I experience His Kingdom realities of faith, joy, and peace uniting my mind and heart, releasing those miracles into my life.*

DREAMS PROMOTE SPIRITUAL TRANSFORMATION

Our dreams are visionary, strongly emotional, and extremely transformational. Nighttime counsel from God comes couched in symbolic

---

45 Alia J. Crum and Ellen J. Langer, "Mind-Set Matters," *Psychological Science* 18, no. 2 (2007): 165–171, doi:10.1111/j.1467-9280.2007.01867.x.

dreams with intense images prompting strong emotions, which occur while you are in alpha and theta brainwave levels.

Thus, dreams can provide huge transformations, especially when recorded and acted upon. Often, the final image or key emotion of the dream is enough to meditate upon and receive a message. I choose to fall asleep asking God to grant revelation, counsel, guidance, gifts, and transformation through the dreams He gives me (see Ps. 16:7).

When you awaken, note any stressful emotions you feel in your dreams. These should be processed during your devotional time, as they are showing areas that need to be given to Christ and healed through His loving touch. Even if you have in the past done a devotional meditation to heal a particular emotion, the fact that it is showing up again means there is a deeper root that still needs to be dealt with or you are now facing a challenge in which you need to re-apply Christ's redemptive power.

Take your time as you go through a "New Creation Celebration: Replacing Emotions" meditation. Resolve this stressful emotion that is showing up in your dream. Jesus can and will *fully* heal it. Discover more about Christian dream interpretation here.[46]

Remember, healing occurs in layers, and as you face new challenges you will be required to apply your faith in a new and perhaps deeper way. Not a problem. That is what the process of life and growth is all about. That is what the Bible calls "working out your salvation" (see Phil. 2:12-13).

---

46 www.cwgministries.org/dreams

MY TESTIMONY: INCREASED FAITH RELEASES A MIRACLE

After using the "New Creation Celebration: Replacing Emotions" for over a week, I switched to "New Creation Celebration: Replacing Beliefs." God wanted to change my beliefs from believing "I can't perform in the area of marketing to groups or networks" to believing "I have an anointing to perform in the area of marketing to networks."

I processed this topic numerous days in a row until I believed and saw myself, during my devotional times, easily and confidently performing in the area of establishing marketing relationships with networks and groups.

Now, remember the statement at the end of the "New Creation Celebration" meditations:

> *God, I ask for and fully expect to see a sign from You today confirming my new-creation reality, which I have just put on. Let it overtake me in whatever **unique** way You purpose. You honor faith! Your faith **is** radiating out through me! I feel it and see its rays reaching out, drawing Your provision to my life. Thank You, Lord! It feels so good (see Ps. 86:17; Matt. 21:22; Deut. 28:1-14).*

Now that my heart was positioned in faith, I was sending out a message into the world for networkers to come to me for their curriculum needs. Within about three weeks I received a call from a curriculum marketer 3,000 miles away, asking if he could enter into a contract with me to market our 100 courses out to 8 million of his contacts!

My answer was yes! This miracle could never have happened in the past because there was no love or compassion in my heart focused on marketing to networks or groups. I believed I couldn't do it. I didn't like to do it, didn't want to do it, and didn't do it. Well, this is death for a businessman or a ministry. *Change your heart, change your life.*

So expect miracles in whatever unique way God wants to reveal them.

As you use the "New Creation Celebration" meditations for several weeks, you will be moving into new faith in key areas in your life. This new faith will result in miracles.

GOD'S ARMOR PROTECTS OUR HEARTS AND MINDS

The Bible warns us not to doubt in our hearts (see Mark 11:23), so we can protect our hearts by filling them with faith and love—putting on the breastplate of faith and love—and protect our minds by filling them with hope—putting on a helmet of hope (see 1 Thess. 5:8), which in Greek means "to anticipate with pleasure" (Strong's G1680).

Faith, hope, and love is the state of Kingdom living (see 1 Cor. 13:13). What a state it is! It's the only state to live in. It's the state that releases health, healing, miracles, and personal transformation, and as such it is the state satan will seek to steal from us and return us to his kingdom's emotions of fear, hopelessness, and anger.

The devotional "New Creation Celebration: Replacing Emotions" brings you into God's Kingdom state on a daily basis. It is worth the time it takes to do it, because living outside God's Kingdom state is barely living at all, for you are living in the kingdom of darkness rather than the Kingdom of light.

ACTION EXERCISES

1. Continue using the devotional, "New Creation Celebration: Replacing Emotions"[47] from last week's assignment.

2. Journaling: "Lord, what do You want to speak to me concerning being single-minded about my destiny and my health? Am I double-minded? How would You have me deal with this?"

3. Practice receiving, writing, and speaking statements that write God's words on your heart. Let the Lord guide you in completing a series of power-packed statements. Each statement is to be 1) personal, 2) positive, 3) present tense, 4) visual, and 5) emotional. "I am

   _____.

4. Journaling: Put your journal next to your bed, and as you fall asleep ask God to give you dreams. When you awaken, immediately record them, then interpret them in the morning and act in obedience to the counsel being received.

5. Examine the vast array of things faith accomplishes.[48]

---

47 cwgministries.org/emotions
48 cwgministries.org/ReasonOrFaith

Chapter 6

ENERGIZED BY POWER FROM THE HOLY SPIRIT

*"Faith **energized by** love."*
—see GALATIANS 5:6

*Discover how to tap into the Holy Spirit's
energy, which is everywhere!*

Faith needs to be coupled with something in order to be truly effective. The Bible talks of "faith *working through* love" (Gal. 5:6). *Working through* is an interesting phrase. It indicates that when faith is joined by love there is some sort of energizing that takes place. The phrase *working through* is the Greek word *energeō* (Strong's G1754), which we shall see literally means "energized by."

In this chapter, we are going to explore *energeō* in depth so we get a feel for this power that energizes faith. What is it? Where is it? Where does it come from? How can it be increased or decreased? Is this energizing actually crucial to releasing faith that moves mountains and casts them into the sea? Do I really need this energizing if I am going to experience miracles and healings?

This energizing, the power of the Holy Spirit, fills everything and is everywhere: *"In Him all things hold together"* (Col 1:17). This energy of the Spirit is the energy or power of God, the Creator and Sustainer of the world. The power or energy of the Spirit is what Jesus drew upon to release miracles in His life. This is the power I passionately desire to become intimately acquainted with so I too can walk effortlessly in the supernatural. The Holy Spirit is more than a power. The Holy Spirit is a Person of the Godhead who is to be honored and loved and who can be grieved.

The Bible says, "God is love" and that God is almighty (see 1 John 4:7; Gen. 17:1). The key to releasing God's almighty power is to be deeply embedded in His love. When I am abiding in His love, then I can experience His power energizing me and flowing out through me to others (see John 15:9; 1 Cor. 13:13; Mark 5:30).

MY STRENGTH *OR* THE EMPOWERING OF THE HOLY SPIRIT?

*Cursed is the man who trusts in mankind and **makes flesh his strength**, and whose heart turns away from the Lord* (Jeremiah 17:5).

***It is the Spirit who gives life**; the flesh profits nothing; the words* [rhemas] *that I have spoken to you are spirit and are life* (John 6:63-64).

Apart from Me you can do nothing (John 15:5).

The above verses are incredibly intense!

If I am going to choose my strength, I am cursed. The strength of my flesh provides *no profit!* The Greek word *rhema* in the above verse means "spoken word," so the alternative to living out of my strength is to live out of God by hearing His voice and receiving His power.

The following verses teach us that our focus needs to be on the energizing power of the Spirit.

> *For the mind set on the flesh is death, but the **mind set on the Spirit** is life and peace* (Romans 8:6).

> *You are not in the flesh but **in the Spirit*** (Romans 8:9).

> ***If by the Spirit you are** putting to death the deeds of the body, you will live* (Romans 8:13).

In this chapter we are going to explore in depth the Holy Spirit and His amazing energy that fills us, surrounds us, and is the very breath we breathe. As we tune to His power, not trusting in the strength of our flesh, miracles happen. So expect miracles to occur as you continue doing the "New Creation Celebration" devotionals.

These miracles can happen in every area, including experiencing transformed emotions, physical healings, relational healings, miracles of provision, and increased creativity. The list is absolutely endless, so widen your expectations. As you grow in faith in area after area, the Holy Spirit will draw to you that which you believe God for.

THE HOLY SPIRIT'S POWER IS ACTIVE *ENERGY*

Energeō is one of the three Greek words translated "power" in the New Testament. The summary below focuses on *energeō*, which includes "the active flow of God's power within us and out through us producing transformation."

GREEK WORDS FOR POWER	BIBLICAL REALITY	CONTEMPORARY EXAMPLE
Authority *Exousia* Used over 100 times	God has given us authority (*exousia*) to cast out demons and heal the sick.	New York Power Authority : *Authorized* to see that power is provided to NYS residents.
Power *Dunamis* Used over 100 times	The Holy Spirit provides us power (*dunamis/* dynamite) from God to perform these miracles.	Niagara Mohawk power plant provides the electric *power* to each home.
Energy *Energeō* Used about 40 times	When I speak and lay hands on the sick, I am actively releasing (*energeō*) God's energy.	A toaster provides an *active release* of this electricity.

The Greek word "Energeo" as Defined from Bible Dictionaries

- *Kittle Theological Dictionary of the New Testament*: Active energy, to be at work.

- *Robinson's Word Pictures:* To energize, God is the energizer of the universe.

- *Thayer's Greek Definitions:* To put forth power, to work for one, to aid one, to effect.

A Working Definition of Energeō:

> *Energeō is the power of God available through the Holy Spirit that accomplishes God's work. I experience it as flowing, active energy. This energy is released when faith and compassion are joined!*

What do *you* believe the energy of the Holy Spirit accomplishes?

I suggest it would be helpful for you to just stop reading for a moment and ask yourself this question: "When do I sense the Holy Spirit? What is He currently doing in my life? What is the Spirit doing in the world today? Is the Spirit's energizing only for miracles or for other things also? If other things, then what would these things include?"

This is what I believe the Holy Spirit accomplishes in my life and in the world today:

_____

_____

_____

_____

_____

Did you stop? Did you make your list of what you believe the power of the Holy Spirit accomplishes in your life?

Let's take a look at the word *energeō* in the New Testament and see if His energy is more or less limited than what you have described above. Because being empowered by God is the core of successful living, it is truly crucial we have a good grasp of what His power accomplishes. So here we go!

WHAT THE ENERGY OF THE HOLY SPIRIT ACCOMPLISHES

Energeō or some form of this Greek word shows up in each Scripture below.

1. God energizes the Christian and is working all things out for good.

God energizes Christians by His Spirit to accomplish His good pleasure. While demons can energize unbelievers, their energizing power is limited by God and will ultimately be overcome by Him (see John 19:11; Eph. 2:2; 2 Thess. 2:9,11). For those who want to be deceived, God energizes them with a strong delusion (see 2 Thess. 2:11).

For example:

> *For it is God who is at* **work** [energizes] *in you, both to will and to* **work** [energizes] *for His good pleasure* (Philippians 2:13).

> *I also labour, striving according to his working* [energizing], *which worketh* [energizes] *in me mightily* [dunamis] (Colossians 1:29 KJV).

> *We have obtained an inheritance, having been predestined according to His purpose who* **works** [energizes] *all things after the counsel of His will* (Ephesians 1:11).

Record a time(s) you have experienced the above energizing by the Spirit:

_____

_____

_____

_____

_____

_____

2. Both the Bible and Spirit-anointed preaching are energized by God.

The Bible is anointed and energized by God and transforming for those who receive its truths (see 1 Thess. 2:13). Spirit-energized testimonies can transform the lives of those who receive and believe them (see Phil. 1:6). For example:

> For the word of God is living and active [energizing] and sharper than any two-edged sword (Hebrews 4:12).

Record times you have received energizing revelation from Scripture or preaching:

_____

_____

_____

_____

_____

3. The gifts and ministry one has as well as the open doors to minister come from divine energizing through the Holy Spirit.

The gifts one has, the ministry one is called to, and open doors to minister are "energizings" from God (see 1 Cor. 12:6,10,11; Gal. 2:7-8; Eph. 3:7). We are to labor according to the energizing of the Holy Spirit working within us (see Col. 1:29). When we operate in the divine gifts

God has placed within us, serving one another with these gifts, we build up and energize the body of Christ (see Eph. 4:16). As we draw upon Christ's life in trying situations, the testimony of His in-working power energizes others (see 2 Cor. 4:11-12). We should pray for divine energizing of our words as we share our testimonies of Christ's work within us (see Phil. 1:6). For example:

> *A wide door for effective* [energizing] *service has opened to me, and there are many adversaries* (1 Corinthians. 16:9).

Record times you have seen the Spirit opening a door for you to minister:

_____

_____

_____

_____

_____

4. *Spirit-energized prayer accomplishes supernatural results, including deliverance and healing.*

The energized prayer of a righteous man is effective, as it imparts God's power (see James 5:16). Divine energizing brings forth divine works (see Eph. 1:29; 3:20; Mark 6:13-14). Faith is energized when coupled with love (see Gal. 5:6). God's energy within us releases God's grace to us and this is *freely* received. The energizing release of power for a miracle comes from God and is not a result of the works of the law but of hearing with faith. It was God's energy that brought forth Jesus from the dead (see Eph. 1:20). For example:

So then, does He who provides you with the Spirit and works [energizes] *miracles among you, do it by the works of the Law, or by hearing with faith?* (Galatians 3:5)

Record times you have seen the Spirit accomplish a miracle in your life;

_____

_____

_____

_____

_____

_____

In summary, *make sure you are experiencing the Spirit in all these ways* so you don't lean instead on the strength of your flesh. This "active energy" (*energeō*) operates in the release of divine power for miracles and gifts of healings, the sustaining of the universe, the energizing of individual gifts within people, the opening of doors God provides for us to minister, as well as when we preach under the Spirit's anointing. This "active energy" is also present in the experience of God's manifest presence, which is sometimes called the "glory" of God. This "active energy" illumines the Scriptures to our hearts and minds and ministers Spirit life to the hearts of those who hear the preaching of the word.

Energeō, the energy of the Holy Spirit, produces personal transformation, miracles, gifts of healings, rising from the dead, opportunities to minister, and anointed ministry, while sustaining every molecule in the universe.

Become an expert on the active energy of the Holy Spirit by carefully meditating on each verse that has *energeō* (or its forms) in it.[49]

WHAT DOES HOLY SPIRIT ENERGIZING FEEL LIKE?

You can *sense* the energizing (*energeō*) of the Holy Spirit in the following ways (especially as you tune to inner sensations);

1. When our *hands* are energized by the Holy Spirit, it is sensed as warmth, fire, heat, tingling, and energy. This is often experienced as we lay hands on the sick (see Luke 5:17; Mark 5:30).

2. When our *hearts* are energized by the Holy Spirit, it is sensed as an inner quickening resulting in a flow of faith, hope, love, compassion, joy, peace, mercy, power, or our hearts burning within. We are experiencing the manifestation and fruit of the Holy Spirit within us (see Gal. 5:22; 1 Cor. 12:7-11; Luke 24:32).

3. When our *lips* are energized by the Holy Spirit it is sensed as a flow of words that come through the instruction of the Holy Spirit and set the captive free (see Luke 12:12; 21:15; 4:32). We are "speaking the oracles of God" (see 1 Pet. 4:11 KJV). It is our hearts instructing our mouths and adding persuasiveness to our lips (see Prov. 16:23); or, another way to say this, the Holy Spirit within is teaching our lips what to say (see 1 Cor. 2:13; Matt. 10:20).

---

49 www.cwgministries.org/energeo

4. When our *work* is energized by the Holy Spirit, it is sensed as working at ease, experiencing flow, creativity, and productivity because we've entered His rest, and is considered a "live work" rather than a "dead work" (see Heb. 6:1-2).

5. When our *mind* is energized by the Holy Spirit, it is sensed as flowing, anointed, creative thoughts and is called "the mind of Christ" (1 Cor. 2:16).

Record times you have experienced these Holy Spirit sensations in your life:

_____

_____

_____

_____

_____

_____

HOW DO WE SENSE THE HOLY SPIRIT'S ENERGY?

The eyes and ears of our hearts see and hear.

We can ask God to show us the flow of His power. We tune to flowing pictures and flowing thoughts and minister what we are receiving (see John 5:19-20,30).

Our hearts feel God's emotions.

We ask the Holy Spirit to manifest God's compassion on the person/situation to whom we are ministering, and then we sense that compassion supernaturally arise within us (see Matt. 14:14).

Hands release power.

Our hands often feel heat, energy, and vibration/tingling in them when the power of God is moving out through them (see Luke 6:19).

> *Light flashes from his* [and my] **hand, there where his power is hidden** (Habakkuk 3:4 GNT).

When I lay my hands on the sick, I see and feel this power flowing out through my touch.

Record times you have experienced these things in your life:

_____

_____

_____

_____

_____

_____

WHAT ACTIVITIES INCREASE THE FLOW OF HOLY SPIRIT'S ENERGY?

1. Inviting the Holy Spirit to Be Present

We can then look and see Him as light and glory shimmering around us, through us and throughout His creation. One way we *honor* the Holy Spirit is by inviting Him to be present and stating our dependence upon His healing power to be released to perform the miracle at hand. This results in Him manifesting Himself in the ways we need—the power to heal or any of the nine fruits or nine-fold manifestations of His Spirit (see Gal. 5:22-23; 1 Cor. 12:7-11).

2. *Praying for Healing*

We ask for the Holy Spirit's power and compassion to be present. We tune to God's compassion arising in our hearts and a sensation of energy being present in our hands, which we may experience as trembling/tingling and often heat. As we touch the sick, we release that energy into them. The Holy Spirit's flow and power can be restricted when any of the following are present: unforgiveness, anger, bitterness, hatred, rage, unconfessed sin, not welcoming and drawing upon the Holy Spirit's presence, and speaking negative words (see Eph. 4:29-32).

3. *Worshiping in Spirit (John 4:23-24)*

We are to see ourselves seated with Him in heavenly places and worshiping before His throne (see Eph. 2:6-7; Rev. 4). As we do this, we soak up the atmosphere of heaven. We are gazing upon God's power streaming from His throne as rays of light. They penetrate our being (see Hab. 3:4). We soak up this power and light. Then as we lay hands on the sick and command healing, we see God's power (*energeō*) as light flowing out from us.

Record times you have experienced these things in your life:

_____

_____

_____

_____

_____

_____

Summary: Maximizing the Flow of the Holy Spirit

In each of the above situations, we enter into a state of rest, ceasing our own labors, while inviting and believing instead for the power of the Holy Spirit to accomplish (see Heb. 3-4). We honor the Holy Spirit by welcoming His presence, and then we turn to the Holy Spirit who is experienced within as a flowing river (see John 7:37-39). This means we tune to flowing thoughts, flowing pictures, flowing emotions, and flowing energy, which are all coming from our heavenly Father's throne room. This River of the Holy Spirit, which flows from His throne, is now flowing out through us (see Rev. 22:1).

DOES SEEING WITH THE EYES OF THE HEART INCREASE THE FLOW OF HOLY SPIRIT ENERGY?

King David wrote about abiding (see Ps. 15:1), and in the following chapter in Psalms he said that the way he did this was to see the Lord at His right hand, all the time (see Ps. 16:8; Acts 2:25). We can choose to do the same thing. Using godly imagination, we can see Jesus at our right hand all the time. As we invite the Holy Spirit to show us what Jesus is doing, and we tune to flow, we get to see visions of Jesus in action in our world today. We join Him, becoming His hands, feet, and body. As we take on Jesus' actions, we are releasing Christ into our surroundings!

Pictures are the language of our hearts. When our heart speaks to us in our sleep, it does so in dreams that are composed of pictures (see Ps. 16:7). The Bible says the issues of life flow from our hearts (see Prov. 4:23). In his letter to the Ephesian church, Paul prayed for the eyes of their hearts to be enlightened (see Eph. 1:17-18). We want to do the same. This invites visions to flow within us.

When Abram, the father of faith, *saw* God's promise fulfilled in a divinely imparted picture ("the stars of the sky"), the Bible says *then* Abram believed (see Gen. 15:5-6). *Seeing* a spiritual reality with the eyes of our hearts *deepens faith* in our hearts. The Bible says that the one who does not doubt in his heart can cast mountains into the sea, and all things become possible to him who believes.

As you declare healing, choose to look and see the flow of God's divine power (*energeō*) as light decimating satan's darkness. Practice tuning to flow so you can feel His power leaving you and entering another.

Record a time you had a clear picture of the promise fulfilled and it produced deepened faith:

_____

_____

_____

_____

_____

_____

Testimonies of Spirit Energy at Work

Many have shared that as they did the "River of Life" meditation they felt energy pulsating through their body. I experience that as well. The same goes for the "New Creation Celebration: Replacing Emotions" meditation. Many have testified to a release of demonic energy and a fresh new energizing by the Holy Spirit. I am confident that as you experience these devotionals, you will sense the same energizing.

Journaling about God's Power

Mark, My power sustains all things. It is the manifestation of My power that releases creative miracles. When you come into My presence you see Me. You see My power. You see My glory as light that shines forth from My Throne and My Presence. And then you command My will on earth as you see it in heaven.

The Kingdom comes to earth because the one who has been breathing in the atmosphere of My heaven releases that atmosphere on My earth through their commands. So it is all about Me. It is about being in My presence and releasing My presence and My authority on My earth. It is about breathing in My glory and then exhaling it on My earth. This is what I have chosen for My Church to do. This is your job. Behold, I have spoken. Behold, it is to be done.

THE HOLY SPIRIT, FILLING ALL SPACE

When I look around, do I see the Holy Spirit everywhere or do I see empty space filled with various items—houses, trees, chairs, etc.?

The 99.999 percent of the atom that is "empty space" is actually the Spirit of God who fills all things (see Col. 1:17, *"In Him all things hold together"*). So don't see this as empty space. See the life-giving Spirit, infused with divine wisdom and power that He is constantly releasing!

> *I choose to see true reality. I see God's energy flowing everywhere, all the time. I see God's Spirit energizing every atom, transforming every molecule, healing all oppressed by the devil.*

As I look to see what the Holy Spirit might look like, I see shimmering waves of light around me. Sometimes I see Him as similar to the Aurora Borealis lights in the northern sky. When I look to the throne room I also see Him as shimmering waves of light and energy, swirling around the thrones of God and Jesus. I see His energy lighting me within.

The Spirit rides out through us on the waves of compassion and gratitude. In releasing healing to ourselves or others, we begin with God's compassion, which He gives us as we ask for it. We extend compassion to ourselves and all others. On the waves of compassion ride

God's wisdom, light, glory, and power to heal. We maintain an attitude of gratitude believing that this amazing energy of the Spirit is real and is present all around us, infusing all things. This energy is transforming everything into the glory of God (see Rom. 8:28).

We see this, feel it, think it, speak it, believe it, and bask in the glow of His radiant light. No wonder we are happy and filled with joy and thanksgiving. Who wouldn't be?

Journaling about God's Glory

> Mark, do not make My manifest presence hard. It is not hard. Yes, it is true that I choose when to manifest Myself. I have chosen to manifest My presence and My glory when I am invited to do so. It is as simple as that. Do not make it any harder. When you ask according to My will, then you receive that which you have asked for. It *is* My will to manifest My glory throughout the whole world. So ask and receive, that your joy be made full. My glory does arise over My people. It does protect and empower them. It is My will to do so and for My world to see this glory.
>
> Mark, the more you live and see yourself seated with Me in heaven, the more you are endued with heaven's atmosphere and are able to release heaven on earth. For that which you live in is what you see, breathe, and soak up. Then it is that which you release to others. So come and live in My heavens, for that is where I have placed you. You *are* seated with Me in heavenly places. Come up here often and see My glory and My Kingdom and then release it on earth. Behold, I have spoken; behold, it is to be done.

BE INTENTIONAL ABOUT CONNECTING WITH THE SPIRIT

Don't be haphazard as you enter into worship, pray for healing, or just walk down the road of life. I don't hope to get into the Spirit somehow, sometime, during the worship service. I choose Spirit emotions, not soulish emotions. I want emotions generated by the Holy Spirit, not the beat of the song or the stirring words of the leader.

I know how to get in the Spirit:

- With the *eyes* of my heart I look for flowing pictures of God, Jesus, and the Holy Spirit. I look to see Him either in heaven or around me or touching others.

- With the *ears* of my heart I ask for His input and then listen to flowing thoughts that light upon me, trusting they are coming from the River that flows within (see John 7:37-39).

- With the *emotions* of my heart I reach out to touch the compassionate flow of His love to me and through me to others.

Airplanes take off 100 percent of the time because they follow the laws that provide lift. We can do the same as we take off in the Spirit. We know what to do and we do it. Plain and simple.

Keep everything simple and childlike so the Holy Spirit can flow. With a smile on our face, we surrender to God's power, love, and compassion. We cease our own striving, our efforts, our thinking, and tune to the flow within, which is the River of the Holy Spirit (see Heb. 3:18-19; 4:1-11; John 6:63). Really, could life be any easier?

ACTION EXERCISES

Meditate on *every* verse with the Greek word *energeō*. Jeremiah 17:5 and John 6:63-64 are so absolute, telling us emphatically that we are cursed if we go with our power and blessed if we go with God's power, that it really makes me passionate to explore every New Testament Scripture that has the word *energeō* in it. We want to fully understand and embrace the power of His Spirit! Miracles occur when God's energy flows through us.

Read this article[50] and meditate with me on *all verses* that contain the word *energeō* in the New Testament. Ask, "What does the release of God's divine energy (*energeō*) feel like, and what does it accomplish?" We want to gain a *full understanding* of how God uses the word *energeō*. By doing this you discover everything God has said about this topic and you ascend to the top 1 percent of the people in the world with a revelation on the active flowing energy of the Holy Spirit. How valuable is that!

Journaling Exercise

> *Lord, what do You want to speak to me concerning the presence and the power of Your Spirit in and through me and the truths presented in this chapter?*

Meditation Exercise

The "River of Life"[51] devotional simply and easily brings you into awareness of the flow of the Holy Spirit's energy, power, wisdom, revelation, and anointing. For each of the next five days, complete the "River of Life," a 12-minute meditation. Do this while sitting in a chair so you experience the full impact of it. You are acknowledging the Holy Spirit,

---

50 www.cwgministries.org/energeo
51 www.cwgministries.org/immersed

tuning to His active flow of energy, and receiving from Him healing, power, miracles, wisdom, revelation, discernment, and transformation. When you do the "River of Life" meditation you are likely to feel your body gently shake and vibrate as this divine energy pulsates through you.

I strongly recommend you be intentional about the "River of Life" meditation. If you need a specific healing, miracle, or release, ask for it during the devotional. Believe for it, ask God for a vision of it happening, and then gaze upon that vision, allowing His healing energy to penetrate your being in the specific area(s) that need it.

As you gaze in faith at God's vision of your destiny or healing fulfilled, you receive. As you turn away from trusting in your own provision (remember blind Bartimaeus who *threw down* his cloak) and trust *only* in God to heal and deliver you, God rewards this faith with miracles. You step out on the water and find supernatural power enabling you to do supernatural feats. The Bible is full of such stories. Create your own story! Practice this daily for several weeks or more and see what miracles befall you. Send me your testimony.

- Listen to this amazing music video—"Greater"[52] by MercyMe—and be inspired by the greatness of the One who lives within you.

- Try this seven-step healing model.[53]

---

52   http://bit.ly/GreaterVid
53   www.cwgministries.org/7StepHealing

Chapter 7

LOVE: GOD'S ON/OFF SWITCH FOR UNLEASHING HEALING POWER

*"Faith energized by **love**."*
—see GALATIANS 5:6

Isn't it interesting that God has designed the on/off switch that releases His healing power to be compassion? The power to perform miracles could have been given to:

- Those ordained in the ministry
- Those with a well-developed theology
- Those with a Bible college degree
- Those with a brilliant brain
- Those who trust in their own righteousness

Instead, healing power is released by those who are moved by faith and compassion. Faith and compassion are available to everyone, including children and brand-new believers. Doesn't that just feel right!

> Love and fear are key emotions contrasted in Scripture: *"Perfect love casts out fear"* (1 John 4:18).

- God's thoughts, when aligned with the emotion of love, release God's power (see Gal. 5:6).

- God's thoughts, when aligned with the emotion of fear, release no results.

- Satan's thoughts, aligned with the emotion of fear, release satan's power (see Job 3:25).

Let's briefly consider how fear and love affect us:

- If my faith is to grow in Christian spirituality and my emotion is *love* and thankfulness that in Christ I am complete, I enter a state of *spiritual growth.*

- If my faith is to grow in Christian spirituality and my emotion is *fear* or guilt that I am not acceptable to God, my growth into Christian spirituality is *stalled.*

- If my faith is for my healing and my emotion is *love* and gratitude for the finished work of Christ upon the cross and the principles of vibrant health, I enter the state of *miracles and gifts of healing.*

- If my faith is for my healing and my emotion is *fear* I will not get well; *infirmity remains.*

- If my faith is to achieve my destiny and my emotion is *love* and gratefulness for the destiny God has designed for me, my *destiny is drawn to me* as God leads me in the way I should go.

- If my faith is to achieve my destiny and my emotion is *fear* that I am inadequate and unable, then my destiny remains *blocked*.

- If my faith is for financial freedom and my emotion is *love* and gratitude concerning God's passion to bless me financially, *financial freedom is drawn to me* as I follow His voice (see Deut. 28).

- If my faith is for financial freedom and my emotion is *fear* that I cannot make it financially, then financial freedom as a blessing from God remains *unobtainable*.

As a point of biblical clarification, it is possible to have a *fear* of God (a reverent respect that causes one to obey Him) while at the same time *loving* Him (see Deut. 10:12; see also Ps. 19:9; 111:10; Prov. 1:7; 8:13; 10:27; 14:27).

When I am immersed in love, I am experiencing and radiating God's heart (see 1 John 4:7). I feel valuable, have hope, and am optimistic. This nourishes faith. I look for the good and I find it. Love moves one toward faith, while fear moves one toward doubt.

COMPASSION

Jesus *"felt compassion for them and healed their sick"* (Matt. 14:14). Compassion! *Really!* I'm not even sure I know how to define compassion or how compassion might be different from love, even though these are two distinct words in the New Testament. Both words sound like emotions to me. I have been taught that emotions are part of my soul and that I am to cut them off, which I quite successfully did in my early Christian life.

There are many reasons I might pray for the sick. As a workaholic, I might do it to get the job done; or I might pray out of the guilt of performance orientation, feeling that if I don't meet people's needs I have failed God. I might pray because there is a biblical law telling me I am supposed to pray for the sick and my goal is obedience to God's laws. Well, *Jesus healed because He felt compassion!*

In Chapter 1, I shared the story of how Jesus restored emotion to my life. Because I am a theologian, He also lovingly revealed to me from Scripture the truth that we have *emotions* in our *spirits* (see Ezek. 3:14), so it was wrong of me to relegate emotions to the soul and then ignore compassion as a foundational piece in Jesus' healing ministry. During the period of my life that I didn't express compassion, no miracles flowed through my hands. (There might be a clue in that as to the importance of emotions!)

> *God's power is released when living in the state of God's abiding realities, which are faith, hope and love (see 1 Cor. 13:13).*

CHARITY

COMPASSION AS THE CARRIER WAVE

I had been pondering Galatians 5:6 on how faith works through love in relation to how Jesus was moved by compassion and healed the sick (see Matt. 14:14). A picture came to me that is analogous in the natural world to what is happening in the spirit realm.

In telecommunications, a carrier wave is what a message is carried on. The message is encoded in the carrier wave by modifying the carrier wave's frequency, amplitude, or phase. The idea I received from the Lord is how we can see compassion as a "carrier wave" of God's healing power.

> *Compassion is the divine frequency upon which God's power is carried and released. For Jesus, emotions were the channel of the Spirit's power.*

THE "CARRIER WAVE PRINCIPLE" REVEALED IN A DREAM

Setting of the dream—I went to bed having just meditated on the need for compassion to be present in order to release spiritual power and energy, and I had the following dream.

The dream—I was at the office and my co-worker, Karen, gave me a homeopathic remedy from a lady I'm ministering to.

Interpretation of the Symbols in the Dream

- *The office* = where I work (so to make healing *work*...).

- *Passed through Karen's hands* = Karen sounds a lot like "caring" and she actually is one of the most caring, *compassionate* people I know (healing works when moving through the hands of caring; it's carried by compassion).

- *Homeopathic remedy* = a healing frequency (i.e., God's healing power/energy).

- *Being given from the person I was ministering to* = miracles begin with a need. (The person to whom I am ministering has a need, and when that is united with care/compassion, then healing occurs.)

Message of the Dream

Compassion was present in Karen, and it was through her that the energized frequency for healing was transferred and flowed. It was in her presence that the gift was given and received. "Caring Karen" was the "carrier" and connector of the gift of healing.

> This dream showed that the divine frequency of compassion must be present for God's healing power to work.
>
> *Compassion is the "spiritual carrier wave" that conveys God's wisdom, healing, power, and gifts to us and through us to others.*

MARK

GREEK DEFINITIONS: "FELT COMPASSION"

Charles Spurgeon said, "The original word [*compassion*] is a very remarkable one. It is not found in classic Greek. It is not found in the Septuagint. The fact is, it was a word coined by the evangelists [Gospel writers] themselves. They did not find one in the whole Greek language that suited their purpose, and therefore they had to make one. It is expressive of the deepest emotion; a striving of the bowels—a yearning of the innermost nature."[54]

As I researched this claim, I found that compassion was a noun up until the time of the Gospel writers, and they changed it into a verb to describe the intensity of Jesus' heart of compassion toward the people. Spurgeon was right—a new word was created. Jesus was moved so deeply that there wasn't even a word in their entire language to describe it! There was a need to create a brand-new verb form specifically to

---

54   Charles Spurgeon, "Sermon No. 3438: The Compassion of Jesus," December 24, 1914, Metropolitan Tabernacle, London, UK.

attempt to capture an emotion that He was experiencing as He released miracles of healing. Amazing! The Greek definition of compassion is as follows:

- *Strong's Hebrew and Greek Dictionary*: "To have the bowels yearn, be moved with compassion" (*splagchnizomai*, Strong's G4697).

- *Thayer's Greek Definitions*: "To be moved as to one's bowels; hence, to be moved with compassion. Part of speech: *verb*."

A practical definition of God's compassion released:

> *God's yearning heart of mercy and care, flowing from the Holy Spirit within, which carries His healing and provision to those in need.*

Become an expert by exploring all 12 occurrences of the word *splankna* (compassion) in the Bible.[55] Compassion is the carrier wave upon which God's healing power flows, so I want to know *everything* the Bible says about this word and the effects it produces.

CHARITY

WAVES OF COMPASSION IN AN OCEAN OF LOVE

Jesus often used natural things in our physical world to describe spiritual realities, so I will use the carrier wave/ocean of love picture and build on it. Everything in the physical comes from the spirit realm, and what is in each of the realms has a corollary in the other (see Heb. 11:3). Pictures are the language of the heart, and we want more and more to

---

55 www.cwgministries.org/Compassion

connect with Kingdom emotions that flow up through our hearts, so let's picture it this way.

It's as if the spirit realm is an ocean. The land is our natural, physical world, and the shoreline is the border between the two dimensions. I had previously understood that it was an ocean of love and the wave was love that carried the power to us, but I want to amend that slightly and offer a distinction between the ocean of love and the waves of compassion.

What's Love Got to Do with It?

Love can be somewhat static at times. Love, like an ocean, can be still and calm. It can just *be*. We can say we love someone, but it doesn't mean we're necessarily planning to move heaven and earth for that person. It's "just" love.

Surely, the writers of the Bible had experienced love. They loved God, they had wives and kids—they knew what love is. *Agape, eros, phileo*—they had a lot of good love words. But whatever they knew about love before was not sufficient to describe what they saw in Jesus. They felt the need to coin a new word form, *splanka,* to describe the emotion they saw come upon Jesus and move Him to action. Wow!

Of course, love is wonderful, and we should love people constantly (in that we're always kind and patient and preferring others before ourselves). But we feel and are moved by compassion not as constantly. Love can just be, but compassion can't. Compassion *moves*. So in the ocean of love, it's the compassion that moves. It's compassion that is the waves.

What's Up with the Waves?

Waves speak of flow and current and intensity. Waves move by definition. They don't stand still. Same with compassion. Compassion moves, by definition. It can't be still. Scripture says Jesus felt compassion and that He was moved by compassion. Compassion is different from love, because compassion always moves us to act, to minister, to help meet a need. Love is always there, but compassion is over and above and more intense than love. It's a very forceful term. It's unmistakable in its intensity that moves us to action.

We saw that when we looked at the 12 verses noting that Jesus *saw* a need, was *moved* with compassion, *and then acted.* But it's even bigger than compassion moving Him to heal people. It's actually incredible because He wasn't just moved with compassion and then healed. *He was moved with compassion—and then did everything.* That was His entire and exclusive motivation for ministry. He didn't do anything outside of it.

We know Jesus worked healing miracles out of compassion. But He also showed mercy ministry (like the Good Samaritan) out of compassion. He ministered deliverance out of compassion (see Mark 9:22). He administered practical needs ministry of feeding the hungry out of compassion (see Matt. 15:32). He even spoke and taught the multitudes out of compassion (see Mark 6:34).

That pretty much covers every type of "ministry" we should be doing! From healing to teaching to deliverance, all out of divine feelings. Because He was *moved* by compassion. Kingdom emotion.

It's been said that "compassion [has] messianic significance for it is only Jesus who shows compassion. In each case what we have is not so much the description of a human emotion but a messianic characterization."[56]

I agree that it's not a human emotion. However, it is not a messianic significance or characterization in that it's only Jesus who can and should and could experience compassion. He is the example showing us how it's done. The Son of God became the Son of Man so that sons of

---

56   G. Kittel, *Theological Dictionary of the New Testament*, vol 1 (Grand Rapids: Eerdmans and Paternoster Press, 1985).

men might become sons of God. As children of the Spirit we are moved by what moves God. We want to live out of His divine emotion, which is what the fruit of the Spirit is—love, joy, peace, etc.

As Rage Is to Hatred

Compassion moves—it moves us and it moves through us. It causes us to take action and *do*. Considering the opposite of it can help make the distinction between love and compassion easier to see. For example, hatred. Someone might say they hate somebody, but they might not do anything about it.

But what about rage? If that person doesn't just hate but is *enraged*—he is moved to action. Rage moves you. Just like compassion, it is a spirit-level emotion and people who are moved upon by rage do stuff. They throw things. They beat people up. They murder. That is an emotion down deeper than our own hearts. Hatred is like love—we can just have it in our hearts. Rage is like compassion—it comes up into us from the spirit realm. It comes upon us, and it moves us.

Coming Against or Coming Alongside

Another significant aspect of rage is that it's always "against" something. Rage against a spouse or parent, etc. It pits you up against someone. Again, that's a great picture to understand the opposite of it, because compassion puts you in agreement with. Just like the accuser of the brethren comes against, the Holy Spirit comes alongside.

We want to come alongside whatever God is doing by coming into agreement with whatever He is feeling. We feel His emotions and align ourselves with them by letting them flow freely through us.

That's the other exciting thing too—it's something done to us. Compassion is a Kingdom emotion that comes over us; or more specifically, it rises up from within us like a flood. Just like it is God who is at work in us to will and do His pleasure; just like it is Holy Spirit who is transforming us as we behold with unveiled face the glory of the Lord; just like it is the love of God that compels and controls us. It is the divinely spirit-realm-initiated emotion of compassion that *moves us*.

Can We Love Enough?

We don't muster it up. We can't! Obviously we would never try to work really hard and generate enough power in our hands to go heal blind eyes. We know that's outside of what we can do in and of ourselves. However, quite often we are tempted to try and "muster up" love for people, to try in our own selves to love enough to release a blessing to them. But we can't generate compassion any more than we can strive to work a power miracle of healing.

It's outside of us. Instead, it is done to us. It comes upon and moves up through us. Only after we have been moved upon are we then moved to action and the miracle is released. So to live like Jesus means we are moved by compassion and everything we do for ministry is out of that Kingdom emotion.

Where's the Kingdom of God?

The innermost being speaks of the belly, the womb, the matrix. Lower than our hearts. Not in our chests, but down even deeper. The Kingdom is within (see Luke 17:21).

Our spiritual heart might be near where our physical heart organ is, and this may be where Holy Spirit is joined to our spirit. But He's bigger than that. And so while He is there, one with our heart, He also goes down deeper into our belly, behind the navel. It is in that place there is a spiritual umbilical cord to the heavenly dimension, to the spirit realm. It's down deep, where the innermost being is, and that is the portal and connecting place from our physical selves out to the spirit realm. I was encouraged when I heard an excellent teaching by the late prophet Bob

Jones who had a similar understanding of the Kingdom within, which I took as great confirmation.

The *splanka* definition makes it clear that it is not an emotion that originates with us. It is God's compassion and His mercy. It originates in the very heart of Love Himself in the spirit world. And then it comes to us and explodes into our physical atmosphere, through where? Our innermost being. Down deep inside, in our belly (see John 7:37-39).

When compassion from the heavenly atmosphere explodes into our world, that moment of impact could very well be described as a "striving of the bowels, a yearning of the innermost nature." That Kingdom emotion invading a human body is a dramatic thing. It *moves* you. It makes some people fall over. Or tremble. Or laugh. Or cry. But when you get good at flowing with it, riding on it, and living out of it like Jesus did, it moves you to ministry action.

Is Compassion a Sovereign Move of God Within, or Can We Learn to Surf These Waves?

We understand that Jesus didn't just heal out of compassion but that He actually did everything out of it exclusively.

> *All ministries originate from the emotion of love initiated by God Himself.*

So what then—if it's a sovereign moving upon by God, what are we supposed to do? What part do we play in the miracle?

When you are beginning to learn how to surf, it can be challenging to position yourself correctly to catch the waves. As you're just starting out, you realize you have never striven in your own strength, never felt your own weakness in relation to a force larger than you, like when you have jumped on your surfboard at the edge of the ocean and tried to paddle out away from the shore in big waves. You fight through surf that is rolling and crashing on top of you, pulling you back toward land, and at first it can seem so futile and take every ounce of focus and strength you have.

Now that can speak to a lot of different things. One is that when we are going against the purposes of God, His heart, and what He wants to do in a situation, it's impossible.

Another obvious characteristic of waves is that they are all about flow, direction, and intensity. Compassion speaks of the intensity of Kingdom emotion too, as it crashes against the shores of our physical existence. And as difficult as it is to fight against those waves, there is nothing more beautiful or exciting than when you are flowing *with* the waves. It's a force so much greater than you carrying you, doing all the work. It is then you discover that you're successfully riding those powerful waves of the spirit, the waves of compassion.

So How Can We Flow with God's Compassion?

We need to get out into the quiet place of the spirit/ocean. At the shoreline, it's loud and waves are crashing and it can be chaotic. But if you can get out away from the material world and quiet down into your spirit and connect with the Spirit in the spirit realm, then that is as if you have paddled your board out through the surf and you're on the other side of the waves and you're just hanging out in the ocean.

Here, you can actually sit on your board for as little or as long as you want, resting and getting strengthened and refreshed before you decide to turn your board around and head back to shore. Just as Hebrews 4:11 describes, we labor to enter into rest (KJV).

It is like Jesus going off to the lonely places to pray and spend time communing with the Father. If even the Son of God needed to have quiet times of meditation, how much more so do we! So we can take a long time relaxing out in the ocean of God's spirit realm and soaking up all that is there for us. We are focused away from shore then as we are face to face with God. But then, once we are sufficiently refreshed, we turn our boards around and we're ready to face man and the natural world and share with them what we have received from heaven.

So compassion is a wave, and it's not constant. It waves and then dissipates, rolls in big and then away. It is not a constant wall of wave, but it *is* constantly waving. It is consistent and continual in its waving. The same is true of God's compassion. Just because it is a sovereign, divinely initiated Kingdom emotion doesn't mean that it is random or few and far between in its coming upon us and waving. No, God's waves of compassion are always there, always flowing. It is just about us getting ourselves in position in order to ride the wave well, all the way to the shore.

How Do We Position Ourselves to Ride His Wave?

We need to line ourselves up with the wave. We need to come into alignment and into agreement with what is already taking place. That is, align ourselves with what God has already begun to do and how He is already moving.

It is easy to see it when we're in the spirit, and so we say yes to that and agree with that. We align ourselves with the force of holy emotion that is already flowing toward the shore by turning our boards around and "watching to see" (see Hab. 2:1). Timing is everything, so at the precise moment, after a time of waiting and watching and looking to see where the wave is going and how it's rolling in, we do get to "do" something.

For just a few seconds, at precisely the right moment, we have to paddle our hearts out. Lying down on the board, the same way we got out there but now headed back in, we paddle with all our might in order to have momentum to catch the wave's force and ride it. If we are just at a standstill, it doesn't pick us up and carry us to shore. We need to be moving with it, in the direction that it's going, in order to catch it and be able to flow with it.

So if we want something to "do," this is it. We do align our gifts and strengths and will and choose to surrender them and line them up with God's purposes and go all out—at least for a few moments.

> *Rather than strive with my flesh's strength, I align myself with the moving of the Spirit.*

We choose to come into agreement with the power of that wave so that we can be moved upon and carried—effortlessly and gracefully—on the wave of Kingdom emotion. And as long as we stay in line with where it's going, it will carry us all the way from the outlying peaceful ocean of the spirit, right up to the sandy beach, waves of compassion crashing onto the shore of the physical dimension in an explosion of spirit realm life and energy and power.

> *Have this attitude in yourselves which was also in Christ Jesus* (Philippians 2:5).

We see then that to pray for someone's healing just because we "should," because there's a biblical command that says to, isn't actually the best motivation. Look at Jesus' example. Lying all around the pool at Bethesda were the lame and blind and deaf—many, many people in need. We have a record of Jesus healing one of them—just one out of all those who were sick.

While we know He healed everyone who came to Him, He didn't heal everyone. When He died on the cross and said it is finished, there were still sick people around. There were still hungry people on earth.

There were still people who needed deliverance. Yet He said His work was finished.

I can learn from this and have Jesus' perspective—that is, that it's not all for me to do either. It is better to live out of the heart of God, and when He moves upon me through His Spirit and I feel that "striving in my inward parts" then I know, "OK, *now* is the time." Compassion is moving me, which means there *is* power present to be released (see Luke 5:17). This makes it exciting because then I have faith that provision and healing are flowing unhindered, carried on that wave of compassion, and I know the person will be met at their point of need.

We surely can't go wrong if we simply follow Jesus' example, exclusively doing what He saw Father do and only moving when He was moved by compassion. Likewise, we shouldn't do anything if it's not out of Kingdom emotion. If it's out of guilt, obligation, or duty, it is not out of faith. And whatever is not from faith is sin (see Rom. 14:23).

What We're Going For

I don't need to think more highly of myself than I ought to think, for there are many members of one body (see Rom. 12:3). We're not an expression of God's fullness each one our own selves. I'm not God, but I'm a part of His body. There are other brothers and sisters and hands and feet and each part of the body specializes in specific things. We work together in unity and connectedness.

If we are all waiting on God and tuned in to His frequency and living out of His divine emotion, then all of the work of the ministry *will* be done. That is the vision. If everyone is sensitive to God and doesn't act until they are moved by compassion, but also just as importantly they *do* act every time they are moved by compassion, then everyone will be taken care of. All the hospitals will be emptied. All the hungry people will be fed. We will all be demonstrating extraordinary power because we will all be living out of extraordinary love.

Love that moves us. Love that's above and beyond and causes us to take action. A deep love flowing up out of the spirit realm and from the very heart of God. A divine emotion so powerful in nature that when it bursts into our physical atmosphere, the impact on the human conduit through whom it flows appears as a "striving of the inward parts," a current so strong we are caught up in it and swept along and moved to ministry by the sheer intensity of it.

A love that moves us—that is compassion.

Emotion of God

Perhaps this is even a key for getting our prayers answered more often. If we want healing released and supernatural power manifested every time we pray, then maybe we should make sure we only pray when we're moved by compassion to do so. According to Scripture, that's what Jesus does.

He doesn't do anything on His own initiative and the Holy Spirit doesn't do anything on His own initiative—so we don't need to either (see John 8:28; 16:13). If we simply move with compassion the way Jesus does, then we'll move in power the way He does too. One hundred percent success rate! By living exclusively out of divine initiative, by ministering always and only out of the emotion of God.

Driven by Compassion

It was in the midst of this biblical research and meditation on compassion that I had two dreams. They encapsulated the truths Holy Spirit had been teaching me in waking life—how Kingdom emotion is what moved Jesus. Compassion is what drove Him.

As we saw in an earlier dream, my compassionate co-worker Karen usually represents "compassion" to me. Her name sounds like "caring" and her dominant personality trait as I see her completely match, so she makes the perfect recurring symbol whenever the Lord wants to teach me more about this Kingdom emotion.

I dreamt that all of the people from our ministry offices were car-avanning together and Karen was in the lead car. She ended up on the side of the road and I followed her. However, the people behind us weren't paying attention and ended up slamming into the back of my car, which in turn crashed me into Karen and made all of us plunge down the embankment. It was pretty scary!

By looking at the main action of the dream, we see the message is that all ministry needs to flow out of, or follow, compassion. Love and compassion need to lead the charge. It is dangerous to lose sight of caring, to let that pure heart motive be relegated off to the side. Just like compassion was driving our lead ministry vehicle in the dream, every-thing was going great until compassion was marginalized and sidelined off to the edge of the road. God was showing through the dream that if we don't keep compassion front and center as our guiding force, we'll crash and burn.

Deliverance, teaching, healing—the various gifts represented by the various ministry staff members following in their cars—all of it needs to be born in the heart of God. It is His compassion that must move our ministry. It is His love that must compel us and His caring that must lead us (see 2 Cor. 5:14). Otherwise, even our best intentions and Kingdom work can become derailed and end up a train wreck—or a car wreck, as the case may be.

Compassion and Her Son

In the previous dream we saw how important it was for God's com-passion to lead us. It has to come first and all ministry should follow that divine emotion. In this next dream, we get to see the other side of that same truth. In this dream I discovered that Karen and her son shared a birthday on not only the same day but also the same year.

We have established Karen represents "compassion" to me, so we then want to ask, "What does it mean if compassion and its fruit have the same genesis?" Normally, fruit comes after a tree is fully grown. Usually, a child is born after a woman has become an adult. But somehow—in a surprisingly matter-of-fact way—this dream showed something different.

God showed how the fruit of compassion, which is ministry, cannot be separated from compassion itself. As we just saw, scripturally speaking, compassion moves us to action. Jesus felt compassion and healed, fed, taught, and delivered. He didn't just feel compassion and walk away; His ministry immediately followed the Kingdom emotion of compassion.

If it is truly compassion from heaven, it will always move us to action. There isn't a long time lapse between feeling and doing. There isn't a distance or break between connecting with God's emotions and releasing His power to meet the need at hand. While it is very important for compassion to be what inspires our actions, it is just as important that action immediately follow. Exactly as depicted in the dream—compassion was born, and so was her fruit. All at the same time, with no distance and no delay.

MARK

ENERGY CARRIED ON THE WINGS OF OUR HEARTS

From examination of Scripture and personal life experience I believe that the flow of God's Spirit out through our hearts is carried on the wings of pictures, emotions, faith, and flow, as these are the language of the heart. To say it another way:

> *God's healing power rides on the wings of revelation, compassion, vision, and faith, which I speak as my personal, present-tense reality.*

Therefore, when ministering healing I want to be looking with the eyes of my heart into the spiritual world and seeing God's Kingdom. As I do, His emotions—His ever-present faith, revelation, and power—flow.

Here's what I do, practically speaking: I look to see how Jesus is ministering grace to the person for whom I am praying (see Dan. 8:2-3; Heb. 12:1-2; 2 Cor. 3:18; 4:18). I embrace His heart of compassion toward the individual and then do and speak that which I see Jesus doing and speaking, thanking Him for the blessings He is releasing, believing that it is done.

LIVING THE TRUTH

What does it mean to *believe* God's truth? The answer is, "to *live* the truth!" Mental assent is not enough. In spiritual transformation, we migrate between the following two lifestyles:

- *From automatically, instinctively doing it wrong.* This is where one is unaware of their unconscious negative inner thoughts, pictures, and emotions.

- *To automatically, instinctively doing it right.* This is where one unconsciously, instinctively releases Christ's character and power (see Rom. 2:13; James 1:22; Gal. 5:22-24; 1 Cor. 12:7-11).

To move from the wrong lifestyle to the right lifestyle we need to:

- *Become conscious* of our automatic negative thoughts, pictures, and emotions.

- *Become conscious* of how to reverse these and do things right.

- *Consciously practice* doing things right (this takes time, rehearsal, and discipline).

ACQUIRING NEW AUTOMATIC RESPONSES

Once I have sufficiently understood the keys to correct a behavior, *I practice them until I do them instinctively.* I give myself several weeks or even several months of intentional, focused practice to acquire a new skill. Once the skill is acquired, I have achieved single-mindedness. I am focused exclusively on God's will and destiny for this area of my life. My eye is single, clear, full of light with no darkness in it (see Luke 11:34).

Practice can include *picturing* God's promised blessings to us. Picturing helps bring us more quickly toward our goal. Those who practice a skill simply by picturing it in detail in their minds have been found to improve in that skill almost as fast as those who physically practice it. A picture truly is worth a thousand words, because pictures are the language of the heart.

For example, God tells us to honor all people (see 1 Pet. 2:17). If in my morning devotional time, I practice visually seeing and honoring the people I will meet during the day, do you think I will come into the reality of honoring all people more quickly than if I don't practice picturing the reality I know God wants me to live in?

If dishonoring people is an issue you need to deal with, then you could use the "New Creation Celebration: Replacing Beliefs" for a week. The beliefs you might want to replace are:

- Day 1: "It is OK to dishonor those I disagree with."

- Day 2: "It is OK to dishonor unbelievers."

- Day 3: "It is OK to dishonor the political party that opposes mine."
- Day 4: "It is OK to dishonor Islam."
- Day 5: "It is OK to dishonor the news media."

Continue until dishonor is fully removed and replaced with honor toward those with whom you disagree. This doesn't mean you now agree with them. It simply means you have not taken up a spirit of reproach (a negative attitude) toward them. It is really hard to interest someone in the salvation message if in your spirit you are dishonoring them. They will feel the contempt and turn away.

During your devotional times, stay tuned to flow, which allows God the opportunity to bring to your awareness the different roots that contribute to your desire to dishonor others. Then use the prayer steps that take you through an effective removal process of these roots.

Note: "New Creation Celebration: Replacing Emotions" deals *most extensively* with the removal of a vast array of various roots to an issue, so use this template for the fullest and most complete transformational process. Yes, it takes 40 minutes to do with the guided audio meditation, but if you experience true heart transformation it will be among the best 40 minutes of your week.

If you use the worksheet alone, without the guided audio, then you can work at your own pace, which is probably best. That means you may do it in 30 minutes, or you may take an hour. If you need to do this devotional for five days in a row, hitting dishonor from many different vantage points, and you root it out, you have spent five hours in a prayer exercise and radically transformed your life. How cool is that!

Eventually, your breakthrough to a new way of life is full and complete. This is Christian spirituality at work. A truth is learned when you are living it.

WHEN TO MOVE ON TO OTHER DEVOTIONAL STYLES

Once you arrive at an automatic, instinctive awareness of Jesus' heart attitude in the area you are praying about, you will discover that when you begin your devotional time by asking God what emotion He would have you let go of, rather than receiving a negative emotion or belief, you will have a positive emotion lighting upon your mind (in my example below it was "union"). That means you have succeeded in dealing with this issue! It is time to move on. You can move on to present to God another demanding situation you are facing or a troubling emotion you are struggling with or a health problem you are battling. Or you can move on to another devotional style.[57]

Repeat the "New Creation Celebration: Replacing Emotions" meditation until transformed. I spent a week of morning devotions seeking anointing and blessing for an upcoming conversation I was going to have with an individual from a large marketing firm with whom I wished to establish a relationship. I was seeking to move from fear of rejection to a conviction we would work together in harmony. I was using the "New Creation Celebration: Replacing Emotions."

For six mornings in a row, *fear* and *separation* were the words that appeared when I asked, "What negative emotion would You have me let go of?" Finally, on the seventh morning, the answer came back, "Union." I realized this was not a negative emotion to let go of. This was the realization that the new reality was now released in my consciousness, in my heart, and in my spirit. I was now sending out waves of faith for union and partnership between me and this marketing firm. The following day, we had an outstanding hour-long phone call that resulted in merging in wonderful, beneficial ways for both of us.

---

57 www.cwgministries.org/devotionals

> *Faith, energized by love, brought me into God's Promised Land concerning this situation!*

That success meant I was ready to move on to another area of need. I had another marketing person I needed to communicate with in the upcoming weeks. I pictured them and asked, "Lord, what emotion would You have me drop?" and we began the faith-building, Spirit-anointed process again for my next miracle. Within a week, I received an email from them inviting me to a phone conversation.

Talk about a *fun* way to do devotions that brings transformation and blessing continuously to our lives! Experience your own "New Creation Celebrations" in *your* life. Take the time to fall in love with your new self in Christ!

In the Fullness of Time, God Brings Forth (Gal. 4:4)

Now of course, I want all miracles to be instant. However, God's timing is not our timing. Abraham received the supernatural birth of Isaac 25 years after the promise was given (see Gen. 21:5). The Israelites entered Canaan 40 years after they were promised the land of Israel (see Num. 32:13). Our responsibility is to *live in faith* and even to die in faith (see Gal. 2:20; Heb. 10:36-39; 11). God's responsibility is to bring forth His destiny for our lives as we walk by His Spirit (see Gal. 5:25).

IS IT OK TO ASK FOR SIGNS?

David asked for a sign from God confirming He was with him. *"Show me a sign for good"* (Ps. 86:17). Gideon asked God for a sign (see Judges 6:37-40). We can ask God for a sign. God is willing to confirm, to a humble seeking heart, that they are on the right path and that He is supporting them.

There is no reason not to ask God for a confirming sign. It can be just about anything—a confirming witness from a brother or sister, a confirming circumstance, a supernatural event, whatever God chooses. He is unique in each and every circumstance, so just keep your heart, ears, and eyes open so you recognize the confirming sign of God's presence and blessing when it happens.

CHARITY

SHOW ME A SIGN

Before the Israelites reached Canaan, Moses asked God to show him His glory (Exod. 33:18). I appreciate verse 15 of this chapter especially: *"Then he said to Him, 'If Your presence does not go with us, do not lead us up from here.'"* It is so remarkable that Moses would have rather stayed in the wilderness with God, than enter the Promised Land without Him (Exod. 33:15). That's how much he treasured God's presence. Like Moses, I only want to go where God is leading, and I only want to go there if He's going too.

Last year before our book *Hearing God Through Your Dreams* came out, I had been wondering what the Lord was up to; how was He going to use it and where was He going to take it? In answer to my heart's question, the Lord blessed me with His version of my situation through a sign given to my friend. Don, a prophetic co-worker, shared a vision God revealed to him about our new book that was soon to be released.

He saw a hummingbird with a mail pouch, and it was delivering my book all over the world. This struck him as especially significant because he had just seen hummingbirds over the weekend and noticed how incredibly fast they were. There one second and gone the next; if you blinked, you would miss them!

Don's vision was a confirming sign of the dreams I had had the two previous nights. Two nights before, I dreamt God was sending mail for me (putting my return address labels on correspondence), and He was on the move (with packed and stacked-up moving boxes). Then the night immediately before Don's vision I dreamt about "taking off."

When we looked up hummingbirds, we discovered that when you take their body length into consideration, they are actually the fastest animal on earth, which was amazing and something I never knew before.

This encouraged me that the message of our book on dream work was going to be well received. God showed me through the signs of my own dreams and the confirming sign of my friend's vision that He's got this. Intimacy with Him through dreams is *His* message and He's the one responsible for getting it out. I'm just responsible for being obedient; the results are up to Him.

Practicing Pondering

So those are the pictures I pondered. I diligently practiced my meditations every day, sometimes twice a day, just because I loved the place it took me and how I felt when I was there in spirit with God.

The fourth chapter of Ephesians talks about "learning Christ," which means to *"put off your old self, which is being corrupted by its deceitful desires; to be made new in the attitude of your minds; and to put on the new self, created to be like God in true righteousness and holiness"* (Eph. 4:22-24 NIV).

What that looked like for me in this situation was that I meditated on the fact that I felt unprepared and nervous. I put off my stress and put on Jesus' strength. I put off my anxiety and put on His anointing. I exchanged those unhealthy thoughts and feelings for more empowering ones by seeing myself as fully equipped with His grace and wisdom.

I spent time feeling how good it would feel to have completed my interviews successfully. I spent time imagining how grateful I would be once I had finished my first conferences and people were blessed by what they learned. I got into that space in my meditation times before these things ever happened in my "real" world. And by observing that positive, victorious version of my life, by God's grace I collapsed it. *Faith attracts and vision collapses*, and what I had only experienced during my meditations then became a reality that I experienced in this natural world too.

Many have prophesied that God's favor is upon this teaching, but I didn't want my insecurities or issues to hinder the advancement of His message. I dealt with that negativity through my times of meditation, actively and purposefully choosing to live to my new-creation self. Once we got the old me out of the way, God's will and perfect plans could be more fully realized.

Now, only one year later, the fruit of these meditations is being seen, and Holy Spirit's sign through my friend's vision of quickly taking this message worldwide has materialized. Our time with Sid Roth was my first TV interview ever.[58] No pressure or anything! Thankfully, it has had a half-million views on YouTube already and we continue to receive wonderful reports of people making sense of their dreams after watching just that one show. Hallelujah!

In the same short span of time I have had the privilege of teaching God's truth about dreams at over forty events in nine countries around the globe. He is passionate about meeting people in their dreams and wants everyone to know it! I am grateful and honored to be a carrier of that word.

Just like a hummingbird, God has seen to it that His message takes off and moves quickly. Every day there is a new opportunity or another

---

58 www.youtube.com/watch?v=DgbR5oydRRw

awesome testimony—so much blessing I can hardly keep up! Life with Holy Spirit is an unfolding adventure full of confirming signs, wonders, and every good thing. He likes to keep the journey exciting for us! All we need to do is pay attention and notice the miracles that are all around us. It is always easiest to see what we are looking for. Or, as Jesus put it—what we seek, we will surely find (see Luke 11:9-10).

MARK

COMPASSION PRECIPITATES MIRACLES OF HEALING

We know that Jesus was moved by compassion to heal (see Matt. 14:14). Well, now HeartMath Institute has proven that those who have heart coherence, meaning they can 1) connect with their hearts and 2) release compassion coupled with 3) the intention to heal are the ones who see miracles of healing occur.

HeartMath Institute conducted an amazing experiment with various people seeking to wind or unwind a DNA strand. Only those who were 1) skilled in the technique of heart coherence, 2) actually entered that state, and 3) intended for DNA to change were able to wind or unwind the DNA strand.

> Individuals capable of generating high ratios of heart coherence were able to alter DNA conformation according to their intention. ...Control group participants showed low ratios of heart coherence and were unable to intentionally alter the conformation of DNA.[59]

---

59 "You Can Change Your DNA," HeartMath Institute, June 14, 2015, Changing DNA Through Intention, http://www.heartmath.org/articles-of-the-heart/personal-development/you-can-change-your-dna.

You can read a full descriptive article of this experiment in the link listed below.[60] (an identical but highlighted version is found in the next link listed.)[61] An extended discussion of heart coherence and its relationship to Christian spirituality can be found in Chapter 11 of this book, along with a link for purchasing a heart coherence monitor if interested.

This provides some absolutely astounding scientific confirmation of these verses: *"He...felt compassion for them and healed their sick"* (Matt. 14:14), and faith energized by love (see Gal. 5:6).

COMPASSION COUPLED WITH *BELIEF* RELEASES MIRACLES

Perhaps this is why, when some people take the communion elements with the intention of receiving healing, they receive a miracle of healing. During communion, they are in a coherent state; they are focused on their hearts, expressing gratitude toward the Lord for His finished work on the cross where He purchased healing for them, which they receive in faith. That stance surely releases God's healing power.

Some people pray intercessory prayers during communion and see amazing spiritual transformations occur. Again, I suspect it is because they have entered the state of heart coherence and felt God's compassion, which they coupled with faith (clear intention).

I recall Kathryn Kuhlman healing services, which I attended decades ago, where I witnessed many miracles take place. She would have the congregation sing over and over, "Jesus, Jesus, Jesus, there's just something about that name."

---

60 http://laszlo.ind.br/admin/artigos/arquivos/
ModulacaodoDNApelaenergiadasmaos.pdf
61 http://fiimplinit.ro/wp-content/uploads/modulation-of-dna.pdf

Well, I'm sure a good number entered the state of heart coherence during this worship. They were tuned to their hearts, at ease, feeling an emotion of gratitude and faith to receive a miracle. The preaching, testimonies, and worship that lifted up Jesus had properly prepared them. God met them with a miracle of healing!

Many have noted that *more* miracles happen when evangelistic healing crusades are conducted in developing nations. I noticed this myself when I went with such a group to India. I laid hands on many who were healed. Reflecting back, I now realize that one added ingredient to my prayers was *increased compassion* as I prayed. Perhaps that is one key reason we see more miracles in such circumstances. Thankfully, I have now been able to bring a heart of compassion back to my home country and see more miracles happen here as well.

I often begin my prayers with a focus on the compassion of Christ that compelled Him to allow His body to be whipped in order to purchase our healing. I ask for that same compassion to be released in my heart toward the person I am praying for. I thank Jesus that by His stripes He has *purchased healing* for the person I am praying for. I declare that I do not regard lightly this sacrifice He made. I honor it. I receive it with gratitude and thankfulness. I speak healing to this body in the name of Jesus. By His stripes this body is healed (see Isa. 53:5). I thank Him for the release of His healing power and receive with gratitude full healing for this body.

I find this focus helps bring the feeling of compassion (Christ's compassion expressed through my heart) into the equation as I pray for people.

ACTION EXERCISES

Meditation exercise: For each of the next five days, complete the "New Creation Celebration: Replacing Emotions"[62] (40 minutes). You may choose to also include the "River of Life,"[63] a 12-minute devotional where you are immersed in the River of the Holy Spirit.

Meditate on *all* 12 occurrences of the word *splankna (compassion)* in the Bible.[64] By doing this you will discover everything God has said about this topic in Scripture and ascend to the top 1 percent of people in the world with a revelation on the compassion Jesus expressed.

Journaling about Compassion

> *Lord, what do You want to show me from the verses that contain the word compassion? Please reveal to me the role of compassion in releasing Your mercy and healing power. What would You have me do to grow in the gift of compassion? What do You want to speak to me concerning the idea that love is an energizing Kingdom emotion, and what is the role of emotions in health, healing, and release of miracles? Thank You, Lord, for what You speak.*

Pray compassionate, healing prayers for several people you meet this week who are in pain. Feel deep compassion as you lay hands on them, speaking that by His stripes this body is healed. See the stripes Christ bore on His back. Feel His compassion, which allowed this to happen. Release this Kingdom emotion with faith, seeing that *Christ's act of compassion has purchased healing* for the one you are praying for. Feel the heat and energy leave your hands and enter their body. It is amazing!

---

62 www.cwgministries.org/emotions
63 www.cwgministries.org/immersed
64 www.cwgministries.org/Compassion

I *love* doing this! When praying for individuals, you may choose to use the seven-step healing process.[65]

> *I am struck with the renewed revelation that God's transforming power is not reserved for the scholarly but available to all who hear His voice. Couple it with faith and compassion and act.*

---

65   www.cwgministries.org/7StepHealing

Part III

~~~~~~~~~~~~~~~~~~

EMOTIONAL HEALING:
THE HEALING STATE

Chapter 8

KINGDOM EMOTIONS
TURN ON HEALING GENES

*Let the peace of Christ rule in your hearts...and be **thankful**.*
—COLOSSIANS 3:15

*Established in your faith...and overflowing with **gratitude**.*
—COLOSSIANS 2:7

The human brain takes in 11 million bits of information every second but is only consciously aware of 50.[66] The true self is the subconscious part of me, what the Bible calls the heart. Out of the heart flow the issues of life (see Prov. 4:23). It consists of my programed automatic responses, some of which are naturally occurring and some of which I have put on as I put on Christ.

---

66 George Markowsky, "Physiology," Encyclopædia Britannica, June 08, 2015, https://www.britannica.com/topic/information-theory/Physiology.

Ten million of those bits of information come in through the eyes, while only 100,000 bits of information come in through the ears.[67] Yes, pictures are the language of the heart, and pictures are where things are at! We are transformed while we look (see 2 Cor. 3:17-18; 4:18). This helps me get a grip on the amazing transformational power generated if I will simply gaze for a few minutes upon my new-creation reality in Christ. Transformation occurs while we look!

How fast can healing occur? A red blood cell can make a complete circuit of your body in 20 seconds, so what I see or picture can affect my health within minutes, if not seconds.[68] I choose to only see the promises of God as being already fulfilled in my life. That picture draws my destiny to me.

BENEFITS OF MAINTAINING KINGDOM ATTITUDES OF GRATITUDE AND THANKFULNESS

There are many benefits to maintaining Kingdom attitudes, including improved relationships, better physical and mental health, increased empathy, reduced aggression, deeper sleep, improved self-esteem, and increased telomere length,[69] to name just a few.

Scriptures commend Kingdom emotions:

1. *"The fruit of the Spirit is **love, joy, peace...**"* (Gal. 5:22).

2. *"The Kingdom of God is...righteousness and **peace and joy** in the Holy Spirit"* (Rom. 14:17).

---

67   Markowsky, "Physiology."https://www.britannica.com/topic/information
-theory/Physiology

68   John Lloyd, John Mitchinson, and James Harkin, *1,227 Quite Interesting Facts to Blow Your Socks Off* (New York: W.W. Norton & Company, 2013).

69   Kissairis Munoz, "5 Thought Patterns Scientifically Proven to Shorten Your Life," Dr. Axe, July 26, 2017, https://draxe.com/thoughts-make-age-faster/.

3. *"Let the* **peace** *of Christ rule in your hearts...singing with* **thankfulness** *in your hearts to God...giving* **thanks** *through Him to God the Father"* (Col. 3:15-17).

4. *"A* **joyful** *heart is good medicine..."* (Prov. 17:22).

5. *"Always* **giving thanks for** *all things..."* (Eph. 5:20). *"**In** everything give* **thanks...**" (1 Thess. 5:18).

6. *"Since we receive a Kingdom which cannot be shaken, let us show* **gratitude**" (Heb. 12:28).

7. *"Having shod your feet with the preparation of the gospel of* **peace...**" (Eph. 6:15).

I demand Kingdom focus, exclusively, in my life! I would *never* meditate on the evil presented by the daily news as it upholds a focus on calamity and fear and can easily leave one despairing. Jesus would have had a hard time living in peace, hope, and love if He meditated on the evils of the Roman Empire. The main reason, as far as I can see, for quickly scanning the news would be to know how to effectively intercede.

Whatever is true, whatever is honorable, whatever is right, whatever is pure, whatever is lovely, whatever is of good repute, if there is any excellence and if anything worthy of praise, **dwell on these things***...and the* **God of peace** *will be with you* (Philippians 4:8-9).

Not being grateful is not even an option.

Because you did not serve the Lord your God with joy and a glad heart, for the abundance of all things; therefore you shall serve your enemies whom the Lord will send against you, in hunger, in thirst, in nakedness, and in the lack of all things; and He will put an iron yoke on your neck until He has destroyed you (Deuteronomy 28:47-48).

The description of the destruction continues on for ten more verses.

CHARITY

JONAH'S ATTITUDE OF GRATITUDE

Second only to compassion, gratitude is the most powerful emotional state in which we can live. We see an example of this in the Old Testament story of Jonah. His experience of being swallowed by a fish and then spit back out is incredible! What we may have overlooked, however, is what Jonah did immediately before he was delivered out of the fish's belly. It's actually quite impressive, because with all the things not going right at that moment in Jonah's world, he still found something to be grateful for.

In the second chapter of Jonah he is praying and says, *"I will sacrifice to You with the voice of thanksgiving...Salvation is from the Lord"* (Jonah 2:9).

We see in the very next verse God's response to Jonah's thanksgiving: *"Then the Lord commanded the fish, and it vomited Jonah up onto the dry land"* (Jonah 2:10).

God is a gracious God and a generous Dad and we know every good gift is from Him (see James 1:17). He loves when His kids appreciate what He's done for them! What father wouldn't? In the life of Jonah we see clearly and powerfully how gratitude moves God's heart, which is why we choose to give thanks in every circumstance, thereby not quenching the flow of His Spirit in our lives (see 1 Thess. 5:18-19).

More Than Healed

Similarly, in Luke 17 we read the story about ten lepers who cried out to Jesus. He told them to go show themselves to the priests, and

Scripture says they were "cleansed" on the way. One of the men, when he realized that he'd been "healed," returned to Jesus to thank Him. It was only then, after gratitude was expressed, that Jesus declared the man made "whole" (see Luke 17:14-19).

In English, we tend to read right over the meaning, but there are three distinct Greek words used in each of these verses. While the first two words (*katharizó* in verse 14 and *iaomai* in verse 15, Strong's G2511 and G2390) do speak of the wonderful miracle of physical healing, the Greek word used in verse 19 is even more comprehensive. The word translated "made well" or "whole" is *sozo*, which speaks not only to physical healing but spiritual and emotional healing as well (Strong's G4982). It's an all-inclusive word that is used to indicate radical deliverance, protection, recovery, and restoration, true salvation in every way.

Jesus healed the leper's body, but what was it that released the complete *sozo* healing from a lifetime of psychological distress and emotional trauma of living as an unclean outcast of society? What spirit-born emotion unleashed heaven's healing power in spirit, soul, and body?

Gratefulness. Faith expressed through a thankful heart.

Clearly, we cannot overestimate the value of living in gratitude. It changes us from the inside out, collapsing the very blessings we appreciate into our world. Only one of the lepers received the full manifestation of complete *sozo* healing. And his secret to releasing that blessing was simply that he was found grateful (see Luke 17:16).

Surrendering the When and How

I had been pondering these truths and the importance of heartfelt thankfulness in releasing God's blessings into our lives, and in that place of meditation I had another dream.

In the dream, the mailman came, pulled into our driveway, and I thought he'd left some packages. I went out to meet him, but he was already gone, having driven up the driveway and down the street. I checked the mailbox, but there wasn't anything there. Obviously I'd been expecting something, but I wasn't worried about it. I started back down the hill to go into the house, but then the mailman came back and drove down our driveway again and stopped right behind me.

He got out and gave me more than I was expecting—three different gift packages. One big one on the bottom was almost shaped like a huge veggie platter, though that's not what was inside (I didn't open them, I just knew). I received all the gifts, and with a loud and joyful shout exclaimed to the mailman, "Happy Thanksgiving!"

God's principle is: *We fully expect great things, but we surrender the when and how.* In the dream I didn't know when or how my gifts were being delivered, and it wasn't when or how I expected. However, I was grateful even before I received the blessings and it turned out even better than I thought.

First, we see that the gifts/blessings actually chased me down! I wasn't striving and yelling after the mailman to come back. I just went about my life, living as if my prayers were already answered and the blessings were on their way. I turned my back and then he came up behind me with the gifts. This is a great dream snapshot of Deuteronomy 28:2, how the blessings come upon and overtake us.

The fact that there were three gift packages is like a picture of my mom at Christmastime—giving just one gift is never enough! For example, we may pray and observe in our meditation a certain blessing and we ask God for something. Well, Father is jealous for our joy and always wants to give us good things. At the same time Jesus also wants to answer our prayers, and Holy Spirit sure doesn't want to be left out of blessing us either! So we get the gifts/blessings/answers times three, which is exceedingly and abundantly more than we could ask or imagine. A trinity of blessing.

My enthusiastic proclamation of "Happy Thanksgiving!" shows that it was as I lived inside Kingdom emotions and the energy of joy and gratitude—un-worrying and fully surrendered to God's when and how—then the blessings were all brought to me. Then the gifts showed up. I didn't have to struggle and work for them. Instead, like the platter I mentioned, it's as if everything I wanted and more was being easily given over and presented, all "handed to me on a silver platter."

First John 5:14-15 says, *"This is the confidence which we have before Him, that if we ask anything according to His will, He hears us. And if we know that He hears us in whatever we ask, we know that we have* (already possess) *the requests which we have asked from Him"* (NASB).

It's easy to be grateful once we have received our blessing, and God is letting us know that we already have. He gave us everything when He gave us Jesus, so it is already ours. We can be thankful and peaceful now and live as if our prayers have already been answered because we have asked according to His will. Because we have asked according to His will, He has heard us, and so we know that we already possess what we have asked of Him.

MARK

> *"Thankfulness is the frequency of receivership."*

HEALING EMOTIONS

By seeing my body already healed, I feel *now* the emotion of *my body already healed, by seeing it done!*

As I behold a picture of God's vision of my future reality, I am living in the future moment now. *I am filled with gratitude* because

I am excited to be alive, experiencing this healed reality or fulfilled destiny now.

The Bible says to end prayer in the emotional state of thanksgiving: *"Be anxious for nothing, but in everything by prayer and supplication with thanksgiving let your requests be made known to God"* (Phil. 4:6). Thanksgiving is not simply a phrase I tack on the end of my prayer, "Lord, I am thankful that You have heard." It is a feeling of thankfulness and gratitude.

This thanksgiving needs to be more than words, and it needs to be more than a fake emotion. It must be a *true emotion*, generated by the thoughts and pictures in my mind. I accomplish this by gazing into the unseen world at the promise of God fulfilled. Remember Abram gazing at millions of stars as being his millions of children? What I gaze upon produces an emotional reaction. My mind signals the emotions of gratitude and thankfulness that flood my being, causing a cascade of millions of healing chemical responses throughout my body so my body is now in a healing mode!

Of course, this in no way negates the spiritual reality that as I gaze at God's promises fulfilled, faith is also being generated, which releases God's supernatural power (see Gen. 15:5-6). I have just activated both miracles and gifts of healings in my life by holding in my mind a picture of God's promises fulfilled (see 1 Cor. 12:28).

Kingdom emotions overwrite hardwired responses in your brain and body.

Miracles occur when there is faith and intensified Kingdom emotions. Together they release the Spirit's power. So receive God's spoken promises and visions for your life. See them fulfilled and the Kingdom emotions of compassion, joy, and thanksgiving burst forth. Now you have 1) opened up new receptors, 2) signaled new genes in new ways, and 3) released the Holy Spirit's power, all of which promote healing.

If I need a healed body, I look up pictures of what the healed organ or body part is to look like and gaze steadfastly on this picture, seeing Jesus restoring the area with His healing power and light. I speak loving encouragement to that section of my body because I know that love and compassion carry God's healing power. I cleanse cellular memories and repent of ungodly beliefs. Then I command evil spirits that are connected to the problem to leave.

The devotional template "New Creation Celebration: Replacing Emotions" guides me through *all* these steps, so none are missed. Airline pilots use a checklist to ensure they have completed every step and will achieve liftoff. I, too, choose to use the "New Creation Celebration" devotional checklist because I want to ensure I have liftoff and soar successfully in the Spirit, receiving my healing and my destiny.

Beliefs and emotions lodge in our cells and not just in our minds.

> *Wash your heart from evil, O Jerusalem, that you may be saved. How long will your wicked thoughts lodge within you?* (Jeremiah 4:14)

> *Do not be eager in your heart to be angry, for anger resides in the bosom of fools* (Ecclesiastes 7:9).

Once our cells are cleaned up and full of God's emotions and His light, our body is in the state of healing.

"Everyone who has this hope fixed on Him purifies himself, just as He is pure" (1 John 3:3). So I am going through a purification process as I cleanse myself of ungodly beliefs and emotions.

CHARITY

LIVING LOVED

God did not create employees for a corporation or soldiers for an army. He created children for a family. That is His heart for us and our reason for being—so He could love us!

Not only that, but because we are made in God's image and He is love, we are, in fact, wired for love. In her book, *Switch On Your Brain: The Key to Peak Happiness, Thinking, and Health*, cognitive neuroscientist Dr. Caroline Leaf teaches how it has been scientifically proven that we have no circuitry for fear; fear is a learned response.[70] We know there is no fear in love; so again we see even through our physiology how God designed us only for love (see 1 John 4:18).

There is actually a term, *optimism bias*, to describe the phenomenal fact that we all naturally and instinctively tend to express positive feelings, think healthy thoughts, and hope for the best.[71] Love, hope, joy, peace—these Kingdom emotions are what we are intended to run on and anything contrary interferes with God's perfect design. Fear, anger and unforgiveness short-circuit our systems and cause stress neurologically and biochemically as well as emotionally and spiritually.

There are so many revealing Scriptures that teach us about our mind/body/heart connection. We know we prosper and are in good health to the degree that our soul is in good health (see 1 John 3). And I especially appreciate what the *Aramaic Bible in Plain English* brings out of Proverbs 14:30: *"He that cools his anger is a healer of his heart, and envy is the decay of the bones."*

---

70   www.youtube.com/watch?v=kazIKVxVo94

71   Caroline Leaf, *Switch on Your Brain: The Key to Peak Happiness, Thinking, and Health* (Grand Rapids, MI: Baker Books, 2015).

Perhaps we have considered these to be more poetic refrains and not taken them literally, but science is finally catching up with ancient wisdom and research studies confirm their truth. The Lord let us know in no uncertain terms that negative emotions bring negative physical repercussions in our body. The empowering insight, though, is that the converse is also true—when we cool our anger, we heal our heart. When we walk in love and forgiveness and positive emotions, it has an equally transformative effect for good in our bodies as well.

God wasn't just giving us rules for the sake of rules; He was literally giving us instructions of how best to take care of ourselves. In fact, the Hebrew word for "commandment" (*mitzvah*) is also translated "prescribed," so we see how God's commands are a prescription for us that turns on healing genes and keeps us healthy. Proverbs 19:16 puts it this way: *"Keep God's laws and you will live longer"* (GNT). His laws really are for our own good!

To summarize, we can consider a simple picture: If we fill the gas tank of our car with chocolate syrup, we know it's not going to fuel the engine and the car isn't going to go anywhere. Similarly, when we fill our hearts and minds with negativity, we won't get very far either.

The fuel of our lives is peace and faith, compassion and gratitude. We were designed first and foremost, above all else, to love and be loved. God's love is the energy we are meant to run on, so we must practice giving and receiving it. Every moment of every day, we must learn to live loved.

MARK

COHERENCE: A STATE OF OPTIMAL FUNCTION

The HeartMath Institute's research has shown that generating *sustained positive emotions* facilitates a body-wide shift which is a measurable state. This state is termed *coherence* because it is characterized by increased order and harmony in our minds, emotions, and body, producing optimal function. There is increased access to intuition and creativity, cognitive and performance improvements, and favorable changes in hormonal balance.

Simply put, our body and brain work better, we feel better, and we perform better as shown by the chart below. Respiration, heart rate variability, and blood pressure all come into coherence with an appreciative heart! We have all experienced the opposite. When we are fearful or angry, respiration and blood pressure increase. When we are embarrassed, our faces turn red. Similarly, the emotional state of appreciation affects the health of the entire body, but in a positive way.

Charts Below Are from HeartMath Institute (www.heartmath.org)

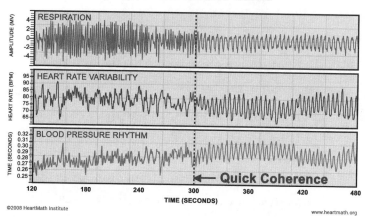

Image courtesy of the HeartMath Institute—www.heartmath.org

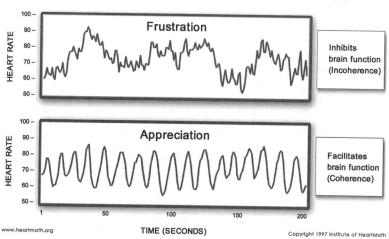

Image courtesy of the HeartMath Institute—www.heartmath.org

Chapter 11 of this book describes my use of the emWave®2 heart monitor, which I purchased through the HeartMath Institute. This device measures one's level of heart coherence and will produce the above charts, showing you your current level of heart coherence or lack thereof. The goal is for this to be a training tool, helping you work and live in the state of heart coherence or what I would call Kingdom emotions.

We have a brain in our hearts!

- The heart sends more signals to the brain than the brain sends to the heart!

- The brain continuously responds to the heart's signals.

- When the heart rhythm pattern is erratic and disordered, the signals traveling from the heart to the brain *inhibit* our ability to think clearly, remember, learn, reason, and make effective decisions. When in these non-coherent heart states we often act impulsively and unwisely (i.e., stress impairs our functions).

From *The Heart-Brain Connecton*[72] by HeartMath Institute

EPIGENETICS: TURNING GENES ON AND OFF

> *Ninety percent of our genes are influenced by their environment, which in turn is influenced by our thought processes.*

- *Epigenetics* literally means "above the gene." This refers to the control of genes not from within the DNA but from messages coming from outside the cell—in other words, from the environment.

---

72 www.heartmath.org/programs/emwave-self-regulation-technology-theoretical-basis/

- *Upregulating* means to turn a gene on; that is, the gene is expressed.

- *Downregulating* means to turn a gene off; that is, the gene is repressed.

GENES CAN AND DO CHANGE!

Identical twins in the same environment have similar epigenetic patterns, while twins separated and living different lifestyles were found to have as much as four times as many differentially expressed genes. Environment affects genes![73]

Amazing quotes about epigenetics:

- "If you change your thoughts, you actually change your biology." —Bruce H. Lipton, PhD. author of *The Biology of Belief.* Here is an eight-minute video from Dr. Lipton.[74]

- "When a gene product is needed, a signal from its environment, not an emergent property of the gene itself, activates expression of that gene." —H.F. Nijhout[75]

- Defective genes cause less than 1 percent of all disease. This article[76] counters the current misconception that we are controlled by our genes.

---

73 M.F. Fraga et al., "Epigenetic Differences Arise During the Lifetime of Monozygotic Twins," *Proceedings of the National Academy of Sciences* 102, no. 30 (2005), doi:10.1073/pnas.0500398102.

74 http://www.learn.hayhouseu.com/biologyofbelief-index1-us

75 H.F. Nijhout, "Problems and Paradigms: Metaphors and the Role of Genes in Development," *BioEssays* 12, no. 9 (1990), doi:10.1002/bies.950120908.

76 www.greenmedinfo.com/blog/defective-genes-cause-less-1-all-disease?page=1

STRESS: ONE OF THE BIGGEST CAUSES OF EPIGENETIC CHANGE

Stress knocks your body out of balance. It comes in three forms—physical stress (trauma), chemical stress (toxins), and emotional stress (fear, worry, stress, being overwhelmed, and so on). Each type can set off more than 1,400 chemical reactions and produce more than 30 hormones and neurotransmitters.[77]

Stress sends blood to our extremities, giving us extra strength in our arms and legs for fight or flight. The "stress response" is designed for emergencies, after which we are supposed to quickly return to normal where blood flows back from our extremities to our internal organs and genes revert back to their normal ongoing work of healing and restoration.

However, if we are living in constant stress then we are keeping our bodies from their normal healing processes. It's like living in a country where 98 percent of the resources are spent on defense, and nothing is left for all the rest of the services needed by a culture. In the case of the human body, the restorative process is shut down. When in stress, the body is constantly asking, "Am I OK? Where is it safe? How long will this threat be present?" The stress mode is the opposite of abiding in Christ, of living in peace, of trusting and surrendering to the loving care of our heavenly Father.

Thoughts alone can turn 2,200 genes on and off.

When 20 volunteers received eight weeks of training on how to meditate, it was determined that when this "relaxation response" took over their bodies, 1,561 genes showed change:

- 874 upregulated (turned on) for health
- 687 downregulated (turned off) for stress

---

77   Joe Dispenza, *You Are the Placebo: Making Your Mind Matter* (Carlsbad, CA: Hay House, Inc., 2015), 96.

The most experienced meditators had changes in 2,209 genes. Some changes occurred after just one session of meditation. Genes that were upregulated involved the immune function and energy metabolism. Genes that were downregulated included those linked to inflammation and stress.[78]

Diet and exercise regulate genes.

THREE MONTHS OF DIET AND EXERCISE REGULATE 500 GENES.	SIX MONTHS OF EXERCISE REGULATE 7,000 GENES.
In three months, 31 men with low-risk prostate cancer were able to upregulate 48 genes (mostly dealing with tumor suppression) and downregulate 453 genes (mostly dealing with tumor promotion) by following an intensive nutrition and lifestyle regimen. They lost weight, reduced their abdominal obesity, blood pressure, and lipid profile over the three months.	A six-month Swedish study of 23 slightly overweight, healthy men who went from being relatively sedentary to aerobic classes an average of twice per week were found to epigenetically alter 7,000 genes—almost 30 percent of all genes in the entire human genome!

Visualizing produces changes in one's body.

In a Harvard study, research subjects who had never before played the piano but *mentally* practiced a simple, five-finger piano exercise for two hours a day for five days made the same brain changes as the subjects who *physically* practiced the same activities. The region of their brains that controls finger movements increased dramatically, allowing their brains to look as though the experience they'd imagined had actually happened. They installed the neurological hardware (circuits) and software (programs), thereby creating new brain maps by thought

---

78 Dispenza, *You Are the Placebo*, 101.

alone.[79] In a French study, subjects who imagined lifting heavier weights activated their muscles more than did those who imagined lifting lighter weights.[80]

Mental rehearsal causes genes to respond in new ways!

If you gaze at an inner picture, it will become more real than the outer environment. The brain responds to what you see internally as well as what you see externally. If you are seeing and falling in love with your new-creation self and see God's promises to you already fulfilled (as did Abraham in Genesis 15:5), then your heart and body will begin to experience this future event in the present moment. You'll signal new genes, in new ways, to prepare for this imagined future event. Your body is turned into a healing machine, and faith is drawing God's miracle-working power to you.

Improper use of the eyes of my heart is to use them in picturing scenes that produce worry, fear, anxiety, doubt, lust, negativity, darkness, or pessimism.

Proper use of the eyes of my heart is to use them in picturing God's promises—Jesus at my side (see Acts 2:25; Heb. 12:1-2), God ruling earth from His heavenly throne with light (see Rev. 4), God working all things out for good, God's Kingdom ever increasing and satan's decreasing (see Isa. 9:7), the Church discipling all nations (see Matt. 28:19), etc.

PUTTING ON CHRIST

If in your daily "New Creation Celebration" meditation you regularly practice a new series of pictures, behaviors, and experiences that

---

79 "Modulation of Muscle Responses Evoked by Transcranial Magnetic Stimulation During the Acquisition of New Nine Motor Skills," *Journal of Neurophysiology* 74, no. 3 (1995).

80 A. Guillot et al., "Muscular Responses During Motor Imagery as a Function of Muscle Contraction Types," *International Journal of Psychophysiology* 66, no. 1 (2007), doi:10.1016/j.ijpsycho.2007.05.009.

are what God has revealed as His destiny for you, then your brain actually physically changes. It installs new neurological circuitry. It begins to look as if the experience has already happened. Your body produces epigenetic changes that lead to structural and functional changes in your body. You are now living as your new-creation self and not as the old self of the past. You have died and your life is hidden with Christ in God (see Col. 3:3).

> *Put on the new self who is being renewed to a **true** knowledge* (Colossians 3:10).

Change your heart; change your life.

Spiritual meditation makes this possible. You close your eyes and see the scene once again of God's promises toward you concerning your life, your health, your family, your future, and your destiny. As you gaze upon this, you are transformed (see 2 Cor. 3:17-18; 4:17-18).

As you rehearse this destiny or promise, it becomes familiar to you. Your heart and mind are rewired to believe and receive and respond in faith and obedience to that which you are gazing upon. Your body changes! Thousands of genes are turned on or off to make this future your possibility today. Gaze upon this new reality, observing every detail, memorizing them, rewiring your mind and heart to receive.

Combine the emotions of compassion, joy, thankfulness, and excitement knowing that what you are seeing on the screen inside your mind is your true reality in Christ! Kingdom emotion bathes your body in the neurochemistry that would be present if that future event were actually happening now. You are experiencing a taste of this future experience *now!*

Your brain and body don't know the difference between having an actual experience in your life and just picturing and pondering the experience. Neurochemically, it's the same. So your brain and body begin to believe they're actually living your new creation in Christ in the present moment.

TRANSFORMATION

By keeping your focus on who you are in Christ and not letting any other thoughts distract you, in a matter of moments you turn down the volume on the neural circuits connected to the old self, which begins to turn off the old genes, and you fire and wire new genes in new ways.

As you keep combining God's *rhema* and visions with Kingdom emotions of compassion and gratitude, your heart and mind are working together, and you are being transformed into His likeness. At this point, your brain and body have been transformed from a record of your past (which it was projecting into your present) to a map guiding you into your future.

Prayer can change cells at great distances, instantly!

When a man's DNA was separated from his body, a change in his thoughts brought instantaneous change in his DNA, which was 350 miles away.[81] Because we are part of the body of Christ, we change each other even from a distance. The Bible clearly teaches this is possible through prayer.

Epigenetic medicine and the new biology of intention

I encourage you to read the fascinating, fun, and fully understandable book, *A Genie in Your Genes: Epigenetic Medicine and the New Biology of Intention* by Dawson Church. It is not a Christian book, and

---

81 Gregg Braden, *The Divine Matrix: Bridging Time, Space, Miracles, and Belief* (Carlsbad, CA: Hay House, 2008), 46–48.

while I don't agree with everything in it I know you will be inspired to create firm intentions to live in faith, hope, and love as the Bible instructs as you rediscover all the healing benefits of such a lifestyle.

Following are just a few statistics and quotes from Dawson's book, which I have followed up with Scriptures.

- People who view God as a judgmental God have a CD4 (helper) cell decline more than twice the rate of those who don't see God as judgmental.[82] *"God is love"* (1 John 4:16).

- Only 23 percent of people see God as a benevolent God.[83] If you are a two-way journaler,[84] I guarantee you have learned to see God as loving and kind.

- Fighting slows healing by 40 percent.[85] That's why we only speak words edifying for the need of the moment and endeavor to live at peace with all men (see Eph. 4:29; Rom. 12:18).

- Those who perform altruistic acts live longer, reducing their odds of an early death by nearly 60 percent.[86] Loving and serving others with our gifts is biblical (see Gal. 5:13; 1 Pet. 4:10).

- "A study of one thousand older adults followed for nine years concluded that people with high levels of optimism had a 23% lower risk of death from cardio-vascular disease and a 55% lower risk of death from

---

82   Dawson Church, *Genie in Your Genes: Epigenetic Medicine and the New Biology of Intention* (Santa Rosa, CA: Energy Psychology Press, 2014), loc. 723.

83   Ibid., loc. 758.

84   www.cwgministries.org/4keys

85   Ibid., loc. 475.

86   Ibid., loc. 826-827.

all causes compared to their more pessimistic peers."[87] Positive older people also have better memories and stay healthier. Overall physical fitness is reflected in walking speed; positive elders were found to walk faster than negative ones. Indeed, a merry heart does good like medicine (see Prov. 17:22)!

- In a 20-year study of 13,000 European subjects, people who believe that happiness is an inside job tend to die of old age, with less than 1 percent of them dying of cancer or heart disease. We know the joy of the Lord is our strength (see Neh. 8:10).

- "A single regulatory gene at the top of a complex network can indirectly launch a cascade of hundreds or thousands of other genes," and, "by compounding and coordinating their effects, genes can exert enormous influence on biological structure." The word he uses, *cascade*, is often associated with regulatory gene expression. The firing of a regulatory gene at the top of a cascade can lead to a massive biological chain reaction. He gives examples of experiments in which "a simple regulatory gene leads directly and indirectly to the expression of approximately 2,500 other genes."[88]

- One study found sudden bursts of high frequency 40 Hz oscillations (gamma waves) in the brain appearing just prior to moments of insight. This oscillation is conducive to creating links across many parts of the brain. The findings suggest that at a moment of

---

87   Ibid., loc. 879-882.
88   Ibid., loc. 1002–1006.

insight, a complex set of new connections is being created.[89] The Bible calls this revelation and inspiration, and it results in true knowledge, not just knowledge (see Acts 9:1-22; Col. 2:2; 3:10).

- The number of new synaptic connections between neurons can double in as little as an hour once the experience-dependent genes are activated. One of the ways in which memories are encoded is when we replay a scene in our minds. Memory is not static, and as we combine old memories with present situations we stimulate neurogenesis. We used to think that memories remained unchanged over time, like taking a photograph out of an album and putting it back in again. We now know that we recombine the old material with bits of information from the current environment. Like printing out a photo on whatever printer is closest, then scanning it back in.[90] King David's eyes would anticipate his pre-dawn prayer times where he would meditate on God's Word, listen for His voice, experience His love, and be revived (see Ps. 119:147-149).

- A normal cell has an electrical potential of about 90 millivolts. An inflamed cell has a potential of about 120 millivolts, and a cell in a state of degeneration may drop to 30 millivolts.[91] When we lay hands on a person and pray for healing, we release the energy of God to them as Jesus did (see Luke 8:43-48).

---

89 Ibid., loc. 1173–1178.
90 Ibid., loc. 1179–1184.
91 Ibid., loc. 1426-1427.

The above information helps me understand the roles of both miracles and gifts of healings (see 1 Cor. 12:28). I now have more insight into the power of inner healing, laying on of hands, and compassion as a carrier wave of God's healing power. I have deepened my commitment to living in faith, hope, and love and setting aside judgment, anger, hopelessness, and other emotions that are not part of my new self in Christ. I am astounded at the healing mechanisms God has designed within our bodies. We are truly fearfully and wonderfully made (see Ps. 139:14)!

Cleansing the Cellular Environment

Genes are turned on and off by the chemicals and instructions provided to them by their environment, so one way we can change the cellular environment is by cleansing cellular memories. This is such an important and powerful concept that the entire next chapter is devoted to it.

Angelic Guardians of What?

Charity has had a lifelong friendship with her guardian angels. She has gotten to know their names, dialogue with them, and have fun with them. Charity has an entire blog series on doing life together with angels, which you will find here,[92] as well as a book on her angelic adventures coming out soon.

Below is one small glimpse into her interactions with angels as it touches on the topic of this chapter, which is living in Kingdom emotions that in turn activate healing genes. Enjoy her testimony of encountering angels of joy!

---

92 www.GloryWaves.org/angels.

CHARITY

THE COMPANY OF HEAVEN

My angels tell me they are "guardians of my laughter" and "protectors of my peace."

So that's kind of their thing. My angels are just like my husband in that they love to hear me laugh. Pojes, Shobis, and Leo all *go out of their way* to elicit a smile or laugh from me, just because they want to see me happy and peaceful and in that good place.

In fact, heartfelt laughter is actually a swipe at the enemy. Satan's strategy is to steal our peace, kill our joy, and bring destruction to our spirit, soul, and body; our laughter is the simplest way to express his total failure in all of those areas. Indeed, that is one reason holy laughter has been such a distinctive element of revival.

Peacekeepers

I was excited when I found Pastor Bill Johnson of Bethel Church shared a similar idea in his book *Hosting the Presence,* and I took it as confirmation that this was a God thought. He said:

> It's important to note that violence in the spiritual realm is always a peace-filled moment for His people. That's how the Prince of Peace can crush satan under our feet (see Rom. 16:20). Another way to put it is every peace-filled moment you experience brings terror to the powers of darkness. Only in the Kingdom of God is peace a military tool.[93]

Yes! That's exactly what the Lord had been teaching me. But honestly, I still needed to have a talk with Jesus about these angels He had assigned to me.

---

93 Bill Johnson, *Hosting the Presence: Unveiling Heaven's Agenda* (Shippensburg, PA: Destiny Image Publishers, 2012), 103.

God, they're really awesome and everything and I don't mean to sound ungrateful, but they are just so into my feelings (of all things!). Guardians of my joy. Seriously? There has got to be a lot more important things for all of us to be concerned with. I mean, isn't there a spiritual war going on? Where are these guys on that anyway?

Jesus Laughed

Jesus just laughed, obviously amused, and assured me that my angels were obeying Him perfectly and accomplishing the mission He'd given them precisely. He then went on to show me how all throughout the New Testament, God-emotion was a decidedly big player.

I already knew about the fruit of the Spirit (love, joy, peace). But then He also reminded me about the "abiding realities"—faith, hope, and love. First Corinthians 13 makes it clear that we must have the fruit of the Spirit in our lives or else the gifts don't count. Spiritual gifts (e.g., miracles and prophecy) are to demonstrate the spiritual fruit of God's feelings—His patience, kindness, and compassion toward us.

What really clinched it for me was when He brought Romans 14:17 onto my radar. Righteousness, peace, and joy in the Holy Ghost are actually the very Kingdom of God. I'm not sure He could put a higher premium on them than that. And if that wasn't enough, Holy Spirit then showed me how all this Kingdom emotion actually even plays a part in our spiritual warfare.

What Kind of Armor?

First there was the realization that it is "only" wrong feelings like anger and unforgiveness that give place to the devil in our lives (see Eph. 4:26-27; 2 Cor. 2:10-11).

Then came the revelation of what the armor for our spiritual battles against the enemy is actually made of—a breastplate of *faith and love* and a helmet of *hope* (see 1 Thess. 5:8). Not to mention feet shod in *peace* (see Eph. 6:15). From head to toe we are dressed in holy Kingdom emotion, and that is what protects and guards us.

It was a great blessing, then, when not long after this I read Pastor Bill's word about peace-filled moments bringing terror to the enemy. Because what is the best outward expression of peace? Laughter sure works for me, which is exactly what my angels had been trying to tell me all along.

If personal revelation, Scripture, *and* Bill Johnson agree? I must be on the right track!

MARK

ACTION EXERCISES

Journaling response: "Lord, what do You want to speak to me about turning on healing genes and turning off inflammatory genes?"

Use this "Evening Prayer of Thanksgiving"[94] five times to get used to the benefits it offers you.

Complete "New Creation Celebration" meditations a minimum of five times this week. I suggest trying one or both of the versions below.

- "New Creation Celebration: Putting on Christ"[95]
- "New Creation Celebration: Possessing Your Promised Land"[96]

Try some "mini-movies" during the day where you take 15 seconds to re-envision your new-creation self, brimming with life and anointing, and Jesus at your side.

---

94 www.cwgministries.org/blogs/evening-prayer-thanksgiving
95 www.cwgministries.org/christ
96 www.cwgministries.org/possess

Chapter 9

CLEANSING CELLULAR MEMORIES

CATCHING A MURDERER

Memories are stored in our cells.

An eight-year-old girl, who received the heart of a murdered ten-year-old girl, began having recurring vivid nightmares about the murder [even though she knew nothing about who her heart donor was]. Her mother arranged a consultation with a psychiatrist who after several sessions concluded that she was witnessing actual physical incidents. They decided to call the police who used the detailed descriptions of the murder (the time, the weapon, the place, the clothes he wore, what the little girl he killed had said to him) given by the little girl to find and convict the man in question.[97]

---

97 Sandeep Joshi, "Memory Transference in Organ Transplant Recipients," Journal of New Approaches to Medicine and Health, April 24, 2011, Cases of Personality Changes Due to Organ Transplants, http://bit.ly/OrganMemory.

Many people who receive organ transplants pick up the likes and dislikes of the person the organ came from. Yes, memories and emotions are stored in our cells.

You have heard the phrase, "That person is a pain in the neck." I have seen the pain of a stiff neck immediately disappear when the person I was counseling forgave another who was "a pain in their neck." The book *Molecules of Emotion* by Dr. Candance Pert lays out scientific evidence that emotions are stored in our cells.

EMOTIONAL TRAUMA LEADS TO 90% OF OUR HEALTH ISSUES

Emotional trauma causes stress on our bodies, which impacts our immune function, brain chemistry, blood sugar levels, hormonal balance, and much more. The US National Library of Medicine hosts an article on stress that indicates up to 90 percent of illnesses are stress-related:

> It is estimated that 80% to 90% of all industrial accidents are related to personal problems and employees' inability to handle stress. The European Agency for Safety and Health at work reported that about 50% of job absenteeism is caused by stress. ...The Centre for Disease Control and Prevention of the United States estimates that stress account about 75% of all doctors visit. ...According to Occupational Health and Safety news and the National Council on compensation of insurance, *up to 90% of all visits to primary care physicians are for stress-related complaints.*[98]

---

98   Razali Salleh Mohd, "Life Event, Stress and Illness," *The Malaysian Journal of Medical Sciences* 15, no. 4 (October 2008): Introduction,http://bit.ly/SickStress.

If stress wreaks that much havoc, imagine how healing it would be to remove stress from the memories of our cells! The prayer experience below guides us in receiving Jesus' healing touch to release stress-producing memories stored on a cellular level.

I have experienced cleansing of cellular memories.

My naturopath had been telling me for years that my adrenal gland (the fight/flight response) was stressed, and I adamantly told her "no" because, after all, I had learned to abide in Christ and even written a book on it.

Well, eventually another naturopath, Kurt Green,[99] told me a skin irritation that kept coming back was the result of a stressed out adrenal gland too. So I decided it was time to get to the root of this and resolve it now, at the tender young age of 63, a good dozen years after first being informed of the problem. (By the way, you don't need to wait 12 years to process your issues as I did. Be wise and choose to get healed when issues pop up!)

My real stressors were historical rather than present tense.

I finally realized that the stress in my adrenals was not necessarily coming from my current life. It was more likely that this was stored stress from past issues in my life and perhaps even stresses that had been passed down through my family line. The stress was being held in the memory of the cells of my adrenal gland. This was a big "wow" moment for me and gave me understanding of a whole new way to pray for healing! Another confirming article I read was called "Do our genes 'remember' pain? Scientists suspect they might."[100]

---

99   www.cwgministries.org/KurtGreen
100   Amy Ellis Nutt, "Do our genes 'remember' pain? Scientists suspect they might," The Washington Post, May 19, 2016, http://bit.ly/GenePain.

Modern medicine tends to have a mechanical view of the body, considering each organ and gland and system as stand-alone components that can function fairly independently of each other and the emotional state of the host body. However, alternative, naturopathic doctors look to the more traditional, ancient understandings of Greek and Chinese medicine, which saw the internal organs as being strongly affected by the emotions, with specific emotions especially affecting specific organs. I embrace this more holistic understanding of the body. Such a view makes the abiding realities of faith, hope, and love take on a whole new significance when it comes to experiencing health and healing (see 1 Cor. 13:13).

MEMORIES TRAPPED IN YOUR CELLS

One great way to discover a root emotional cause of an infirmity is to ask, *"Lord, what happened in my life just before this infirmity began?"* The thought that immediately lights upon your mind is a word of knowledge and will reveal a trauma and a stored cellular memory that needs to be processed in prayer.

Another great way to discover a trapped memory is to notice when you have a negative reaction that is disproportionate to the stimulus that triggered it. The reason your reaction is so extreme is because of the stored energy and memories in your cells.

Let's Define Some Terms

- **Miracles and gifts of healings:** The Bible says, *"God has appointed in the church...miracles, then gifts of healings"* (1 Cor. 12:28). Cleansing cellular memories is an example of one of God's "gifts of healings." I am passionate to experience both miracles and gifts of healings. I am not going to turn down anything God has offered to me. I have seen far too many people suffer with infirmity because they wanted a miracle and did not get it and then would not pursue His gifts of healings. They might go to the doctor and receive a drug to mask the symptoms but refuse to explore gifts of healings.

- **No self-effort allowed**—only prayer guided by the Spirit (see Eph. 6:18). Rather than digging through your past on your own, you will receive words of knowledge as Jesus speaks and highlights things to you (see John 6:63; Ps. 139:23-24; 32:5).

- **Words of knowledge** and words of wisdom are received by you through:

  - Jesus' *voice*—spontaneous, flowing thoughts that light upon your mind.

  - Jesus' *vision*—spontaneous, flowing pictures that light upon your mind.

  - *Jesus' healing touch*—spontaneous, flowing energy and release that you feel in your body.

- **Inner healing**: Inviting Jesus into the scene where the trauma occurred, seeing what He is doing, hearing what He is saying, feeling His touch, and saying "yes" to His instructions.

- **Two-way journaling**: Recording your visions and dialogue with Jesus on paper or an electronic device.

- **A healed hurt**: A hurt is healed when you can see the gift God has produced in your life through the experience (see Rom. 8:28).

- **Tapping:** Some may add EFT tapping, also known as Emotional Freedom Techniques,[101] to release locked up emotions and cellular tension, and it may also facilitate the flow of revelation of root causes.

PAST TRAUMAS RESULTED IN STORED CELLULAR MEMORIES

In my case, I knew what needed healing—my stressed out adrenal gland. So I quieted myself in the Lord's presence and asked, "Lord, what events in my life produced trauma that is stored as memories in my cells and putting stress on my adrenal gland?" I then tuned to flow and jotted down one-line phrases of 11 events from my past that lit upon my mind over the next several minutes. Wow! So now I had 11 traumas to process and pray through. I spent several days working through them, using steps four through eight of the prayer approach below.

The first three steps of the prayer approach were already accomplished in what I have just described above: 1) I had already quieted myself before the Lord, 2) asked for His input, and 3) received and recorded spontaneous thoughts coming from Him. So now let's see what steps four through eight had me do.

Eight Steps for Clearing Cellular Memories and Experiencing Healing

1. **I get in spirit**: I become still in God's presence, loving Him through soft, soaking music and/or praying in tongues, putting a smile on my face and picturing Jesus with me (see 2 Kings 3:15-16; 1 Cor. 14:15; Acts 2:25). I tune to His flowing thoughts, flowing pictures, and flowing emotions (see John 7:37-39).

---

101   www.cwgministries.org/eft

2. **I ask Jesus what needs healing**: "Lord, what needs healing in my life today? What stressed body organ or infirmity or abnormal emotional response needs to be dealt with?"

3. **I receive words of knowledge**: "Holy Spirit, please bring to my attention any event(s) that occurred at the inception of this physical, emotional, or spiritual infirmity in my life or that added to it later on." I tune to flow and make a list of one-line titles for each of the various events that light upon my mind. These are words of wisdom and words of knowledge revealing a root experience that will need to be resolved so the infirmity can be healed. A spouse or close friend can assist me in recalling traumatic events that need healing. *After* this list is created, we then apply steps four through eight to each event. Use the downloadable worksheet to make it easy.

4. **I invite Jesus into the scene (inner healing)**: "Jesus, remind me of what I was feeling and show me where You are in this scene. What are You saying, doing, and asking me to do?" I follow His voice and visions by repenting, forgiving, releasing, honoring, and blessing as He instructs. Pastor John Arnott tells of asking a woman to forgive her horse for falling on her and crushing her hip. As soon as she forgave the horse, her hip pain vanished! So forgive yourself and the event as well as other people involved in the trauma, and even God, for allowing this to happen. Record each inner healing experience in your journal as a part of your spiritual memorials.

5. **Cellular emotional trauma is released by Jesus**: "Jesus, please remove the memory of this trauma that is stored in my (state specific body part)." Breathe out deeply a couple of times. Pause, watch, look, listen, and feel as Jesus ministers healing grace, sweeping out the memory as He cleanses the cells.

6. **Demonic entanglements are renounced in Jesus' name**: "I renounce and break off all demons, in the name of Jesus, that were attached to these events." I pause, watch, look, listen, and feel as Jesus ministers deliverance to me. Breathe out a couple of times forcefully and feel the release. Record what demons are rebuked and what you sense and see happening. The names of the demons will light upon your mind as spontaneous flowing thoughts, and they generally correspond with what they are causing—anger, hatred, fear, inferiority, condemnation, shame, infirmity, arthritis, pain, etc.

7. **Physical healing is received through Jesus**: "Lord Jesus, would You shine Your light upon (name body part)?" Watch Jesus touch, heal, and restore the damaged body part. Then thank Him: "Thank You, Jesus, for Your healing, restorative touch. I receive it with gratefulness." Record what transpires.

8. **Divine gifts are revealed by Jesus**: "Lord, what is the gift You have produced in my life through this trauma/event?" Record what this gift is and see and speak *only* of this gift from now on! A hurt is healed when you can see the gift God has produced in your life through it.

Now we apply steps four through eight to each trauma.

Process each trauma on your list in a relaxed, 20-minute prayer time, performing all five steps (numbered four through eight) for *each* trauma. We have created a prayer journaling worksheet to make this easier. It may be downloaded free.[102] We have a sample of a completed worksheet that you may also download.[103]

Seeing the gifts God has produced in your life through these traumas is the final step (see Rom. 8:28). Here are a couple of the gifts God showed me He had produced from the traumas in my life. *"I am perfectly designed and positioned to fulfill God's destiny for my life"* and *"God used separation (being fired from numerous jobs) to bring me into my own, to function in the role He has called me to, and to lead the ministry I have headed up for the last 25 years."*

COMPLETE HEALING

After processing the 11 scenes the Lord had given me, I was impressed to go back through my life, stage by stage, asking the Lord for any additional experiences that had produced stress in my system. *"Holy Spirit, reveal traumas from my life during...* (state each specific period)." In the womb, birth through age five, elementary school, middle school, high school, college, marriage, after marriage. Jot down one-line titles for each scene that lights upon your mind. For me, this resulted in a list of another 21 traumatic events that popped into my mind in less than 30 minutes (i.e., words of knowledge). Wow, 21 more events to process in prayer. Are you kidding?

Remember, no thinking is allowed as you do this exercise. You are to stay tuned to the flow of the Holy Spirit, allowing *Him* to reveal

---

102   www.cwgministries.org/CellWorksheet
103   www.cwgministries.org/CellWorksheetSample

what needs healing rather than digging around using self-effort (see John 7:37-39; 6:63).

Now, process your list of events by applying the prayer worksheet that covers steps four through eight to each event. I found this takes 20 to 25 minutes per event, so I processed two scenes per day during my daily devotional time, covering all 21 traumas in 11 days. The growing freedom and release I was experiencing was absolutely thrilling and very encouraging, which of course motivated me to continue on.

HOW ABOUT A SECOND OPINION?

The day after I completed praying through the 32 traumas (11 from my first list and 21 from the second list), which had been producing stress on my adrenal gland, I had the opportunity to experience a Spectravision body scan from Rocky Steinert, a doctor of nutrition who was in attendance at a weekend seminar I was conducting. The computerized results said my adrenal stress was down below any critical stage! Yay God!

Because I believe in a multitude of counselors, I checked back with Kurt Green, and using his form of guidance, which is to receive words of knowledge, Kurt told me that 90 percent of my adrenal stress was gone and the remaining stress was coming from a few memories still stuck in my cells.

So I checked with God again, and He gave me two additional traumas to pray through plus He brought up one that I had already prayed about. Obviously, the healing for that one hadn't been complete because He was mentioning it again.

The trauma He highlighted this second time was when I was caught by a policeman in my youth doing something I shouldn't have been doing. God said He is the one who brings calamity (see Isa. 45:7), and He had worked it out for good! Well, I had accepted that idea mentally and theologically, but I did not *feel* it emotionally.

If you don't have a new Kingdom emotion, then the issue is not yet healed.

As I processed the trauma a second time, I discovered that I needed to *look more intently* at the Scriptures and revelation that declared God's perspective so I could *fully feel* God's emotions concerning the situation.

To deepen the revelation, picture, and emotion, I went back to Isaiah 45 and read and meditated on the entire chapter, picturing it and praying over it and *feeling* it. This intensive Bible meditation produced a full emotional healing of that partially healed trauma.

We gain a fuller revelation of God's perspective by meditating on relevant Scriptures, asking Him to explain them so our heart burns with revelation (see Luke 24:32). If we don't clearly *see* God's perspective and *feel* His emotions, the hurt is not yet healed. As we soak in the picture He is showing, emotions and faith are stirred up.

HEALING THROUGH DREAMS

Emotions can be created by Kingdom pictures God gives you during the day or in your nighttime dreams. The Bible shows that it is wise to pay attention to your dreams, journal them out, and receive God's guidance and empowerment through them (see Num. 12:6; Ps. 16:7). Your body and brain respond the same whether you're experiencing the scene in waking life or dream life. Have you noticed that your heart races if you have a scary dream?

I experienced ongoing revelation through my dreams. I went to sleep asking God to reveal any additional scenes that left trauma in my body, and I would awaken each morning with one or two more. Thus the process continued until finally I awoke with no more scenes on my mind or in my heart.

AFTER THE CELLULAR CLEANSING WAS COMPLETE

This healing of my adrenal gland allowed me to begin sleeping a full eight hours every night, something I knew was healthy but had not been able to do for 20 to 30 years. And yes, the skin irritation completely disappeared over the three weeks it took me to process these 35 traumas!

Additionally, before this healing my back would tighten up whenever I sat for several hours. I had needed to go to a chiropractor every two weeks to have my back and neck put back in place. Now I can sit for hours without either one tightening up, and I only go to the chiropractor every six weeks. Even then, it is not because my back is tight or out of place, but because I believe in having my skeleton in maximum alignment for maximum health. Since my healing of cellular memories, my chiropractor says my back is in great shape.

Nutrition

During these three weeks I doubled my daily nutrition, took milk thistle to cleanse my liver, and added a few additional items my naturopath had recommended. I was truly ready to resolve these issues and do whatever was necessary.

GENERATIONAL SINS AND CURSES

Kurt Green, my naturopath, stated, "I have personally found 30 percent of the events that I needed to release were ancestral." Exodus 20:4-6 speaks of things affecting future generations.

Prayer to Remove Generational Sins and Curses

Relax and take your time, see what you are praying, feel it, tune to flow, and allow the Holy Spirit the opportunity to move within the prayer so it is more than rote words. You will pray this for your father's side of the family first and then pray through it a second time for your mother's side of the family.

Picture your father/mother and pray this out loud:

> *I choose to forgive my father/mother and his/her ancestors for all generational sins and curses that flowed through him/her to me and are contributing to (state infirmity, e.g. "the stress in my adrenal gland"). I picture myself as a baby in my mother's womb. I place the cross of Christ between my father/mother and that baby. I command all negative energy that is flowing from him/her to me and (state infirmity, e.g. "stressing out my adrenal gland") to halt at the cross of Christ and to fall to the ground powerless at the foot of the cross.*

Repeat this statement while seeing the negative energy hitting the cross of Christ and falling to the ground powerless.

> *I release that baby in the womb—you are set free, you are set free, you are set free. Those whom the Son sets free are free indeed. I lay my hand on the body part (e.g. adrenal gland). (Speak name of body part), you are set free to function normally in Jesus' name. Function normally, in Jesus' name. Come to peace in Jesus' name. Be healed in Jesus' name.*

See and feel this new freedom.

I speak the blessings of Calvary over that baby in the womb. I bless you with health, with healing, with life. I thank You, Jesus, for Your healing power that is restoring my (name body part). I am healed, in Jesus' name! I am healed, in Jesus' name. I am healed, in Jesus' name.

Breathe in and out deeply a couple of times, feeling the full release and new life flowing within you.

I thank You, Jesus, for Your healing touch.

Repetition

Because things are deepened through repetition, I would encourage you to pray the prayer twice for your father's side of the family and then twice for your mother's side.

Get your release from generational garbage! I did! It is a simple prayer and it felt good. This release should also be effective for your children who have not yet reached the age of accountability.

IS IT A TRUE MEMORY?

Have you ever wondered if a memory is true or false? Was this only a false memory and should I blow it off? Is it just a figment of my imagination? Is it too little, too big, too long ago?

My experience is that if it came to your attention during prayer, you should deal with it. It doesn't matter if it is a false memory or not, because if it is on your mind then you are already engaged with it and these prayers will allow you to disengage. People have received healing from memories they are not even sure were true. Even as the heart transplant patient received memories of the donor's murder, we can carry memories in our DNA from previous generations.

Stop trying to figure out if you need to pray for the issue that came to your mind. Just pray the prayer that is appropriate (breaking generational sins, cleansing cellular memories, etc.). If the prayer was not necessary, your greatest loss was a few minutes in prayer. If the prayer was necessary, then you are free of one more negative energy field within you.

FIVE TAKEAWAYS ON CLEANSING CELLULAR MEMORIES

1. **I am committed to wholeness:** living in His presence, which releases within me His love. I will take whatever time and effort is necessary to apply His healing presence to all emotional traumas and come to the state of peace.

2. **I use repetition to deepen the healing:** I review my journaling, asking God to deepen and expand what He has shown me. I may choose to use "tapping," as taught in Emotional Freedom Techniques (EFT), as I process a traumatic scene.[104]

3. **Once healed,** I will gaze only upon pictures of the *gifts* God has produced in my life through these traumas.

4. **I will see, feel, and confess**, "I am healed. Body, function normally in Jesus' name."

5. **I restructure my thought processes:** I pull down unbiblical thought processes and replace them with biblical thoughts that I arrive at by hearing God's voice, seeing

---

104 www.GloryWaves.org/eft

His visions, feeling His emotions, and conducting Bible meditations on topics that are relevant to maintaining my new position of health (see 2 Cor. 10:4-5).

SATAN'S TOP LIES TO ENSURE WE STAY SICK

	SATAN'S LIES	GOD'S TRUTH
1	This prayer approach takes too much time.	This devotional method makes your prayer times revelation-based healing encounters with Almighty God, which bring transformation to your life. Could anything be better?
2	The prayer worksheet is too methodical for me.	Pilots use detailed checklists before takeoff to ensure everything is done perfectly. Isn't that a worthwhile endeavor? Do we want pilots to stop using checklists because they are too methodical?
3	I started with my biggest scene and it was too traumatic. Now I'm stuck.	Start with something smaller and work your way up.
4	No one can be perfectly healthy.	Sure you can. Jesus purchased your health with His broken body on the cross (see Isa. 53:5).

Some find an excuse why they can't.
Others find a way they can!

CHARITY

TAPPED OUT

At our EFT workshop I tapped with a pastor who was a counselor and who had also received a great deal of counseling herself.[105] She never understood her weight issues and why she had them, but after a few minutes of tapping it "came up" that it started when she was a child, the year her parents got divorced.

She had tried to control her parents' relationship and help fix it but couldn't. She then began gaining weight, another negative thing and also a cushion to separate and insulate her from the situation. She realized the connection in that she had felt helpless in controlling her eating and fixing her weight, in the same way she felt helpless about her parents' divorce.

She was amazed that the root underlying issue just "came to her" when years of talk therapy never touched it. It reminds me of Isaac taking the Philistines' earth out of the wells (see Gen 26:15). The rivers of living water are deep in the innermost being, and tapping lets them bubble up to the surface.

MARK

TESTIMONY OF HEALING THROUGH RELEASING CELLULAR MEMORIES

I was previously unfamiliar with EFT tapping. I used it on working with my fourth trauma. It definitely made a difference. I felt healing as I worked through the steps and

---

105 To learn more about biblically based EFT, visit www.GloryWaves.org/eft

Jesus gave me a new perspective on the situation, which involved my mother.

As I worked through the stages of life, He showed me my mother and He showed me the many years of deep heartache and quiet desperation she has suffered. She will be 91 in 3 weeks. Jesus opened my heart to see her in a way I never have before. He showed me her incredible beauty, talent, and love. He showed me so many blessings she has given me. Even through the mental health issues, she was amazing. She had her first set of shock treatments when I was ten.

I now have an appreciation for her that fills my heart with love and awe for her. I am deeply grateful that Father selected her to be my mother. Thank You, Father, for my mother! Father is healing my heart toward my dad, too. I am deeply grateful.

Healing is very hard and it takes a lot of courage, but man oh man, is it worth it! Healing is truly an incredible gift of our loving Father! He is so amazing! I am deeply humbled with being so blessed!

Resting in Father's embrace,

Linda

Epilogue from Linda: Her Story Continues

I have worked a little bit more with healing the cells of my body. Jesus brought up another memory that I thought I had completely addressed. As I went through prayer steps four through eight, which you outlined, there were very deep emotions that surfaced and then I felt a release and calm.

Jesus gave me a new picture with Him in it. Something seemed to really be different. My health immediately improved. Infirmity I had been putting up with because I believed I needed to vanished immediately. Jesus brought up a couple more situations and I will work with them as soon as I can. I can see that it takes Jesus showing us the emotions that the cells are holding on to. This has made a huge difference.

Even if you feel you have processed a hurt already, if Jesus brings it up again, process it again, making sure you *do all eight prayer steps listed above*. Partial healing can occur by doing some of the steps. Full healing can occur using all of the steps.

ACTION EXERCISE

Do a complete journaling retreat (or series of daily devotions) and process emotions stored in your cells. Use the method and worksheet provided in this chapter. Take the time necessary to experience the release. No need to rush and not get your breakthrough. If it takes you three weeks to do this assignment, then take three weeks. You are worth it! Jesus died for *your* healing.

Chapter 10

INNER HARMONY: CASTING OUT DEMONS

When evening came, they brought to Him many who
were demon-possessed; and He cast out the spirits with
a word, and healed all who were ill. This was to fulfill
what was spoken through Isaiah the prophet: "He Himself
took our infirmities and carried away our diseases."
—MATTHEW 8:16-17

DELIVERANCE FROM DEMONS: ONE OF THE BLESSINGS PROVIDED AT CALVARY

Jesus truly is the perfect pattern and the One whom I choose to imitate. Jesus cast out demons, and people were healed (see Acts 10:38). Twelve of forty-one of Jesus' recorded prayers for healing were prayers for deliverance, meaning almost one third of His prayers involved deliverance. I choose to follow that example and plan on about one third of my prayers being deliverance prayers also.

Not that I have always held this position. I began with the assumption that much of the Bible wasn't for today. However, Jesus has convinced me I can live the Bible from Genesis to Revelation. I have written about deliverance extensively elsewhere, so I am only going to briefly review those concepts in this chapter, and if you decide you need more you can access those materials either in hard copy form[106] or through our electronic School of the Spirit.[107]

The Greek word in the New Testament translated "demon-possessed" is *daimonizomai* and literally means "under the influence of" (Strong's G1139). Therefore, I reject the idea of demon *possession* as it is not an accurate translation of the Greek text, and it is an unacceptable picture of a Christian. Christians have the Holy Spirit joined to their spirits (see 1 Cor. 6:17), so there is no way they could be possessed by a demon. However, they could have some area of their life that was *under the influence* of a demon as we shall see in the example below.

HEART WOUNDS ATTRACT DEMONS CAUSING MAJOR DEBILITATION

Demon of Fear

"I want to be healed of fear. Fear *never* goes away! Everything makes me afraid. I am afraid of financial ruin and declining health. I am afraid for my children and my spouse and for our nation. I am fearful of evil men, the IRS, the antichrist, and persecution. I am fearful of rejection and failure. If I decide I want to pray for healing of the sick, I am afraid the prayer will not work and I will look bad, God will look bad, and

---

106   www.cwgministries.org/store/prayers-heal-heart-dvd-package
107   www.cluschoolofthespirit.com/courses/prayers-that-heal-the-heart

people will be discouraged and fall away from the Lord. Jesus, help! Remove this fear!"

Solution

Fear is a big problem. Fear is mentioned 313 times in the New American Standard Bible and unbelief/unbelieving 33 times. Fear and unbelief began with the whisper of satan, the voice of the accuser, in the Garden of Eden when he suggested, "Has God said...?" (Gen. 3:1). He is still saying the exact same thing, trying to influence us through the thoughts in our minds on a daily basis.

What Is a Heart Wound?

I consider fear a heart wound. I define heart wounds as *any attitude that is an opposite of faith, hope, and love* (see 1 Cor. 13:13). So fear, hopelessness, and anger would be the opposites of faith, hope, and love and would be considered three different heart wounds. (There are others.)

SEVEN PRAYERS TO HEAL A HEART WOUND

I have learned to apply seven prayers to a heart wound so that it is fully processed and fully healed. They are: 1) breaking generational sins and curses; 2) severing ungodly soul ties; 3) repenting of ungodly beliefs and 4) inner vows and replacing them with godly beliefs and godly purposes; 5) inner healing to resolve traumatic pictures; 6) breaking off word curses; and finally, 7) now that the demons' house is torn down and anchors removed, casting out accompanying homeless demons.

The first six prayers are removing the legal entry points that demons used to gain access to you. These legal rights become anchors demons attach to. If I remove all the legal rights (anchors) first, then when I command the demon to leave it is easy because it has no right to stay.

It took me more than ten years to learn this simple lesson! Now that I have learned it, deliverance is easy and fun. It is a comprehensive and thorough healing process, and we provide a simple, free, download-able worksheet that you can use to pray through these seven prayers.[108] Thousands have been set free using them.

Let's apply these seven prayers to just one fear that we all likely have: "I am afraid to pray for the sick because they may not get healed." The following is a *sample only* of how these prayers can be applied.

Holy Spirit, please guide us as we pray. Now tune to flowing pictures, flowing thoughts, and flowing emotions, as these are the language of your heart.

---

108   www.cwgministries.org/free-resources-prayers-that-heal-the-heart

First Prayer: Breaking Generational Sins and Curses

Picture your father and say:

> *I forgive you, Dad, for the unbelief you passed on to me. I choose to love you, honor you, and release you in Jesus' name. I place the cross of Jesus Christ between you and me, and I command all generational sins and curses of fear, doubt, and unbelief to halt at the cross of Christ and fall to the ground, powerless. I bless that baby in the womb (me) with the blessings of Calvary. I bless you with life. I bless you with faith. I bless you with belief. Faith, come alive in Jesus' name (repeat three times). Thank You, Lord. I see Your light cascading down upon that baby in the womb.*

Repeat the above prayer until it comes from your heart with flow, emotion, and passion. Then repeat the entire process, picturing your mother and applying the prayer to her.

Second Prayer: Severing Ungodly Soul Ties

Picture a person with whom you have a very close relationship who has fed fear to you, and say:

> *I choose to forgive you, release you, and bless you in Jesus' name. I take the sword of the Spirit (take it up in your hand), and I cut the ungodly soul tie between you and me in Jesus' name (swing your hand with the sword in it and see yourself cutting through the chain that connects the two of you). I cut it (repeat five times). I command all negative energy that was passing from you to me to fall to the ground. Lord, I ask that You circumcise my heart. Cut out the fear and unbelief that was placed there through this relationship and give me a new heart, a heart of faith and belief. Thank You, Lord. I receive. I receive. I receive.*

Repeat this prayer picturing others you have soul ties with who have nurtured fear and unbelief in your heart.

Third and Fourth Prayers: Repenting and Replacing

Repent of ungodly beliefs and corresponding inner vows while replacing them with godly beliefs and godly purposes.

> *I repent for believing that I am alone and that God is not with me. I repent of my inner vow to protect myself and defend myself and rely on myself. I accept the truth that You are always with me at my right hand, guiding, protecting, and empowering me with Your Spirit. Thank You, Lord, for Your presence.*
>
> *I repent for believing it needs to be my power and my ability that heals the sick and my inner vow not to try as I obviously do not have such power. I accept the truth from Your Word that it is Your power, flowing through Your Holy Spirit, that releases healing to the sick.*
>
> *I repent for taking false responsibility on myself in the healing process and getting all stressed out, rather than relaxing, putting a smile on my face, and realizing that all I am doing is applying Your completed victory from the cross to the situation that stands before me. By Your stripes we **are** healed!*
>
> *Thank You, Lord, that health has been purchased and the debt has been paid. I am freed from satan's grasp. I bring this person into freedom and out of satan's darkness. I release them into the light of Your Kingdom. Your power flows through my hand, driving out darkness. Thank You, Lord. I receive. I celebrate; I dance for joy! You have won the victory. Blessed be the name of the Lord!*

Pray the above prayer again, inserting other ungodly beliefs you have that fuel fear within you.

Fifth Prayer: Experiencing Inner Healing

Picture a scene where fear of praying for healing entered you:

> *Lord, would You please walk into this scene now and let me see You present in it, ministering Your grace and truth to me.*

Tune to flowing pictures and flowing thoughts and record what Jesus says and does. It will be powerful. If He touches you, feel His power enter your being, restoring and transforming you.

For example, I see Jesus walking into the traditional church where I was saved and hearing the pastor teach that signs and miracles are not for today. Jesus is placing His hands over my ears. He says, "Let's go for a walk. You don't want to listen to this. It will defile your heart and mind."

He takes me outside the church and we enjoy His creation as He speaks words of truth to me and sets me free to believe that I am a co-creator with Him of all this wonder and beauty. Jesus has seated me with Him to rule and reign over the earth, and He is calling me to take up that position and that responsibility and not to live under satan's cloud of darkness and death. I say:

> *Yes, Lord, I will follow Your lead. I will rule with You. Together we will reign over the forces of darkness. Thank You, Lord, for this honor You have bestowed upon me. I am grateful for it.*

Pray the above prayer again, inserting other scenes where fear entered you.

Sixth Prayer: Breaking Off Word Curses

Picture the person who spoke something negative about your abilities (and this could be you):

> *I choose to forgive you and release you and bless you in Jesus'*
> *name. I repent for believing this word curse and I break off*
> *any power it has had over me. I break off all spiritual forces*
> *connected with it. I am a child of the King. All that the*
> *King has, He has placed at my disposal. I rule and reign*
> *with Him. I speak forth His Kingdom and His glory, and*
> *His Kingdom is manifest on the earth and the works of*
> *darkness are destroyed. Thank You, Lord, for entrusting*
> *me with such awesome power and authority. I will use it*
> *wisely. I will use it only as You instruct me to.*

Seventh Prayer: Casting Out Demons

> *I repent for agreeing with thoughts of fear and inadequacy,*
> *which demons have whispered in my mind. I turn away*
> *from these thoughts. From this day on, I will only dwell on*
> *those things which are lovely, just, and pure and are in full*
> *alignment with Your Word. I command all demons of fear,*
> *doubt, and unbelief to leave me now in Jesus' name and*
> *never return (repeat three to four times).*

> *Lord, come and fill me with Your light. Faith, come alive*
> *within my heart. Overwhelm me. Transform me. Make*
> *me a new person. A different person. A child of faith. A*
> *worker of miracles that the world may know that God*
> *sent His Son and His Son is glorified by the mighty works*
> *that pour forth through my hands. Bless the name of the*
> *living Lord!*

It is often wise to have one or two friends pray the above deliverance prayer over you. That was the New Testament pattern. It demonstrates humility and their added input helps destroy the demons' hold in your life.

Testimony from Paul Mortimer in England

> I've been a Christian for 25 years and I'm pretty well read. I've been struggling for many years with a terrible wound in my heart, which has dominated my life. Like you, I was able to minister in the power of the Holy Spirit but was dogged by fears and dominated by traumatic pictures.
>
> I've read many, many books on curses, healing, and deliverance, and whilst I've had...demons cast out, the key root issues didn't seem to be dealt with. After only a couple of days with your teaching, I have found amazing healing through the prayers, and in particular using vision to revisit traumatic experiences of the past and see Jesus begin healing my wounded heart.
>
> As an example, I had a dream of a deep sea diver slowly descending into the deep darkness of the ocean with no rope; I woke up in great fear. So I journaled this, and Jesus explained that the diving suit was my self-protection and vows and the heavy boots were my sins and that He was going to jump in to set me free and swim to safety. This is being fulfilled through your teaching.
>
> For instance, after going through some of the prayers through vision, Jesus took me back to my childhood home; He took me through the house and upstairs into my parents' bedroom. I saw myself standing next to their bed; they were asleep. I had a knife in my hand, and my hands were covered in blood. Then Jesus took me downstairs and out into the garden. We sat and chatted, and

then I wiped my hands clean on His white robe. Amazing. This is only one instance.

I'm opening the eyes of my heart to see Jesus in everything I do; I can now sit for hours and see Jesus come and heal and speak. Incredible. Priceless. Glorious. My life is being transformed daily, from one degree of glory to another. Your teaching (divine flow, life in the spirit, journaling, etc.) is vital to anyone who truly wants to become all that Jesus is. For the first time I have real hope that Jesus can (and is) setting me free. Thanks again.

—PAUL MORTIMER

Demonic Deliverance While Watching a DVD

I have just finished watching the last DVD for the *Prayers That Heal the Heart* course, the DVD on the Model Healing Prayer Session where you minister to Heidi. As background to my testimony, I need to let you know that I have had an issue with fear of abandonment. While I've gone through deliverance for several demons, the problem I've had with the fear of abandonment was not, to my knowledge, ever addressed head-on.

Well, as you prayed for Heidi, I was thinking about how much I identified with her pain and how much compassion I had for her. Then suddenly, I began to cough very forcefully and almost to gag. I knew instantly that a spirit of the fear of abandonment had come out of me! I had to write to tell you that, even though you were not personally ministering to me, that demon of the fear of abandonment had to obey the Name of Jesus. Glory to God!

—DR. MARYANN DIORIO,
a Christian Leadership University Graduate

> Maintain victory over demons by experiencing a unified spirit, soul, and body.

Next, Charity will provide you the keys to maintaining victory over demonic influence by demonstrating how to live in harmony and agreement both within yourself and with God.

CHARITY

THE POWER OF AGREEMENT WITHIN

We know a threefold cord is not quickly broken (see Eccles. 4:12). A single cord is breakable. Two cords is a bit more difficult to unravel. But three entwined together are not easily torn apart. Naturally, we understand that there is strength in unity.

In metallurgy (the science of metal technology), metals are heated, melted, and combined to create new ones with desired properties called alloys. The reason this is done is to make it stronger than each metal is individually and to protect against corrosion. Steel, the most famous of metals, is an alloy with iron as the foundational material. This is another example in the physical world of synergistic strength, where the total is greater than the sum of its parts.

What does that have to do with our journey of faith? How does this type of synergy affect our ability to walk in supernatural victory in every area of our lives?

We know the Lord is three in one, a Trinity. That is one of the unique aspects of Christianity—the unity of the Godhead. For unity to exist, separate and individual members become one, become united. The Father, the Son, and the Holy Spirit exist as one. Everything that happens in heaven happens because the three of them are in agreement and unity.

We were made in the image of God: *"Let Us make man in Our image"* (Gen. 1:26). We also are three in one: *"Now may the God of peace Himself sanctify you entirely; and may your spirit and soul and body be preserved complete, without blame at the coming of our Lord Jesus Christ"* (1 Thess. 5:23). We are a triune being—spirit, soul, and body.

In Mark 3:25, Jesus said, *"If a house is divided against itself, that house will not be able to stand."* What would that look like? Obviously a divided house has squabbling, in-fighting, and conflict. It's not in unity, which makes it weak and vulnerable.

Each one of us is that house with three members—the spirit, soul, and body. When our spirit doesn't agree with our soul or our body is not on the same page with our spirit, we lack synergy and can't stand strong. In order to lead an overcoming life, this trio must be in agreement and seamlessly joined together, forming a united and impenetrable force, undefeatable by the enemy.

To maintain and live in the victory Jesus already won for us, our goal is simply to live in a place of congruence and alignment where we are undivided within ourselves, where we have a "united house." That inner coherence and harmony make us steadfast and immovable as we become that three-old cord that is not quickly broken.

Let's look at each of these three parts of ourselves and see what Scripture has to say. We'll begin with the soul, which includes the mind.

SOUL: THE FIRST MEMBER OF OUR TRIUNE BEING

Dr. Caroline Leaf teaches that no thought entering our mind should ever go unchecked.[109] We don't want to allow a thought to pass

---

109 See Chapter 11 of *Switch on Your Brain: The Key to Peak Happiness, Thinking and Health* by Dr. Caroline Leaf.

by our awareness unless we want to experience it, because as a man thinks in his heart, so is he (see Prov. 23:7). Pastor Bill Johnson puts it this way: we don't want to allow a thought in our minds about ourselves that God doesn't have in His mind about us.[110] If Jesus isn't thinking it, we shouldn't be either because we're in Him and He's in us.

> *For though we walk in the flesh, we do not war after the flesh: (for the weapons of our warfare are not carnal, but mighty through God to the pulling down of strong holds;) casting down imaginations, and every high thing that exalteth itself against the knowledge of God, and bringing into captivity every thought to the obedience of Christ* (2 Corinthians 10:3-5 KJV).

It is fascinating that in Paul's conversation about spiritual warfare, he discusses taking thoughts captive and casting down ungodly imaginations. To effectively win our battles with the enemy, we are told to capture and get rid of those words and pictures that don't agree with God's Word and His vision and version of our lives. We don't look at those pictures with the eyes of our hearts, nor do we entertain those lies in our minds. Many times we think of spiritual warfare as something that happens outside of us. But more often than not, it is happening within us on the battleground of our minds and hearts.

The reason God instructs us to be mindful of the thoughts we engage is because really that is all satan has to work with. He is the father of lies, the truth is not in him, and when he speaks lies he is speaking his native language (see John 8:44). The Bible reveals that the serpent was the most subtle of all the beasts in the field, and this is how he works (see Gen. 3:1).

---

110   See Chapter 2 of *God is Good: He's Better Than You Think* by Bill Johnson.

Obviously, the devil doesn't loudly announce that he's satan and here to deceive us! Instead, he subtly introduces a thought, a little fiery dart, to our mind. He just deceptively drops it into our awareness, and in that moment we must take it captive. If we engage that thought, meditate on the lie, and picture it with our imagination, then we're not going to have the victory.

Satan's Strategy

To understand the enemy's battle plan, let's examine what he did in the Garden. His goal was to destroy that perfect fellowship man had with God, and at such a critical moment in human history he would have pulled out the strongest, deadliest weapon at his disposal.

So what was the devil's big, scary weapon? Words. That's all he's got. Just lies and deceptive ideas. All he could do was make some subtle suggestions: *Did God really say...?* He tricked Eve into questioning God's word to her as well as her own identity.

The tempter asked if she wanted to know good and evil. However, Eve *already* knew good from evil because God told her the difference as she lived out of her conversational relationship with Him (see Gen. 2:16-17). In the same way, the tempter asked if she wanted to be like God, but the truth was she was *already* like Him because she was created in His image.

Consider carefully the progression: satan introduced a thought; Eve latched on to it and began thinking it as if it were her own thought. In her mind she wondered, *Hey, wait a second. God is withholding something from me?* And as she pondered those thoughts, she began imagining a picture in her heart based on the lies. She imagined that God wasn't as loving as she had believed Him to be. She pictured a bad father who was denying her good things.

Those false pictures in her heart caused her to feel negative emotions. By engaging the doubtful thoughts in her mind and imagining them as true, Eve then began experiencing the emotions of ingratitude and pride in her heart.

Pictures move our emotions, and emotions move us to action. The pictures gave birth to feelings of rebellion, rebellion to evil desires, and desire to sin. James agrees with this progression: *"Each one is tempted when he is carried away and enticed by his own lust. Then when lust has conceived, it gives birth to sin; and when sin is accomplished, it brings forth death. Do not be deceived"* (James 1:14-16).

SLIPPERY SLOPE

That is the slippery slope. First it was thoughts in Eve's mind that she pondered. The thoughts were exalting themselves against the knowledge of God, so she should have arrested them and taken them captive to the obedience of Christ. Instead, Eve meditated on these pictures in her heart, began feeling sorry for herself, and acted on those wrong emotions. That was her sin, which brought forth death.

While this is certainly an example of what *not* to do, it is still quite encouraging. We've seen that satan didn't make her sin. He didn't twist her arm or force anything on her. He just tricked her into thinking that God didn't care for her, and it was all downhill from there.

From this story we see the importance of guarding our souls—the first member of our triune being. Adam and Eve didn't guard this member, and that led to the Fall. So we understand that our mind and soul must first be aligned with the mind of Christ and thinking God's thoughts in order for our "house" to be strong.

SPIRIT/HEART: THE SECOND MEMBER OF OUR TRIUNE BEING

The second part of our triune being is our spirit. Having looked at the battleground of our mind, now we will focus on the other main arena of battle within us, which is our heart. Whereas thoughts are the language of the mind, emotions and feelings are the language of the heart.

We have mentioned already that it is, in fact, God's *emotions* that are His armor. First Thessalonians 5:8 reveals that our breastplate is faith and love, so those holy feelings guard our hearts. The verse goes on to tell us that our helmet is hope, which is another Kingdom emotion, and that protects our minds. And we know that walking in peace is what protects our steps (see Eph. 6:15).

God is revealing an incredibly powerful truth that can change every area of our lives—physiologically, emotionally, and spiritually—once we understand and apply it. With this description of His armor, God is letting us know that by living in His Kingdom emotions we are safe. We are strong. We are invincible against the attacks of the devil.

When we live in love and faith and peace, he can't touch us. The enemy can't reach through God's armor and harm us, and that impenetrable armor is made of God's very own emotions, the fruit of His Spirit alive in us (see Gal. 5:22).

Million-Dollar Question

This leads us to the big question. Of course we want to live happy, peaceful lives, but we need to know how. This all sounds great, but how do we tangibly experience God's emotions? How do we feel His feelings?

Simply by seeing our life the way God sees it.

We know God sees the end from the beginning, so that is what we must do as well (see Isa. 46:10). We need to see ourselves already experiencing the blessings that Scripture says are ours. We want to live as if our prayers have already been answered—because they have been. First John 5:14-15 tells us that *"This is the confidence which we have before Him, that, if we ask anything according to His will, He hears us. And if we know that He hears us in whatever we ask, we know that we have* (already possess) *the requests which we have asked of Him."*

Practically, this means we purpose to look at the pictures Holy Spirit gives us, both by day and by night through our dreams, and live out of them. This develops our godly imagination. Godly imagination is picturing things God says are so. That is, we ponder pictures of our bodies healed and whole. We look only at pictures of ourselves experiencing blessed relationships. We meditate exclusively on pictures of ourselves walking in favor and abundance (never sickness, brokenness, or lack).

Progression of a Miracle

We see this example demonstrated in the life of Jesus when He fed the multitudes of men, women, and children. Scripture says thousands were hungry, and there were only a few loaves of bread and some fish. We know that the food was multiplied, but there were critical steps of progression in that miracle that we can learn from and model.

Luke 9:16 shows us that Jesus didn't look at the need; He wasn't consumed with this natural world and its version of reality. In this world there were problems and lack, but Jesus didn't live to this world; He lived to a different Kingdom. While the disciples' hearts were troubled because they were looking only at the material realm, Jesus' heart was peaceful and thankful because He was looking at the unseen.

Taking the five loaves and the two fish and looking up to heaven, he gave thanks and broke them. Then he gave them to the disciples to distribute to the people (Luke 9:16 NIV).

When Jesus was given the lunch, He did three things. First, he looked into heaven. Well, in heaven there is no lack. There is no hunger. There is no need. So Jesus saw the truth that abundance and provision were available and that there was more than enough. That was number one.

The second step Jesus took was to thank the Father. Jesus agreed with the vision and was grateful for the provision even before the provision was manifested.

The third and final step in the progression of this miracle was that Jesus gave bread to the disciples who passed it out to the multitudes. We see then that the food was not multiplied before He thanked Father for it; it was multiplied after. To use quantum scientific terms, Jesus "observed" the potential provision of heaven, thereby "collapsing" those resources into His world.

This is a key principle for us. We can live like Jesus and look to see what Father has provided for us. When we see that picture, our hearts are filled with Kingdom emotions of peace and gratitude. We're not stressed out; our hearts aren't troubled because we see the end from the beginning. We see what God sees and we are confident that we already have the requests we have made known to Him (see 1 John 5:14-15). We observe God's version of our situation, are grateful for His blessing, collapse that glory into our lives, and bring heaven to earth.

Jehoshaphat and Judah's Praise

We see from the example of Jesus feeding the five thousand so many important principles. One that we must not overlook is the power of gratitude. Whatever we are grateful for multiplies; whatever we are thankful for increases in our lives. Jesus was thankful for the food, and He received more of it. This model of proactive thanksgiving is seen throughout Scripture, so let's briefly consider just two more examples, this time from the Old Testament.

In Second Chronicles 20, we see that King Jehoshaphat sent the Tribe of Judah into battle first, before anyone else. The word *Judah* means praise, and that is what this tribe was known for—they were the worshipers in Israel, and this was their battle strategy. Jehoshaphat sent Judah in first, thereby giving God praise for the victory, before they had the victory, in order to receive the victory.

This was not an isolated incident, nor was it simply Jehoshaphat's good idea. God Himself gave the blueprint for victory to His people in Judges 20:18, *"Now the sons of Israel arose, went up to Bethel, and inquired of God and said, 'Who shall go up first for us to battle against the sons of Benjamin?' Then the Lord said, 'Judah shall go up first.'"*

Again we see that they were grateful and thanked God for their military success, before they had the success, in order to achieve the success. They got into gratitude and praise by seeing the vision the Lord promised as already accomplished. The combination of their thankfulness and observation collapsed heaven's glory into their world, allowing them to walk in the victory God intended for them.

BODY: THE THIRD MEMBER
OF OUR TRIUNE BEING

We have discussed our soul and how we must get our thoughts aligned with God's thoughts, living into the mind of Christ. We have learned that our spirits/hearts must be aligned with Holy Spirit's emotions and in agreement with the heart of God. Those are two aspects of our house in unity and harmony, which brings us to the final one.

We are spirit, soul, and body, and now we will consider the body, the third part of our triune being. We have learned that the language of the mind is thoughts, and the language of the heart is emotions and feelings. Naturally, the language of the body is words.

The tongue is either a weapon or a tool and can either destroy or create. The late Derek Prince taught that a right confession is to say exactly, and only, what God says about our situation, and to keep on saying it! Every word we speak should be in agreement with God's word about us, our situation, our health, our relationships, and our finances.

Proverbs 18:21 tells us that life and death are in the power of tongue, and we know that when we declare a thing it is established for us (see Job 22:28). This is why the Psalmist prayed, *"Set a guard, O Lord, over my mouth; keep watch over the door of my lips"* (Ps. 141:3). He understood that by our words we are either justified or condemned (see Matt. 12:36-37).

Every one of us is a child of God in that He is our Creator Father and we were made in His image. What is extraordinary about our confession as Christians, though, is that we take it to the next level, because our spirits are also joined with the Holy Spirit (see 1 Cor. 6:17). Biblically speaking, the word for "breath" and "spirit" are interchangeable in the original languages, so when we declare something, we have the breath and Spirit of God enforcing it, expressing that word, declaring and decreeing it into the atmosphere.

We know what God's Word and Spirit do—they create. God created the world with His words (see Heb. 11:3). This is why we must only speak His words and express His thoughts, because His Holy Spirit animates and enforces those words. It is His Spirit within us, released out through us, that backs up what we say.

Satan's Only Weapon

We looked previously at the temptation of Eve in the Garden of Eden and saw an example of what not to do. Let's fast-forward down the timeline of history. Now we have Jesus, the Son of God, on His rescue mission to save the world from their sin. Satan shows up to derail God's plan. If there were ever a crucial moment in this battle, ever a time for the enemy to pull out his big guns, his most powerful supernatural ballistic missiles, this would be it.

So what huge, deadly artillery does satan use when he encounters Jesus in the wilderness? What are his big, scary weapons? Words. He tempted Jesus with words to question His own identity. *"If You are the Son of God..."* (Matt. 4:6).

The enemy does the same with us, trying to trick us into being afraid of him, as if he can actually harm us. But these are just subtle words and manipulative lies and they are not a threat to us. All satan used with Jesus were lies, deception, and words. That's all he used because that's all he had. Jesus showed us what we are supposed to do with the enemy's words and lies—we take them captive and declare God's Word instead.

Cognitive neuroscientist and behavioral pathologist Dr. Caroline Leaf is a Spirit-filled Christian, and I love how she explains this: All satan has are lies, which can't be measured. All he has is darkness, which can't be measured. Only light can be measured. So satan's lies have no substance. It is only when we accept his lie and begin thinking it ourselves that we give substance to it. Satan needs us to believe him. Faith is the substance (see Heb. 11:1). When we engage satan's lie, we create an electromagnetic flow of energy in our brain that is very much real and measurable. However, when we take that thought captive and speak God's Word instead, we destroy the lie. We no longer believe it, and when that happens, physiologically speaking, the lie actually "dies." It is no longer a flow of electromagnetic energy; instead, it is released from our mouth as hot air, converted to heat energy, and dissipates. It no longer exists.[111]

Wow! As we can see, satan is no match for us—especially when we have coherence between our heart, mind, and the words of our mouth. Next, we will look at what Scripture says is available to us once we have achieved this inner harmony.

GOD'S KIND OF FAITH

Let's examine two biblical examples that illustrate the mountain-moving power of our united triune being. What kind of potential and possibilities are available to us when we actually live in coherence and congruence within ourselves?

A familiar passage of Scripture is Mark 11:22-24 where Jesus explains how to have God's faith, the God kind of faith. We have often focused on the importance of "saying" to the mountain *be moved,* and indeed that is one important aspect. However, there are two other members of our triune being playing a part in the miracle recorded in this verse, so let's look carefully at the secret Jesus is revealing.

> *And Jesus answered saying to them, "Have faith in God. Truly I say to you, whoever says to this mountain, 'Be taken up and cast into the sea,' and does not doubt in his heart, but believes that what he says is going to happen, it will be granted him. Therefore I say to you, all things for which you pray and ask, believe that you have received them, and they will be granted you"* (Mark 11:22-24).

There are three things coming into agreement in this passage, and now that we know what we're looking for it's easy to see. "*Whoever*

---

111   This is my summary of her words. The full presentation can be found here: www.youtube.com/watch?v=_C5dZ8Nk2ck.

says"—that is our body getting the words of our mouth in line with God's truth. *"And does not doubt in his heart"*—that is our heart and spirit aligned with Father's heart. *"But believes that"*—that is our mind and soul renewed to the mind of Christ. Body, spirit, and soul—all three in congruence and unity.

In case we missed it, Jesus repeats the concept, again highlighting the three aspects of our triune being, in the very next verse. *"All things for which you pray"*—it is our hearts and spirits that commune with Father. *"And ask"*—with our mouths we make requests (that is, our body). *"Believe that you have received them"*—we purpose with our mind, in our soul, to believe that we *have already* received our answer. Then, after we are thinking, feeling, speaking, and living as if we already have our miracle, it is in that place that the miracle manifests. *"They will be granted you"* is Jesus' promise to us (Mark 11:24).

Once these three members—spirit, soul, and body—are in agreement within ourselves and in agreement with God's word and His purposes and will, nothing is impossible. The prayer is answered and the mountain is moved.

ABRAHAM'S "UNITED HOUSE"

We have used the analogies of a threefold cord, synergistic metal alloys, and a united house. The last picture we'll look at to help us understand the critical importance of all three aspects of ourselves is to view it as a combination lock with a set of three numbers. In order to open, we must have the correct numbers in the correct sequence. Once they align, it is easy to unlock victory and swing wide the door to God's promised blessings.

Let's consider the example of our father of faith himself, to see how this unity in his house and combination of three unlocked God's miracle in his life. God told Abram he would be the father of a multitude. So

Abram began thinking God's thoughts about his descendants—getting his soul/mind in agreement with God's perspective. That's number one.

Then, God gave Abram a picture of his promised future—stars in the sky and sand on the seashore. Genesis 15:5-6 tells us, *"He took him outside and said, 'Now look toward the heavens, and count the stars, if you are able to count them.' And He said to him, 'So shall your descendants be.' Then he believed in the Lord; and He reckoned it to him as righteousness."*

That picture created faith in Abram's heart, so now his heart and spirit were in agreement with God's heart. That's number two.

Finally, out of the abundance of his heart Abram spoke God's truth when his name was changed to Abraham, which means "father of a multitude." This was a demonstration that the third member of Abraham's house was in unity—his body and mouth were now declaring God's version of his situation. Every time Abraham said his name, he was speaking God's promises over his life: "I am the father of a multitude!"

He achieved inner harmony within his triune being—spirit, soul, and body. He had agreement in his heart, mind, and the words of his mouth. It was personal, present-tense, and positive, and it was the part he played in God's miracle.

Heaven is the Lord's, but the earth He has given to the sons of men (see Ps. 115:16). We partner with God in releasing heaven's promised blessings to earth when we live in alignment with His heart, mind, and word. Thinking God's thoughts, feeling His emotions, and speaking His truth. When our triune being is living in harmony with the Trinity Himself, we are a conduit positioned and prepared, ready to release His glory into our world.

WHY IT HAS NEVER BEEN GOD VERSUS SATAN

This all begs the question then—if we are so powerful and have such tremendous potential to move mountains and live the abundant life, why don't we experience it more often? When we struggle and don't see the victory the Bible says is ours, we try to explain that. One common excuse we give is that it must be satan. *He's attacking me and that's why I'm sick, that's why I'm defeated, that's why this bad thing happened to me.*

We say it's the devil's fault, but really we give him far too much credit. He doesn't have the ability to do all the things we blame on him. Likewise, we call natural disasters "acts of God," and again we assign blame to the wrong place.

When bad things happen in this world, it is not really satan's fault, and it sure isn't God's fault. It's on us. These things happen on our watch, and it is because we've let them. Earth is waiting with eager expectation for the revealing of the mature sons and daughters of God (see Rom. 8:19). Creation itself has been subjected to futility as a slave of corruption and is anxiously longing for the freedom of the glory of the children of God (see Rom. 8:20). The world waits on us.

Let's examine carefully what Scripture has to say about us as well as our enemy. Obviously, evil and satan exist; however, they really shouldn't have much influence in our lives. This is the crux of the problem. We see ourselves as small and satan as big and powerful. He's the scary giant and we're just the little guy he's always picking on. Poor us!

Often we see two teams—God is the captain of His team of holy angels and satan is the captain of his team of fallen angels. Without even realizing or recognizing it, we have just put God and satan on equal footing.

We have this fatally flawed picture of spiritual warfare—that it is somehow God versus satan, good versus evil, heaven versus hell. To imagine that there is some type of duality or equality in the rivalry between God and satan is obviously a skewed version of reality that does us an extraordinary disservice as we seek to live in Christ's resurrection power.

Instead, we must see God for who He is. God is the Uncreated One. He is omniscient—He knows everything. God is omnipotent—He has all power. God is omnipresent—He is everywhere all the time.

Unemployed Cherub

Satan is none of these things. He doesn't know everything, he is not powerful, and he's certainly not everywhere at all times. We would never ascribe these qualities to Gabriel or Michael or any other angel. But we have been deceived into inadvertently attributing such a God-like nature to satan himself.

We must get on the same page with God on this and see our enemy for who he really is, as Scripture describes him. As my friend Dr. Jim Richards says, *satan is an unemployed cherub.*[112] That's the revelation we need to understand and the biblical picture we must wrap our hearts around.

Hebrews 2:14 tells us that through His death, Jesus rendered the devil completely powerless. Satan is thoroughly defeated and any power he did have was voided when he was disarmed at the cross and made a public disgrace as Jesus triumphed over him (see Col. 2:15).

Wizard of Oz

In fact, the current state of our enemy reminds me more of the Wizard of Oz than anything else. In the original version of the film

---

112   See *Satan Unmasked: The Truth Behind the Lie* by Dr. Jim Richards.

with Judy Garland, everyone was terrified of the wizard. He was known for his huge size and loud, menacing voice, and Dorothy and her friends were very afraid to meet him.

They gathered their courage and at the end of the movie faced their fear and had an encounter with the wizard of Oz himself. However, what they found was not a big scary threat. Rather, the wizard turned out to be an extremely short man behind a curtain using light and shadows to project a large image.

Furthermore, they discovered he had such a quiet, squeaky voice that he had to use a megaphone in order to even be heard. When they saw the wizard for who he really was, they realized he was never any threat to them. It was all just smoke and mirrors. It was just a great deception.

And so it is with satan.

Isaiah 14:14-16 records satan's rebellious diatribe right before he was kicked out of heaven, as well as the Lord's response to it:

> *"I will ascend above the heights of the clouds; I will make myself like the Most High." "Nevertheless you will be thrust down to Sheol, to the recesses of the pit. Those who see you will gaze at you, they will ponder over you, saying, 'Is this the man who made the earth tremble, who shook kingdoms?'"*

When we see satan for who he is, we'll wonder why we were ever so scared of him in the first place. Is this the one who made us tremble? Is he the one who made us shake? We'll finally understand that the only weapon he ever really had was words. That his power over us was an illusion and his authority in our lives was just a deception. Once we see satan as he really is, we will never be afraid of him again.

WHAT ABOUT US?

Jesus said, *"All authority has been given to Me in heaven and on earth"* (Matt. 28:18). And He gave all of that authority to us: *"I have given you authority to tread on serpents and scorpions, and over all the power of the enemy, and nothing will injure you"* (Luke 10:19; see also Luke 9:1).

While knowing our enemy and his place is obviously important, even more than that we must know ourselves. We must understand our identity and know who we are in Christ. Now that we see God in His rightful place, far above all principalities and powers, where are we on this spectrum?

In Psalm 8:3-6, David asks this very question and reveals the extraordinary answer:

> *When I consider Your heavens, the work of Your fingers, the moon and the stars, which You have ordained; what is man that You take thought of him, and the son of man that You care for him? Yet You have made him a little lower than God, and You crown him with glory and majesty! You make him to rule over the works of Your hands; You have put all things under his feet.*

We are crowned with glory, created to rule, and made *"a little lower than God"* (Ps. 8:5). Some versions of this verse read that we have been made a little lower than "angels," but that is a mistranslation. The Hebrew word is *Elohim*, which is always the name used for God Himself.

This revelation of our identity is confirmed throughout Scripture, as we know that we are children of God (see 1 John 3:1). Our spirit has been joined with the Holy Spirit (see 1 Cor. 6:17). We are seated with Christ in heavenly places (see Eph. 2:6). We are partakers of the divine nature, and we have been filled with the fullness of God (see 2 Pet. 1:4; Eph. 3:19).

Little "g" gods

In fact, there is another amazing passage in Psalms that speaks to our true identity as well. Psalm 82:6 declares, *"You are gods, and all of you are sons of the Most High."*

Really? While we don't usually think of ourselves in this way, it actually dovetails seamlessly with the Genesis account of our beginning.

We know we have been created in the image of God (see Gen. 1:27). Scripture also makes clear that everything reproduces after its own kind (see Gen. 1:21-25). That is, the children of birds are little birds and the children of zebras are little zebras.

It follows naturally then that the children of God would be little gods. Certainly not God Himself, but absolutely children made in His divine likeness with His own DNA, little copies of Him (see 1 John 3:9). He breathed into us His very breath; it is His Spirit flowing through us that gives us life (see Gen. 2:7).

Lest we are tempted to relegate this revelation as confined to some obscure passages in the Old Testament, Jesus actually highlights it for us in the Gospels to be sure we don't miss it. *"Jesus answered them, 'Has it not been written in your Law, "I said, you are gods"?'"* (John 10:34). He even went on to say that this truth is the word of God and Scripture can't be broken (see John 10:35). Indeed, we are the supernatural progeny of God Himself (see 1 Pet. 1:23). We are not of this world (see John 17:16).

WHAT PICTURE ARE YOU LOOKING AT?

So that is what we must see—satan under our feet, God leading us in victory. What does victory and triumph look like? How does it feel to be more than a conqueror? How does it feel to have our prayers already answered? That's what we want to look at and live to.

We all move through life with a picture in the back of our minds—either of defeat or victory. Usually this is on a subconscious level, but nevertheless it is the vision we live from and it informs everything we say and do and every decision we make.

Do we see ourselves as weak and small and afraid of the big scary devil, constantly waiting for the other shoe to drop and looking for what bad thing will happen next? What we seek we will find, so if we're looking for the negative we will always find it. We will attract that to ourselves, because according to our faith it will be done to us (see Matt. 9:29). Our fear is faith in reverse, and what we fear comes upon us (see Job 3:25).

Instead, we need to hold God's true picture of ourselves in our hearts and live from that. That is why we must have the right mindset, which is the mind set on the spirit, living into the mind of Christ (see Rom. 8:6). We cast down any imagination of defeat or sickness or lack and choose instead to envision the biblical promises of success, healing, and provision.

We purpose to see through heaven's lens and ponder God's version of reality—His perspective of us and our situation. He sees us seated with Him in heavenly places. He sees us ruling and reigning with Christ. These are the pictures we need to imagine in our hearts and meditate on. A vision of victory. A picture that we are mighty overcomers (see Rom. 8:37). An image of always being blessed, because Christ always leads us in triumph (see 2 Cor. 2:14).

Those are great verses, but what does that truth look like in our lives, and more importantly how does it feel? Well, once we picture it and imagine it, the feelings will follow. Once we see the truth, we'll feel it as true, and it will become our truth and we can live from it.

IMPOSSIBLE IS NOTHING

Remember what happened at the Tower of Babel? *"The Lord said, 'Look! They are one people with the same language for all of them, and this is only the beginning of what they will do. Nothing that they have a mind to do will be impossible for them!'"* (Gen. 11:6 ISV).

So they are one people (spirit), they all share one language (body), and they have one mind (soul). And God said the result of this unity is that nothing will be impossible for them. Wow!

I like the King James Version of this verse because it says nothing will be withheld from them *"which they have imagined to do."* Again, we see how imagination is a huge player, that our success is largely determined by the picture at which we are looking. That picture we're pondering informs our feelings, thoughts, and the words of our mouth, and this verse confirms the incredible importance of cultivating a godly imagination.

It is significant too that the Lord said He could derail their whole ungodly plan by simply confusing their language. Just one aspect of our triune being going offline and our powerful momentum comes to a screeching halt.

Conversely, when we are unified in our godly endeavors, we understand that the enemy just needs to get one of these areas out of alignment. He doesn't have to impair all three; all he must do is interfere with one of them, as the members are interrelated. When our thoughts aren't right, our feelings turn sour and our confession follows.

But now we know how to defeat the enemy because we recognize his strategy. Now we understand that we have the power and ability to win these battles every single day. When our thoughts are the thoughts of God, our mind and soul are united with His. When our emotions and feelings are what God has in that situation, our heart and spirit are united with His. And when our confession, the words of our mouth, agrees with God's Word, we have brought our entire triune being into agreement with God. In this state, we are not a house divided against itself but a united house that will stand. And because we are united as one, nothing will be impossible for us (see Gen. 11:6). We are unstoppable.

LIVING FREE

In conclusion, to stay free of the enemy's lies and not re-empower him in your life, ask God about His perspective of your situation. We all have challenges and "mountains" that we're facing. What is your mountain? Perhaps it is a doctor's report, a prodigal child, or the need for a new job or promotion at work.

We must get on the other side of the mountain for a moment. Imagine that huge issue you've been struggling with is behind you now. Go over to that side of the mountain with Jesus and see what it's like. Look to see His picture of your healed self, blessed family, or abundant finances. What does that look like? How does it feel?

Ponder that picture, meditate on that godly imagination, and don't get up from your place of prayer with the Lord until you can go throughout your day living as if your prayer has already been answered. How relieved will you feel on the other side of the mountain? How grateful will you be? Experience the end from the beginning and live into those promises now. When you observe God's version of reality and feel it as true, you will collapse His blessings into your world, release His glory into your here and now, and bring heaven to earth.

MARK

ACTION EXERCISE

Download the "Contributing Strands Worksheet" below and complete it for at least one heart wound (allow for three hours). Because most of us have several heart wounds, come back on other days and complete it for others. Healing is a process. It is worth taking whatever time is necessary to do the process well. Going through the three-month interactive "Prayers That Heal the Heart" online module with your family or home Bible study is well worth the time and an excellent way for a group to experience healing together.

The resources below can be downloaded from here.[113]

1. The electronic "Contributing Strands Worksheet"

2. Blog: "Deliverance from Demons Through a Revelation-Based Power Encounter"

3. Blog: "Teaming Up for Deliverance: A Prophet and Teacher Minister Together"

4. *The Prayers That Heal the Heart* DVD module provides a complete learning and healing experience for individuals or groups to explore this healing pattern in depth.[114]

5. An interactive online *Prayers That Heal the Heart* module is available here.[115]

---

113   www.cwgministries.org/prayers
114   www.cwgministries.org/store/prayers-heal-heart-dvd-package
115   www.cluschooolofthespirit.com/prayers

Part IV

UTILIZING KINGDOM EMOTIONS

Chapter 11

HEART RATE VARIABILITY

*I have hungered for years for a simple tool that could
provide clear feedback that I am postured properly
internally. I want to move from head to heart and
from stressful emotions to Kingdom emotions.*

We know that negative emotions such as fear and panic throw our
body into chaos. Our heart races, our thoughts become scattered, our
respiration becomes short, and holding such emotions damages our
health, our peace, and our ability to commune with God. We know
God's Kingdom emotions of love, joy, peace, and gratitude counter the
destructive emotions of fear, anger, and regret.

A TRAINING TOOL FOR HEART-BASED EMOTIONALLY AFFIRMATIVE LIVING

The emWave®2 is a small handheld device that can be used on its
own or plugged into your computer that allows you to view graphs

of information it outputs. Its specific function is to measure "heart coherence," which is a state of inner consistency within your heart and between your heart and your mind.

When you clip the sensor to your ear lobe, it measures heart rate variability, letting you know if:

1. You are tuned to your heart;

2. You are at ease and in the moment;

3. Your mind and heart are functioning together in harmony (coherence);

4. You are expressing a Kingdom emotion such as gratitude or compassion;

5. You are projecting those emotions out to others.

This is truly amazing. So far I have completed over 150 sessions with this unit and I can personally vouch that it verifies you are experiencing the above five realities.

What does the emWave®2 software actually measure, and by what means?

The direct physiological function being measured is the pulse of your heartbeat as sensed in your ear lobe. A small LED (light emitting diode) shines light into the skin, and a photosensor records the changes in the reflected light as each pulse travels through your ear. The unit measures the interval between each pulse and computes your heartrate after every new pulse. Most people's heartrate varies constantly, speeding up and slowing down. The emWave®2 charts your heartbeat as it changes.

Heart rate variability (HRV) is also called heart rhythm. In general, a smoother HRV pattern indicates a more synchronized autonomic nervous system. Researchers at HeartMath Institute discovered that negative emotions disrupt heart rhythms and positive emotions create increased harmony and coherence in the heart's rhythms as well as improved balance in the nervous system overall. A much deeper understanding of HRV is available here.[116]

HEART COHERENCE DEFINED

THESE TRAITS	BIBLICAL DEFINITION AND BENEFIT	SCIENTIFIC DEFINITION AND BENEFIT
A heart focus: It is the heart that is transmitting energy out from your being.	Out of the heart flow the issues of life (see Prov. 4:23). *"It is the Spirit who gives life; the flesh profits nothing"* (John 6:63). Power flowed from Jesus to heal those reaching out to Him in faith (see Luke 6:19). People touched by Peter's shadow were healed (see Acts 5:15).	The heart is 60 times greater electrically and up to 5,000 times stronger magnetically than the brain. Its electromagnetic field extends three feet out from our bodies, carrying information that synchronizes our body systems and interacts with others.
Experiencing positive emotions	Experiencing Kingdom emotions— love, joy, peace, thankfulness, and compassion.	Activates beneficial hormones, boosting our immune system, well-being, creativity, and intuition.

---

116 www.heartmath.org/research/science-of-the-heart/heart-rate-variability/#soh

THESE TRAITS	BIBLICAL DEFINITION AND BENEFIT	SCIENTIFIC DEFINITION AND BENEFIT
System-wide synchronization and harmony	*"Love the Lord your God with all your heart, and with all your soul, and with all your strength, and with all your mind; and your neighbor as yourself"* (Luke 10:27).	Mind, heart, and body functioning in harmony with each other releases optimum energy and information.
At ease and in the moment	Not striving (see Heb. 4:9-11). Abiding in Christ (see John 15; Ps. 15).	A more synchronized autonomic nervous system (energy saving).
Releasing life to others	Give your life away and you receive life (see Matt. 10:38-39).	Those who perform altruistic acts live longer, reducing their odds of an early death by nearly 60 percent.

The Bible tells us to rest from our labors or to cease striving (see Heb. 4). Living at "rest" is a state of health as you are letting your body enjoy the "relaxation response" rather than the "stress response." It is the state of trust as you believe God has all things under His control, and He is watching out for you. Heart coherence is the state of rest. It is a state of ease. It is being at peace and tuned to the flow of the Holy Spirit within you, letting Him live His life out through you. It is dying to self and coming alive to Christ.

The word "heart" shows up 732 times in the New American Standard Bible and is considered the central organ of the human being. The Bible says that out of the heart flow the springs of life (see Prov. 4:23).

HeartMath Institute offers a free downloadable book[117] that overviews 25 years of their research on the heart. It is amazing to peruse. I have found nothing like it on the planet! It does not have a New Age or cultish slant. It is simply scientific research.

THE VALUE OF LIVING WITH HEART COHERENCE!

The Bible and science both reveal that heart coherence increases intuition, creativity, mental clarity, emotional balance, and personal effectiveness, which are all things we desire and need. With stress contributing to 80 to 90 percent of all doctors' visits, heart coherence is a must.

Living tuned to your heart, which you keep filled to overflowing with compassion toward others and gratefulness toward God, is key to divine healing, to experiencing health, and to living an effective Christian life (see Matt. 14:14).

Scriptures surely require we abide in Kingdom emotions, which are stress-reducing:

- *"A joyful heart is good medicine, but a broken spirit dries up the bones"* (Prov. 17:22).

- *We give thanks in and for all things* (see Eph. 5:20; 1 Thess. 5:18).

- We are to love one another; He who does not love abides in death (see 1 John 3:11,14).

- The one who does not love does not know God, for God is love (see 1 John 4:8).

---

117 www.heartmath.org/research/science-of-the-heart/

- *"If we love one another, God abides in us, and His love is perfected in us"* (1 John 4:12).

- *"There is **no fear in love**; but perfect love casts out fear, because fear involves punishment"* (1 John 4:18).

Some people struggle with expressing emotions because they:

1. Have been told to cut them off as they are soulish;

2. Have stuffed them in order to deal with negative emotions;

3. Don't have many because they are naturally thinkers rather than feelers or because they live in the western world, which has elevated reason and devalued emotion, and now they are totally out of touch with their hearts and their feelings.

All of these problems must be resolved if we want to be like Jesus, who was moved to heal by compassion (see Matt. 14:14).

LESSONS FROM THE EMWAVE®2

If miracles, healing, and spiritual transformation occur more readily when I am tuned to my heart, feeling compassion, and in the state of ease, then the emWave®2 can serve as a powerful learning tool, showing visually on a screen when I am in this coherent state. I do assume Jesus didn't live "rattled." I assume He lived at peace, full of faith, and reaching out with a compassion that carried healing on its wings.

The emWave®2 unit taught me that I was mistaking *thinking* thoughts of gratitude with *feeling* gratitude. Thinking thoughts about peace was being substituted for feeling peace, etc. The emWave®2 unit taught me I must *feel* emotions, not just think them. That in itself was priceless, as feeling compassion is a key to releasing miracles, and stress-free living is a key to my body's own healing mechanisms.

MISSING THE MARK	HITTING THE MARK
Thinking gratitude	Feeling gratitude
Thinking love	Feeling love
Thinking abiding	Experiencing abiding
Thinking thankfulness	Feeling thankful
Analyzing	Being
Striving and laboring	Experiencing rest
Thinking peace	Feeling peaceful

The emWave®2 forced me to gain a better definition of what an emotion is. It is something *felt*. It also taught me how to generate and sustain a heart emotion.

RELAXED GRATITUDE AND HIGH HEART COHERENCE

Looking upward indicates that I am engaging my visual faculties. Up and to the left is visually remembering, while up and to the right is visually constructing. The Bible speaks numerous times of looking up and seeing God's provision (see Ps. 121:1; 123:1; Isa. 40:26; Zech. 5:5; John 8:28; Acts 2:25; Rev. 4:1-2). So looking up to the heavens and seeing Jesus seated on His throne and you worshiping in His presence should bring peace, ease, gratitude, love, and worship, all of which are healing, stress-reducing emotions that help produce heart coherence.

Emotions are by-products of pictures, so gazing upon a picture is going to help me experience emotions. I have discovered that if my pictures include Jesus present with me and I am smiling, I enter the *state of ease.* At this point the emWave®2 tells me I have just entered into *high* heart coherence. I find this really neat! I am now ready to experience flow (see John 7:37-39).

Specific Postures to Produce High Heart Coherence

- Lifting up my eyes and seeing Jesus at my right side, laughing and glad to help. I ask for His help, relax, and enter the state of ease, joy, and laughter.

- Healing Prayer: Looking up and seeing Jesus and inwardly seeing, speaking, or feeling:

*You allowed Your body to be whipped in order to purchase healing for me. This gift of compassion is priceless. I will not squander it. I receive it with intense gratitude. By these stripes I **am** healed! It is done! It is done! It is done! Thank You, Lord!*

- Looking up and seeing Jesus and inwardly seeing/speaking/feeling my gratitude for the many things Jesus has done for me.

- Looking up and picturing Patti, and appreciating the joy of being married to her.

- Looking up and seeing Jesus and inwardly seeing/speaking/feeling with heartfelt appreciation: *"I abide in You, the vine. Jesus, You are my life, my source, my all."*

- Looking up and seeing Jesus and expressing heartfelt, emotion-filled worship before His throne.

- Looking up and worshiping God as I pray in tongues (see Acts 2:11).

- Looking and creating in my spirit, being lost in thought, eyes up and to the right.

- With vision and heartfelt emotion inwardly speaking/feeling: "I breathe in Your divine anointing, and I breathe out Your gift of favor."

- Inwardly seeing/speaking/feeling: "I can do all things through Christ who strengthens me."

- Inwardly seeing/speaking/feeling: "I am more than a conqueror in Christ."

- Inwardly seeing/speaking/feeling: "All things are possible to them that believe, and I believe."

- Inwardly seeing/speaking/feeling: "I triumph in Christ as I praise Him for His almighty grace and power toward me."

This blog[118] includes samples of charts produced by the emWave®2 showing heart coherence.

Striving is *out!* It became clear to me that any struggling or striving gave me a poor coherence score. This, of course, lines up with Hebrews 4 and living in Sabbath rest and ceasing our labors. I discovered years ago, when I used biofeedback, that I needed to smile if I wanted the meter to show I was relaxed.

Well, now I discover that a smile does not automatically mean I have an attitude of appreciation, and if I want the emWave®2 monitor to show high coherence, yes, a smile is helpful as it is evidence of being relaxed, but that is not enough. I must be holding a Kingdom attitude such as appreciation, which I am extending out to another, and be using

---

118 www.cwgministries.org/blogs/grateful-heart-healing-heart

heart-focused breathing. By doing all these things, I register as having high heart coherence.

CONCLUSIONS

In addition to using the emWave®2 for 150 sessions, I have reviewed in depth the research on their website.[119] I now understand how coherence works and can define and experience living at rest and in peace. I now can move into coherence within 15 seconds, as confirmed by the emWave®2 unit. However, I almost threw the emWave®2 away during my first 50 tries, some of which were successful, but many of which were not and I could not at first identify what I was doing wrong.

Four Negative Stances

I did identify the *four issues* that produced poor coherence and corrected them.

1. I cannot be tuned to my mind.

2. I cannot strive.

3. I must not "think" gratitude, compassion, etc.

4. I cannot live with a focus on self.

Also, focusing on what I am *not* going to do will never show up on the emWave®2 as being in heart coherence. I *cannot* drive out darkness by focusing on it or attacking it. I drive out darkness (or in this case, stress) by bringing in the light. The four negative stances above were struggling to beat out the darkness, which is why they consistently failed.

---

119 www.heartmath.org/research/science-of-the-heart/

Four Positive Replacement Stances

Let's turn the above four negative statements into four positive statements. The four positive postures below (confirmed by Scripture and the heart coherence monitor) are bringing in the light, which produces high heart coherence:

1. **I tune to my heart:** I picture my breath coming in through my heart and out through my solar plexus.

2. **I tune to the Spirit's flow within:** I tune to the state of ease, acknowledging the Holy Spirit who flows effortlessly within me, receiving His life with each incoming breath.

3. **I feel Kingdom emotions:** I tune to the feelings of gratitude, love, compassion, and joy.

4. **I direct Kingdom emotions to others:** I receive life when I give life to others, so when I breathe out, I intentionally release love, appreciation, and peace to the people I am with, praying for, or picturing in my mind.

> *A consolidated statement of the posture of heart coherence:*
> *I am tuned inwardly to my spirit, a relaxed smile on my face, breathing God's compassion and gratefulness into my heart and releasing it out to others.*

A LEARNING CURVE

I recognize that as I work at my computer and walk through my day, I still have habits that must be replaced—living in my mind, not feeling emotions, and, to some extent, striving. I expect it will now take a period of time and focused attention to change my lifestyle[120] so I live tuned to my heart, in the state of inner ease, expressing emotions of gratitude, and focused on the Holy Spirit flowing freely in and out of me as I pour out love, joy, and peace to all whom I am picturing, praying for, or currently with.

> *Biblical characters spent years learning this lifestyle, as do monks. I believe this process can be sped up by the continuous, instant feedback of the emWave®2.*

So I have my work (whoops, I mean play!) cut out for me, but I am convinced it is worth it. The Bible and science both confirm that the benefits of this grateful, restful, heart-based lifestyle are enormous!

The biblical term for this lifestyle is "abiding." Explore the benefits of abiding as recorded in John 15. Here are a few of them:

> *I am the vine, you are the branches; he who abides in Me and I in him, he bears much fruit, for apart from Me you can do nothing. ...If you abide in Me, and My words abide in you, ask whatever you wish, and it will be done for you. My Father is glorified by this, that you bear much fruit, and so prove to be My disciples* (John 15:5,7-8).

In what way would holding any other stance be of value to me?

If it takes me three months or a year of focus to learn to live in this attitude continuously, it will be one of the greatest periods of growth in my entire life. Staying hooked up to the emWave®2 monitor as I work, create, write, and pray will surely speed me forward in this lifestyle!

---

120   www.cwgministries.org/habit

What a wonderful way to use modern technology. Praise God for this amazing gift! I have waited a long time for such a helpful tool.

My victory has begun! Just two months in and I was already writing and working at a higher level of heart coherence than when I began. Thank You, Lord! I also started to become aware of when I had tension or frustration or impatience or anger in my system, and when I put on the heart monitor ear clip it instantly confirmed that I was in *low* heart coherence. As soon as I repented; gave the tension, frustration, and anger to the Lord; and breathed in His peace, joy, and love, emWave®2 registered high coherence. This can all happen in as little as 30 seconds, which is encouraging and exciting.

I am now more aware of when I am not walking in Kingdom emotions, and I have learned how to quickly return to the experience and expression of Kingdom emotions. The fact that there is an external monitor that will objectively evaluate my heart's condition in real time and show me where I stand in radiating Kingdom emotions is truly amazing.

Wow, heart technology being used for the glory of the Lord and the building up of His Kingdom! They even have research showing how heart coherence *could precipitate miracles of healing.*[121] I probably wouldn't have believed it was possible had I not experienced it myself. Nice thing about the emWave®2, it comes with a 30-day money-back guarantee, so you can actually try it out with no risk and see for yourself.

I would suggest it is worth it to take the time to learn heart coherence. It seems to me that those who have developed powerful, miracle-filled ministries went through a significant learning curve before entering into these ministries. My hunch is that they were learning skills such as heart focus, faith focus, and experiencing gratitude that

---

121   http://fiimplinit.ro/wp-content/uploads/modulation-of-dna.pdf

Jesus has already done the work and purchased our healing through His sacrifice (see Isa. 53:5).

Is it worth it to press on to learn a new way of living, or is it just too much work?

Living with stress causes cortisol levels to increase in your body. This, in turn, causes a chemical called IgA to go down. IgA is responsible for the healthy function of your body's immune system, which is constantly fighting a barrage of bacteria, viruses, and organisms that invade your body. During the course of a four-day workshop with Dr. Joe Dispenza, 120 study participants were asked to move into an emotional state such as love, joy, or gratitude for nine to ten minutes, three times a day. By the conclusion of the event, cortisol levels of the participants dropped by three standard deviations, and their IgA levels shot up on average from 52.5 to 86.[122]

Such research convinces me one more time that a merry heart does good like medicine and that if we want to celebrate old age in health, for heaven's sake, relax and get filled with joy, love, and peace.

So how about simply doing the 13-minute meditation "New Creation Celebration: Putting on Christ"[123] morning and evening for a couple of weeks and see where it takes us. Not only will we have improved health as described in the paragraphs above, but the spiritual benefits will be out of this world.

ACTION EXERCISES

Intentionally practice heart coherence. Practice tuning to your heart, being in the state of ease, feeling Kingdom emotions, and extending them out to others. Do this in your devotional times, while you are at

---

122 www.drjoedispenza.com/blog/health/the-power-of-gratitude/
123 www.cwgministries.org/christ

work and at play. See where this takes you. As you know, practicing the right skills allows you to step forward in God, in life, and in health. So this skill is worth practicing. Moses took 40 years, Jesus took 40 days, and Paul took three years. Monks take an entire lifetime.

You may decide to purchase the emWave®2. I bought the emWave®2 and use it to help me more consistently maintain heart awareness and an emotion of gratitude. Review this article[124] on brainwave activity levels and this article,[125] which defines the language of the heart.

---

124   www.cwgministries.org/Brainwaves
125   www.cwgministries.org/Language

Chapter 12

THE TREASURE CHEST: A SPIRIT-LED PRAYER ORGANIZER

There is more than one way to pray. "If all you have is a hammer, then everything looks like a nail."

I BUILD HOMES—PHYSICALLY AND SPIRITUALLY

I worked on construction crews in my teens and twenties and have built a home that we lived in for many years. So I have a fairly extensive workbench and tool box in my garage, containing tools that I know how to use.

The more than 40 tools that I own and used to build my physical home include—hammer, sledge hammer, nails, crosscut saw, skill saw, jigsaw, hacksaw, chisels, flat screwdrivers, Philips screwdrivers,

Allen wrench, various size crescent wrenches, pliers, needle-nose pliers, adjustable pliers, trowels, mixing pails, paints, various size paintbrushes, various adhesives, stepladder, extension ladder, tool belt, face mask, sandpaper, wood files, metal files, stipple brush, paint roller, utility knife, measuring tape, square, level, pipe wrench, locking pliers, tin snips, hole punch, stilts, extension cords, power drill, power staple gun, and caulking gun.

Below are 40-plus tools (prayer approaches) God has taught me over 40 years, which I have used to build strong spiritual homes for myself and others. I certainly want to be as adept with tools to build a spiritual house as I am with tools to build a physical house, so I have taken the time to learn to use these as needed. I encourage you in a similar endeavor.

Yes, I still hire specialists to help me with jobs in my physical or spiritual home that I feel are outside my area of expertise. However, these 40 tools will allow the construction of a magnificent castle, which the Lord and you may live in and which will shine with His glory.

40-PLUS PRAYER APPROACHES TO MEET YOUR SPECIFIC NEEDS

Prayer takes many forms. So far in this book we have introduced you to the "River of Life" and the "New Creation Celebration" devotionals, available in four versions. We have explored seven prayers that heal the heart, which offer an effective approach to experiencing deliverance from demons. We have also looked at "Cleansing Cellular Memories" and "Seven Steps in Biblical Meditation."

As I was writing this book, I felt the Lord impressing me to review and list the various prayer approaches that I have used over the years with great success. I came up with a list of more than 40. I have written a short blog about each one so you may explore and use these prayer styles as necessary.

In listing them below, I begin with the heart need being experienced, followed by the name of the recommended prayer model and a link to the blog which describes that prayer approach.

Holy Spirit, which prayer approach shall I use today?

Let the Lord help you select the Spirit-led devotional you should use on any given day. You may focus on one specific issue for several days, using different prayer approaches each day so that you examine the issue from different perspectives. Address your issue multiple times from every possible vantage point *until you experience your breakthrough!*

	MY NEED TODAY IS...	DEVOTIONAL TO USE	DESCRIPTIVE BLOG
1	To grow in intimacy with God. To receive wisdom, guidance, faith, hope, and love	*Communion with God*	cwgministries.org/ 4keys
2	A general pattern prayer	*The Lord's Prayer*	cwgministries.org/ lords-prayer
3	To be thankful for the day I have just lived	*Evening Prayer of Thanksgiving*	cwgministries.org/ evening
4	To release God's creativity—to birth something new	*Creative Prayer*	cwgministries.org/ creative
5	A deepened revelation from Scripture in order to establish a truth firmly in my heart	*Biblical Meditation*	cwgministries.org/ meditation
6	A miracle of divine healing	*Miracle Healing*	cwgministries.org/ 7StepHealing

	MY NEED TODAY IS...	DEVOTIONAL TO USE	DESCRIPTIVE BLOG
7	An issue reappears— heart wounds that need complete healing	*Prayers That Heal the Heart*	cwgministries.org/ 7prayers
8	To remove emotional roots of illness	*Healing Cellular Memories*	cwgministries.org/ cellular
9	To interpret a dream so I receive God's counsel and revelation through it	*Dream Interpretation*	cwgministries.org/ daesi
10	To experience throne room worship	*Throne Room Worship*	cwgministries.org/ throne
11	To soak in God's presence	*Soaking Prayer*	cwgministries.org/ soaking
12	To receive a healing divine radiation treatment	*Healing Soaking Prayer*	cwgministries.org/ soak
13	To be immersed in the Holy Spirit	*River of Life*	cwgministries.org/ immersed
14	To experience Kingdom emotions by putting on my new self in Christ	*New Creation Celebration: Replacing Emotions*	cwgministries.org/ emotions
15	To experience Kingdom beliefs by putting on my new self in Christ	*New Creation Celebration: Replacing Beliefs*	cwgministries.org/ beliefs
16	To be fully alive by putting on my new self in Christ	*New Creation Celebration: Putting on Christ*	cwgministries.org/ christ
17	To possess my promised land	*New Creation Celebration: Possess Your Promised Land*	cwgministries.org/ possess

	MY NEED TODAY IS...	DEVOTIONAL TO USE	DESCRIPTIVE BLOG
18	To enhance my anointing and success as a manager, marketer, and leader	*Spirit-Anointed Business Journal*	cwgministries.org/ business
19	To tune my heart to hear God	*Approaching God Through the Tabernacle*	cwgministries.org/ tabernacle
20	To fine-tune my heart to hear from God	*A Fine-Tuning Dial*	cwgministries.org/ tuning
21	To break off invisible forces hindering me from experiencing God's destiny	*Dismantling Curses in Heaven's Courtroom*	cwgministries.org/ court
22	To intercede while being led by the Holy Spirit	*Spirit-Led Intercession*	cwgministries.org/ intercede
23	To engage faith, power, and victory over the enemy	*Roaring, Crying Out, and Prophetic Gestures*	cwgministries.org/ roar
24	To release negative emotions	*Emotional Freedom Techniques*	cwgministries.org/ eft
25	To build up my spirit	*Pray in Tongues*	cwgministries.org/ tongues
26	To improve a relationship	*36 "One Another" Commands*	cwgministries.org/ one-anothers
27	To block a person who is on a path toward evil	*Praying a Hedge of Thorns*	cwgministries.org/ thorns
28	To intensify prayer for a major breakthrough	*Fasting*	cwgministries.org/ fast
29	To put on *all* Christ provided at Calvary	*Honor the Power of the Cross*	cwgministries.org/ cross

	MY NEED TODAY IS...	DEVOTIONAL TO USE	DESCRIPTIVE BLOG
30	To pray from my heart, not my head	*Honor the Language of the Heart*	cwgministries.org/ language
31	To interact with Jesus in a scriptural passage	*St. Ignatius Spiritual Exercises*	cwgministries.org/ ignatius
32	To make a wise decision	*The Leader's Paradigm*	cwgministries.org/ paradigm
33	For our leadership team to make a wise decision	*Leadership Teams Led by the Spirit*	cwgministries.org/ leadership
34	To deepen love and joy in my marriage	*Enriching My Marriage*	cwgministries.org/ marriage
35	To hear the heart behind what another is saying	*Hear People's Hearts*	cwgministries.org/ hearts
36	To be anointed	*Stepping into the Anointing*	cwgministries.org/ anointing
37	To ensure I am maintaining Kingdom attitudes	*Kingdom Be-attitudes*	cwgministries.org/ attitude
38	To have someone to share my two-way journaling with	*Who to Share Two-way Journaling With*	cwgministries.org/ share
39	Help Resolving Multiple Personality Disorder	*Freedom from DID*	cwgministries.org/ did
40	Crisis, I need urgent help!	*Jesus, Help!*	cwgministries.org/ jesus-help
41	Improving digestion	*21 Days of Prayer for Digestive Healing*	cwgministries.org/ digestion
42	I need a healing miracle	*Taking God's Word as Medicine*	cwgministries.org/ ThreeTimes

Get comfortable with each of the above prayer approaches by trying any you have not already done. It is best to try anything that is new a *minimum* of three or four times so you get over that uncomfortable feeling that initially accompanies every new activity. Discover the benefit each prayer approach can provide. Now they have become useful tools in your work belt to meet future needs. David's slingshot was powerful against Goliath because he had practiced using it.

Take a couple of months and become skilled in each of these 40 ways to pray. In the final analysis, you need to *do what works* for you, and you may settle on one primary prayer approach that is best for you while having another dozen you use as necessary. Just remember, no soldier would ever practice shooting a gun *only* three times, decide it doesn't work for him as an effective weapon, and put it down in favor of another weapon. If a prayer approach is found in Scripture, then we practice using it until we are comfortable with it.

Build a strong spiritual home through the effective use of the many prayer methods God has given to His Church. Then train others in these amazing tools. Thank You, Lord, for Your gifts to Your Church!

The effective prayer of a righteous man can accomplish much (James 5:16).

Taking time to master prayer is the best gift you will ever give yourself!

RESOURCES FOR SMALL GROUP AND CLASSROOM USE

Twelve teaching sessions by Mark Virkler on DVD corresponding with the 12 chapters of *Unleashing Healing Power Through Spirit-Born Emotions*. Each teaching is 20-25 minutes long. Also included is a 45-minute video teaching by Charity Kayembe on *Coherence: The Power of Unity Within* as well as a bonus workshop by Mark entitled, *Roaring, Crying Out and Prophetic Gestures*. This is 75 minutes, which includes 45 minutes of training, 20 minutes of a guided meditation, and 10 minutes of testimonies, where three people share miracles that took place during the meditation experience. Order: *Unleashing Healing Power Through Spirit-Born Emotions DVDs* at 1-800-466-6961 or www.cwgministries.org/emotion-dvds.

New Creation Celebration Meditations can be purchased as a CD set containing all four New Creation Celebration meditations from the CWG website, or listened to freely from the links provided at the close of each chapter. Order: www.cwgministries.org/creation-cds.

Electronic Training module *Unleashing Healing Power Through Spirit-Born Emotions*. Includes downloadable ebook, digital videos, MP3s, course syllabus, online self-scoring quizzes and *Certificate of*

Completion plus college credits with CLU. Order: www.cluschoolofthe-spirit.com/emotions.

FREE downloadable PDF containing weekly activities for small group application and interaction. Classtimes are to be experiential in nature. Each meeting will contain a teaching segment, a meditation experience. and conclude with discussion and sharing. Small group activities and discussion questions are provided on our website. Download link: www.cwgministries.org/UnleashingGroups.

Book: If the book *Unleashing Healing Power Through Spirit-Born Emotions* is passed out the week before class begins, then students should read the Introduction and Chapter One before the first class. If books are passed out during the first week of class, then the assigned reading due on week two will be to read the Introduction and Chapters One and Two, so they are prepared on week two to discuss Chapter Two.

RESOURCES TO DEEPEN YOUR WALK IN THE SPIRIT

4 Keys to Hearing God's Voice[126]

Training on how to hear God's voice so you can have daily communion with Him. This allows you to live in heart faith, as Abraham did (eLearning Module here[127]).

Counseled by God[128]

Two-way journaling where God speaks to you about the beliefs and emotions you are holding, replacing negative beliefs and emotions with Kingdom beliefs and emotions (eLearning Module here[129]).

Naturally Supernatural[130]

Learn how to live aware of the Holy Spirit within, so you can release His indwelling power (eLearning Module here[131]).

---

126 www.cwgministries.org/store/4-keys-hearing-gods-voice-dvd-package
127 www.cluschoolofthespirit.com/courses/hearing-gods-voice/
128 www.cluschoolofthespirit.com/courses/counseled-by-god/
129 www.cluschoolofthespirit.com/courses/counseled-by-god/
130 http://www.cwgministries.org/store/naturally-supernatural-complete
-discounted-package
131 www.cluschoolofthespirit.com/courses/living-naturally-supernatural/

How to Walk by the Spirit[132]

Explore 500 Scripture verses on the Spirit so you learn to walk comfortably by the Spirit. Gain a biblical vocabulary to define your heart/spirit sensations so you can cooperate with them and communicate them to others (eLearning Module here[133]).

Prayers that Heal the Heart[134]

Expanded biblical training on applying the language of the heart to seven specific, complementary Spirit-anointed prayers to heal heart wounds (eLearning Module here[135]).

Hearing God Through Your Dreams[136]

Explore 50 dreams from the Bible and over 50 dreams from people living today. Learn how to understand and interpret your own dreams, translating the messages God is speaking to you nightly (eLearning Module here[137]).

Take Charge of Your Health[138]

Your body, soul, and spirit are intricately connected, so learning how to keep your body in optimum shape is part of keeping your spirit soaring (eLearning Module here[139]).

---

132 www.cwgministries.org/store/how-walk-spirit-complete-discounted-package

133 www.cluschoolofthespirit.com/courses/how-to-walk-by-the-spirit/

134 www.cwgministries.org/store/prayers-heal-heart-dvd-package

135 www.cluschoolofthespirit.com/courses/prayers-that-heal-the-heart/

136 www.cwgministries.org/store/dream-your-way-wisdom-complete-discounted-package

137 www.cluschoolofthespirit.com/courses/hearing-god-through-your-dreams/

138 www.cwgministries.org/store/take-charge-your-health-complete-discounted-package

139 www.cluschoolofthespirit.com/courses/take-charge-of-your-health-2/

About Dr. Mark Virkler

Dr. Mark Virkler has written more than 50 books in the areas of hearing God's voice and spiritual growth. He is the founder of Communion with God Ministries (www.CWGMinistries.org) and Christian Leadership University (www.CLUOnline.com), where the voice of God is at the center of every learning experience. Mark's teachings on developing intimacy with God and spiritual healing have been translated into over 40 languages, and he has helped to establish more than 250 church-centered Bible schools around the world.

ABOUT
DR. CHARITY VIRKLER KAYEMBE

Dr. Charity Virkler Kayembe has worked with her parents in ministry for 20 years and is passionate about bringing heaven to earth through restoring the supernatural to believers' everyday lives. She writes about doing life together with God on her blog (www.GloryWaves.org), sharing the unfolding journey and adventure that is walking by the Spirit. Charity's international outreach has taken her to all corners of the globe, traveling to over 50 nations on six continents. She and her husband live in upstate New York.

Discover More from Mark Virkler

Your How-to Coach for the Spirit-Led Life

Mark and Patti Virkler have *written 60 books* demonstrating how to take God's voice into area after area of life. These are available at: CWGMinistries.org/catalog.

They have also developed *over 100 college courses* for Christian Leadership University that put the voice of God in the center of your learning experience. These classes can all be taken from your home. View the complete catalog online at: cluonline.com.

Would you allow the Virklers to recommend *a coach to guide you* in applying God's voice in every area of your life? Information about their Personal Spiritual Trainer program is available at: CWGMinistries.org/pst.

You can even host Mark Virkler or Charity Kayembe in your community for *a weekend seminar.* Details can be found at: CWGMinistries.org/seminars and GloryWaves.org/seminars.

Mark Virkler and Charity Kayembe are *blogging regularly* at: CWGMinistries.org/blog and GloryWaves.org/blog.

Discover a Salvation website which *honors the role of the Holy* Spirit: www.BornOfTheSpirit.Today.

Did you know that *Scripture and science agree* on how you can live long enough to fulfill your destiny in vibrant health? Find out how: www.TakeChargeOfYourHealth.Today.

Interactive Online Training from **CLU School of the Spirit**

How Far Could **You** Go with a Bible School in Your Pocket?

Can I really experience a "School of the Spirit" in my home? **Yes, you can!**

- ☑ You don't have to go away to Bible school or a School of Ministry.

- ☑ You can live in any city in any country, attend any church, and still earn a Diploma in Applied Spirituality from Christian Leadership University's School of the Spirit! CLU provides *interactive* Spirit Life Training Modules that feature video training experiences and online quizzes, all of which can be downloaded directly to your laptop, tablet, or smartphone.

Don't you think it's time YOU team up and focus with a coach at your side so you speed forward and enter your Promised Land?

There is no easier way to grow than to get into a group of like-minded people, and focus intently, under the direction of the Holy Spirit and a coach who is ahead of you in the area you are pursuing. "A cord of three is not quickly broken" (Eccles. 4:12 NIV). You support one another through the training process and by "focusing intently," you become a doer of the Word and not a hearer only (see James. 1:25). No one wants to die in their wilderness, so make sure you are taking the proper steps which will allow you to experience your promised land!

**Learn more and try our
FREE Course Sampler today:
www.CLUSchooloftheSpirit.com**

Unleashing Healing Power Through Spirit-Born Emotion
Interactive e-Learning Course

Coaching speeds you to *mastery*

We guarantee you *will* learn how to recall and interpret dreams! We can teach you in just three months what it took us years to learn because we have gone ahead and prepared the way. And these exercises are so spiritual in nature you can easily complete them as part of your daily devotional time.

When you meditate on revelation truths in the context of a CLU School of the Spirit course, you are required to fully integrate the life-changing principles. Nothing is left to chance. You will learn what you are supposed to learn, and your life will be transformed by the power of the Holy Spirit.

Look at ALL you will receive in this interactive Spirit Life Training Module!

- ☑ Entire series of downloadable videos
- ☑ MP3 audio sessions
- ☑ Complete PDF ebook
- ☑ Two bonus digital video workshops
- ☑ *New Creation Celebration* and *River of Life* meditations
- ☑ Step-by-step guidance from the Interactive Learning Management System
- ☑ Certificate of Completion awarding 5 CEUs
- ☑ Coaching

Learn more and enroll today at
www.CLUSchooloftheSpirit.com/emotions